The GOLDEN AGE of Rock Instrumentals

STEVE OTFINOSKI

BILLBOARD BOOKS
An imprint of Watson-Guptill Publications/New York

This book is dedicated to
Ernie Freeman, Plas Johnson, Rene Hall, Earl Palmer
and all the other unsung session musicians—both white
and black—whose skill, talent and energy helped to make
the golden age of rock instrumentals truly golden.

Senior Editor: Bob Nirkind
Edited by: Lester Strong
Book and cover design: Bob Fillie, Graphiti Graphics
Production Manager: Ellen Greene

First published by Billboard Books,
 an imprint of Watson-Guptill Publications,
a division of Billboard Publications, Inc.,
at 1515 Broadway, New York, NY 10036

Library of Congress Cataloging-in-Publication Data
Otfinoski, Steve
      The golden age of rock instrumentals: a loving tribute to the
    pioneers of the instrumental era, from Dick Dale and Sandy Nelson
    to Booker T. & the MGs and the Ventures/Steve Otfinoski
          p.   cm.
      Includes bibliographical reference and discography.
      ISBN 0-8230-7639-3
      1. Rock music—History and criticism.   I. Title.
    ML3534.O84 1997
    784. 166' 09' 045—dc21   97–21919
                                                          CIP
                                                          MN

Manufactured in the United States of America

First printing, 1997

1 2 3 4 5 6 7 8 9 / 99 98 97

ACKNOWLEDGMENTS

I would like to thank my two editors at Billboard Books, Paul Lukas, whom I started the project with, and Bob Nirkind, with whom I finished it, for their encouragement and support. Thanks also to Jim Pash of the Surfaris. Bob Spickard of the Chantays, Paul Johnson of the Belairs, Buck Ormsby of the Wailers and Clem Cattini of the Tornadoes for their reminiscences, pictures and recordings. Thanks as well to Alan Taylor of *Pipeline* magazine, Joel Whitburn and Bill Hathaway at Record Research, Jeff Smith and Tim Livingston at Sundazed Music, Steven K. Peeples at Rhino Records, John Crosby at Ace Records, Marc Fenton at Razor & Tie, Michael Caprio at Varese Sarabande, Billy Miller at Norton Records, Pamela Goshman at Taragon Records, Art Mariano at Boogie Music, Mike Silverman, Ron Buono and John Lambrosa for helping to fill in the gaps in my research and record and CD collection. Also thanks to Dave "Daddy Cool" Booth at Showtime Archives and Michael Shulman at Archive Photos for their help in gathering the pictures for this volume.

A very special thanks to my good buddy Dewey Ewing for his generosity in sharing with me his amazing music collection and his deep love of all pop music of the rock era.

Finally, thanks to my long-suffering wife Beverly and my children Daniel and Martha for putting up with my obsession and enduring hours of instrumentals on the car tape deck. They made the supreme sacrifice.

Contents

Introduction

They say the music of our youth, like so much else of popular culture, haunts us all our days. As this was true for my parents' generation who came of age in the days of the big bands, so it is for this aging baby boomer. Too young to remember the appearance of Elvis and the other first generation of rockers, I was first fixated on the radio during those so-called "fallow" years of the early sixties, before the Beatles put rock 'n' roll back on the right track. Fortunately, critical opinion has shifted mightily in recent years to give this often misunderstood era its due.

The so-called "girl groups" in all their glory have been lauded by critics and performers alike, along with the talented tunesmiths of the Brill Building who gave them such beautifully crafted pop to sing. Roy Orbison and Sam Cooke have been the subjects of several biographies. Phil Spector. The Beach Boys. Early Motown. They have all been appreciated, analyzed, dissected and reassessed by a host of rock pundits.

But of all the genres to flourish in this incredibly fecund period of pop music, one has been consistently ignored by the critical establishment—the instrumental. The last rock genre to emerge in 1956, the instrumental reached its peak of popularity in the years 1960-63. From 1956 to 1966, nearly two hundred fifty of them charted on the *Billboard* Top 40. Hundreds more made the lower sixty of the Hot One Hundred. And yet instrumentals have been given short shrift in even the most comprehensive of rock chronicles. Only a few instrumental artists (Duane Eddy, Link Wray, Herb Alpert) and even fewer instrumental groups (the Ventures) are more than mentioned in these works, leaving many readers with the impression that twangy guitars and a stray trumpet were the heart and soul of the rock instrumental in its heyday.

In reality, instrumentals were the most diverse and eclectic genre in this age of pop diversity. There were rhythm and blues instrumentals, big band instrumentals, easy listening instrumentals, jazz instrumentals, soul instrumentals, surf instrumentals and even country and western instrumentals. To say nothing of the occasional movie and TV theme.

Although rock instrumentals make up only a fraction of the instrumentals that charted in the fifties and sixties, I have decided to use this term for the title of my book. While all the other instrumental subgenres will be examined and given their due, the rock instrumental, in all its rich variety, lies at the creative heart of the genre.

Why has the instrumental gotten so little respect? First, and most obviously, it was largely the province of artists who hit the jackpot once and were never heard from again. In a business largely populated by one-hit wonders, the instrumental boasts more of them than any other pop genre with the exception of novelty songs. Yet at the same time the number of instrumental artists and groups who were consistent hit makers or who, with only one or two hits under their belt, managed to have long and productive recording and performing careers, is impressive. Duane Eddy, Link Wray, Bill Doggett, Sandy Nelson, the Ventures, Booker T. and the MG's, Bill Black, Ramsey Lewis, Herb Alpert and the Tijuana Brass. And that's just for starters. Not only were many of these artists successful, their music strongly influenced younger artists, both instrumentalists and vocalists.

The second argument used against the instrumental is that the music itself, including many of the biggest hits, were mere novelties, often employing a musical gimmick or sound effect that caught the public's ear long enough to sell a few records. In other words, it was eminently disposable dreck, hardly material to be enshrined in the pantheon of rock. Again, this is a half truth. While novelty has undeniably been a central ingredient in pop instrumentals going at least as far back as "Kitten on the Keys" by Zez Confrey (1923), the best instrumentals were more novel than novelty.

Indeed, the history of the pop instrumental can be seen as a search for new and unique sounds. Sounds that would expand the ears of listeners, create a new vocabulary for pop and rock music and influence generations of rock musicians to come. From the pioneering electronic wizardry of Les Paul to the ground-breaking studio work of Duane Eddy and his producer Lee Hazlewood to the rich, rhythmic sound of Memphis soul created by Booker T. and the MG's at Stax and Willie Mitchell at Hi Records, the best of these sound-makers revolutionized the recording industry not just in terms of instrumental music but of all rock.

Even those faceless, forgotten one-hit wonders of the late fifties and early sixties played a more significant role than most of the history books allow. Obscure groups like the Rock-a-Teens, the Ramrods and the Rockin' R's (just to pick three that begin with one letter) kept the primal beat of rock alive when vocal groups and solo artists were going soft. By 1961, even Fats Domino was adding strings to his heavy New Orleans beat while groups like the Ventures and the Fireballs were keeping the faith with one rocking guitar instrumental after another.

The third and perhaps most convincing argument against the instrumental as art is the low esteem it was held in by the music industry itself. Without a voice or a good-looking lead singer, instrumental groups had no identity for the teen listener to latch onto except the music itself. More often than not, these artists were poorly promoted by their record labels and sometimes not even pictured on their album covers.

Instrumentals were often used as lead-in music for the radio news, as any AM listener in the early sixties can tell you. Disk jockeys cued them in to "fill out" the hour right before the news. Unlike vocal records, instrumentals could be faded out neatly without irate listeners complaining that their favorite song had been cut off in mid-phrase. However, there was an upside to this indignity. Listeners who happened to like the snatch of music would call up and ask the disk jockey what it was called and who performed it. Enough such calls might cause the record to be added to the playlist and eventually make it onto the charts.

In many instances the group was a group only in the loosest meaning of the word—an amalgamation of studio musicians brought together by chance or the canny machinations of a studio executive. Trying to figure out at this late date who the Marketts were on any given day would test even the savvy of Joe Saraceno, the mastermind who created the group.

For all the anonymity and neglect they suffered, the instrumentals of rock's first decade have proven to have as much staying power as any other music of that era. When I look back at my earliest radio-listening memories, many of the songs I remember most fondly weren't songs at all, but instrumentals. Without a lyric or a good-looking teen idol or girl group, they still managed to set a mood, evoke a feeling, create a vivid picture in music that still lingers in the mind's ear. "Telstar," "Pipeline," "Stranger on the Shore," "Green Onions," "Cast Your Fate to the Wind" (the Vince Guaraldi original of course), just about anything by Jimmy Smith and his electrifying organ. These were great records and great sounds whose power has not diminished in the three decades since they were first heard.

So sit back for a journey into the golden age of a genre. It is a journey filled with unsung heroes, eccentric characters, canny producers and singular sounds. Bring your curiosity, your sense of humor and certainly your nostalgia. But most of all, bring your ears.

Chapter One

Dream Music and Theme Music

Rock 'n' roll's appeal to youngsters is the equivalent of those "confidential" magazines to adults. This is the first time in the history of our business that records have capitalized on illiteracy and bad recording.
MITCH MILLER

We establish a mood by stressing melodic content and highlight it with novel effects.
MARTIN DENNY

The beauty of the instrumental is that it takes people places without words. You can go to Spain, Italy or anywhere the music takes you.
JOHN TESH

ineteen-fifty-five was the year that rock 'n' roll, percolating for several years in the hillbilly South and the black inner cities of the North, burst into the mainstream of American commercial music. Chuck Berry, Fats Domino and Bill Haley and the Comets (with no less than five entries in the year's *Billboard* Top 200) all broke into the commercial charts that year. So did rhythm and blues artists like Johnny Ace and LaVern Baker and doo-wop groups like the Penguins, the El Dorados and the Moonglows. While the Hit Parade still dominated pop music in 1955, the tide was turning as many of these white pop artists began "covering" rhythm and blues (popularly called r & b) and rock songs first sung by black artists.

Rock 'n' roll was flexing its muscles, preparing for the major assault on the national consciousness that would be led the following year by Elvis Presley, Little Richard and a slew of other first-generation rockers.

But while vocal pop music would never be the same, instrumental music was barely affected by the new sounds of rock 'n' roll. The #1 song of the year was not "Rock around the Clock" but "Cherry Pink and Apple Blossom White," an unabashedly romantic Latin instrumental by a short, pudgy Cuban band leader named Pérez Prado.

Pop instrumentals were, as they had been since the decade began, the exclusive domain of lush orchestras, cocktail lounge combos and a handful of solo musicians, most of them keyboard artists. The orchestras evolved from the big bands of the forties, largely replaced by the solo vocalists who had originally been mere appendages to them. In the post-war decade the crooners reigned supreme, but instrumental music, if no longer the center of attraction, was still very much in demand, albeit to fulfill different needs.

The World War II couples, who had jitterbugged and fox-trotted to Glen Miller and the Dorsey Brothers, had settled down in the suburbs and started families. They were looking for music to calm them down with a cocktail or two after a long day at the office or at home with the kids. Mellow mood music, enchanced by the improved high-fidelity sound of long-playing record albums, filled the airwaves and the couples' new home entertainment centers. Listening today to these instrumentals of the early and mid-fifties is like entering an aural time machine which transports the listener to a never-never land of romantic dreamscapes where the air is filled with soaring strings, tinkling pianos, thumping jungle drums, crooning male choruses and phantom whistlers.

Nearly all of these best-selling instrumentals came from twin worlds of make-believe—a tired businessman's vision of faraway vacation dreamlands or the more recognizable dreamland of Hollywood, whose fantasies were growing more extravagant to compete with the more mundane world of that new threat to the movies—television.

THE ALLURE OF FARAWAY PLACES

While Bill Haley and the Comets were rocking around the clock, the easy-listening orchestras of the fifties were literally whizzing around the world, in search of romantic ports of call and the forbidden fruit of exotic climes. The very titles of the tunes conjure up a world of fairy-tale places: "Caravan," "Harem Dance," "Lisbon Antigua," "The Poor People of Paris" (who like all poor natives in the travelogues are content and merry), "Port au Prince," "Martinique," "Calcutta," "Isle of Capri," "The Enchanted Sea," and "Around the World," which covered the world in a romantic quest for love, not on a gentlemen's bet as in the Jules Verne novel on which the 1956 movie and its title song were based. This movie theme was composed and performed by veteran film composer Victor Young, who had the great misfortune to die suddenly six months before it became a Top 20 hit. Like many of the craftsmen who rode the crest of the pop instrumental wave in the fifties, Young was a multi-talented man of music, for whom a hit record was the crowning touch to an already distinguished career.

NELSON RIDDLE, FOR INSTANCE, was a triple threat as a conductor, composer and masterful arranger who singlehandedly hoisted Frank Sinatra from music oblivion with a clutch of classic albums. Riddle's last assignment before his death in 1985 was arranging some of these same standards on three memorable albums for Linda Ronstadt.

In 1956 Riddle took a 20-year-old tune by three Portuguese writers, arranged it for quivering strings and a perky little piano riff, and used it as the theme music for a minor spy movie, *Lisbon*, starring Ray Milland and Maureen O'Hara. "Lisbon Antigua" ("In Old Lisbon") quickly shot to #1 on the charts for four weeks in early 1956. Six years later, Riddle used the same formula—strings and a catchy piano figure—to craft one of the best TV themes of the 1960s, "Route 66" (#30), his last Top 40 hit. The producers of the CBS drama series had wanted to use the well-known Bobby Troup song of the same name, but were talked out of it by the resourceful Riddle.

LES BAXTER'S "The Poor People of Paris" took over the #1 slot from "Lisbon Antigua" in February 1956—the only instance of back-to-back instrumentals in that lofty position before or since. The composer of over one hundred film scores, Baxter also created the subgenre of instrumental exotica with a string of mood-drenched albums set in island paradises. The man who made *Ritual of the Savage* showed a more benign side in "The Poor People of Paris," his biggest single. He set the simple, gliding French melody to pizzicato strings and a whistling male chorus, on which he cleverly faded out the music and then abruptly woke up the listener with a brash big band rendition of the melody. It was jaunty with a capital "J." It didn't matter to anyone that the English title was a travesty of the original, "The Ballad of Poor Jean," mistranslated by a careless Capitol Records rep in Paris who wrote "gens" for "Jean."

In an interview with Joe Smith in his candid collection *Off the Record*, Baxter took credit for creating the low male unison chorus and (surprise, surprise) the beat of rock 'n' roll. "It was like a stripper's beat," Baxter recalled. "I don't know if I got it from Africa or Cuba, but it went, 'Boom, ch, boom, boom, ch, boom, boom' which became rock 'n' roll." Roll over, Chuck Berry.

LAWRENCE WELK, WHO TOOK no credit for rock 'n' roll, did rightly lay claim to the bubbly orchestral style he called "champagne music." This choppy style of music-making apparently came about when Welk found that short clipped phrases were easier to master for the inexperienced pick-up musicians he first used in his ensemble. His #1 hit, "Calcutta" (1961), is less bubbly than floaty, buoyed up by a "lalaing" female chorus and a sprightly harpsichord played by Welk stalwart Frank Scott. "Calcutta" had nothing to do with the teeming Indian metropolis and was originally titled "Tivoli Melody" by its German

Among the orchestra leaders of the fifties, few enjoyed the chart success of Lawrence Welk. His biggest hit, "Calcutta," featured Frank Scott on a harpsichord with an internal microphone. Scott had to wear earphones in order to hear himself play. (Photo courtesy of Showtime Archives, Toronto)

composer Heino Gaze. Two years and several title changes later, it became "Kalkutta Leight am Ganges," which was shortened by Dot, Welk's record label, to "Calcutta." Like Rick Nelson, Welk had the added advantage of being able to plug his tunes on his long-running television series, which may help account for his string of over twenty Top 100 singles from 1956 to 1965.

··

AS THE FIFTIES PROGRESSED, adult listeners' jaded tastes required more exotic settings for their instrumentals. Although Les Baxter started the craze for exotica, it was Martin Denny who truly capitalized on it. Denny's stripped down version of Baxter's "Quiet Village" (#4) was an amusing contradiction where raucous jungle life cawed, hooted and croaked behind every grass hut and hanging vine. Denny, born and bred in exotic New York City, started life as a student of classical piano, who, like so many of his peers, developed a soft spot for cool jazz. He toured South America with a jazz group, ending up at Don the Beachcomber's in Honolulu in 1959.

This was the year that the mainland went "Hawaii crazy." James Michener's epic novel about the islands was a best-seller, Andy Williams' "The Hawaiian Wedding Song" was a hit and in August Hawaii became the fiftiethth state. Denny got on the bandwagon and formed a jazz combo called The Exotic Sounds of Martin Denny. It featured not only Latin and Polynesian instruments like the marimba, bongos, congas and vibraphone, but bird calls, faithfully reproduced by group member August Colon, and croaking bullfrogs ingeniously imitated by grinding on a grated cylinder. Denny's group, ensconced in

Part of exotica's appeal, as this album cover confirms, was sexual. "Quiet Village," the genre's biggest-selling single, was, in the hands of Martin Denny, anything but quiet. (Photo courtesy of Showtime Archives, Toronto)

Henry Kaiser's Hawaiian Village nightclub in Honolulu, became as much a tourist attraction as Pearl Harbor.

Denny's vibes player, Arthur Lyman, left the group in 1957 and formed his own exotic franchise, the Arthur Lyman Group. A native Hawaiian from the island of Kauai, Lyman added whooping monkeys and chirping insects to the jungle mix in his first charting record, "Taboo" (#55). He had his biggest hit in 1961 with the tender, calypso-tinged, folk song, "Yellow Bird" (#4), which gratefully featured no bird calls, only a sweet guitar and Lyman's seductive vibes. Both Denny and Lyman forsook exotica for a cleaner, sparer style in their last charting singles, jazzy renditions of, respectively, "A Taste of Honey" (#50) and "Love for Sale" (#43).

Exotica may have reached the pinnacle of absurdity with "The Enchanted Sea" (#15), a dreamy piece of ersatz concocted by jazz arranger Frank Metis and moonlighting dentist Warren Nadell (aka Randy Starr) who called themselves the Islanders. Their accordion-guitar duet featured a phantom whistler, lapping waters, a San Francisco lighthouse foghorn and surf sounds from Nantucket Bay (both courtesy of a CBS sound-effects man), making this the first bi-coastal instrumental. For the record, the lapping waves were made by the sound man splashing his elbow in dishwater. "The Enchanted Sea" sounded like nothing so much as a movie soundtrack, which is the next stop on our musical travelogue. . . .

THE THEME FROM . . .

The appearance of bigger and splashier movies to counteract the growing threat of television to the film industry in the early fifties had a profound effect in the world of pop music. Hollywood studios worked overtime to lure patrons out from in front of their TV screens with such new technologies as Cinemascope and Three-D, the use of big-name stars they couldn't see on television and the introduction of lush soundtracks, featuring memorable musical themes. People who enjoyed a movie could now go out and buy an album of the music from it. If the title theme was catchy or melodic enough, it could even become a hit single. Top songwriters were hired by Hollywood studios to write a main title tune for non-musical dramatic films, which could be recorded in both a vocal and instrumental versions. A prime example is Victor Young's "Around the World" (#13), whose B-side, a vocal version by Bing Crosby, went to #25. It was one of the pop crooner's few hits in the rock era.

....

SOME MOVIE THEMES became so inextricably linked with the films they came from that success was almost guaranteed. A prime example of this was Mitch Miller's perky, whistling rendition of the "March from the River Kwai and Colonel Bogey" (#20) from the Academy Award-winning movie *The Bridge on the River Kwai*. The music was used extensively in the film as English and American prisoners-of-war helped build a bridge for their Japanese captors during World War II.

A staunch opponent of rock 'n' roll, "The Beard," as Miller was known in the business, used elements of rock, particularly its steady beat and bass man voice, in many of the Hit Parade songs he produced and arranged for Columbia in the fifties. On his own records, however, Miller eschewed any hint of rock and stuck to old American songs and that squeaky clean "Sing along with Mitch" sound in such hits as "The Yellow Rose of Texas" (#1) and "The Children's Marching Song" (#16). His "Theme from 'Song for a Summer Night'" (#8) in 1956 was one of the first hit themes from a television program, a dramatic production from *Studio One*.

....

THE SAME YEAR SAW the appearance of one of the most memorable and deftly crafted of the big movie themes, "Moonglow and Theme from *Picnic*." Morris Stoloff, a pop song composer, classical violinist and musical director for Columbia Pictures since the 1930s, was musical director for the film version of William Inge's juicy small-town drama. He wove an intriguing medley of the Picnic theme and the 1934 pop song "Moonglow," heard during the famous dance scene between William Holden and Kim Novak. The instrumental opens quietly with a small cocktail combo of piano, bass, and drums playing "Moonglow" until a tremulous string section breezes in with the *Picnic* theme. The contrast between the understated, jazzy piano and the sentimental, soaring strings makes for an achingly beautiful counterpoint. Number one for three weeks, the theme was so popular that George Cates, musical director for Lawrence Welk's TV show, managed to have a million seller with it as well.

....

MORE INNOVATIVE WAS the bold, exciting "Themes from *The Man with the Golden Arm*," one of the first Hollywood movies to feature a jazz score. Composer Elmer Bernstein's own brash, big band treatment of this title theme was a Top 20 hit, but was outsold by a cover version by band leader Richard Maltby, father of Broadway director and lyricist Richard Maltby, Jr., which went to #14. Perhaps the strangest charting movie theme of the decade was a third version by TV's *Your Hit Parade* musical director Dick Jacobs called "Main Title and Molly-O" (#22), which sandwiched a corny love ballad from the film sung by a male chorus between the jazzy theme music.

....

SOME INSTRUMENTAL MOVIE HITS weren't actual theme songs. The most famous example appeared in Howard Hughes' 1954 epic *Underwater!*, a disaster of oceanic proportions, the fifties' equivalent of the more recent *Waterworld*. For the full story of this expensive flop and its incredible underwater premier, see Harry and Michael Medved's highly entertaining *The Hollywood Hall of Shame: The Most Expensive Flops in Movie History*. Interestingly, the authors fail to note in their account that out of this prize turkey came the #1 instrumental hit of the decade. Cuban band leader Pérez Prado, a frequent comic character in Mexican

Latin bandleader Pérez Prado was known as "King of the Mambo," a dance he virtually invented. While embraced in the United States, the mambo was less well received in other countries. The Roman Catholic cardinal of Peru warned his flock that anyone who dared do the dance would be denied absolution. (Archive Photos/Frank Driggs Collection)

films, appeared briefly as himself in the film, playing "Cherry Pink and Apple Blossom White." Prado, a big seller with RCA International's album line, was known as "King of the Mambo," a dance he invented on the dance floors of Mexico City. "Cherry Pink," however, was a cha-cha, the first to be heard widely in the States. Easier to master than either the mambo or the rumba, the cha-cha brought more non-dancers onto the floor than any dance until the emergence of the twist. The cha-cha craze and an outrageously romantic trumpet solo by Billy Regis, who knew how to hold a note, kept "Cherry Pink" in the #1 position on the *Billboard* charts for an incredible ten weeks.

Off-stage, Prado was a quiet, private man who spoke little English; but on the podium he was a showman who could have taught Little Richard a trick or two. He wore tux and tails, jeweled gloves (decades before Michael Jackson donned them) and cavorted around the stage, leaping and kicking in time to the music. His trademark, however, was the mostly unintelligible sounds he would utter to urge his musicians to blow harder on their horns. These grunts and groans became so popular on his records that they became obligatory for every subsequent mambo record.

Three years after "Cherry Pink," Prado had his second #1 hit, "Patricia," a more hip dance tune with a bouncy melody played on an electric organ that showed the influence of rock on the Latin music maker. It was, as Peter Grendysa writes, "the last hurrah for the big Latin bands," although Prado continued to tour the United States until the early seventies when he moved back to Mexico.

··

THE RISE OF ROCK MAY have finished off Latin big band music in the late fifties, but instrumental movie theme music continued on its profitable path. An article headlined "Film Themes Spark Multi-Coverage in Singles Field" in a September 1960 issue of *Billboard* pointed out that Hollywood studios "are more aware of the exploitation value of records today (and their appeal to young movie-minded fans) than ever before in the history of the medium."

The point had been well made earlier that year by the incredible success of "Theme from *A Summer Place*" by Canadian band leader and arranger Percy Faith. It remains the only instrumental of the rock era to be the #1 song of its year and was the third best-selling single of the sixties. The theme was written by veteran Hollywood composer Max Steiner for a big screen soap opera that propelled Troy Donahue and Sandra Dee to fleeting fame. Steiner pleaded with his publisher to released the theme song as a single. "[He] wouldn't touch that song," Steiner recalled years later. "Said it was nothing. Then Percy Faith did it and sold 10 million copies."

Faith's superb arrangement may have done as much to sell the record as Steiner's memorable melody. He opened the piece with mesmerizing triplets that ushered in the main theme with the silkiest of string sections and then kept

No other movie theme of the rock era is as embedded in the public consciousness as "Theme from A Summer Place." As a young man, Percy Faith badly burned his hands putting out a fire on his sister's clothes. Unable to play the piano for five years, he decided to try conducting, with spectacular results. (Photo courtesy of Showtime Archives, Toronto)

upping the ante with brass and a haunting chorus of French horns. The upbeat arrangement, according to Joseph Lanza in his fascinating study of mood music, *Elevator Music*, disturbed many Faith fans at the time, who accused him of selling out to rock 'n' roll! Faith himself never much cared for the song that will forever be associated with him and preferred the more rhythmic style of other successes, such as his 1952 Latin hit "Delicado." Yet he could never escape "Summer Place" and even recorded a disco version ("Summer Place '76") shortly before his death from cancer in 1976.

Movie themes entered a new age with the emergence in the late fifties of Henry Mancini. Mancini was raised in Aliquippa, Pennsylvania, where his steel worker father Zuinto played flute on his lunch breaks. It was at the senior Mancini's urging that the talented Hank went to Carnegie Technical Music School and later Julliard in New York. He moved to Hollywood in the early fifties and became staff composer and arranger at Universal Studios, where he served his apprenticeship scoring over one hundred fifty pictures, including vehicles for Abbott and Costello, Francis the Talking Mule and the Creature from the Black Lagoon. In 1955 he was nominated for an Oscar for his score for *The Glenn Miller Story*.

An eclectic composer with an abiding love for all kinds of popular music, Mancini's talent embraced everything from romantic title songs ("Moon River," "Days of Wine and Roses") to humorous instrumentals that featured novel instrumentation ("Baby Elephant Walk" from 1962's *Hatari*, "The Pink Panther Theme") to surf music ("Banzai Pipeline," a surprisingly decent surf instrumental from 1963). As gifted a composer as he was a conductor, Mancini brought a rare intelligence and dramatic flair to movie themes.

Perhaps the most recorded theme music of the fifties, however, wasn't from a movie at all but from an Off-Broadway revival of Kurt Weill and Bertolt Brecht's twenties' musical drama *The Three-Penny Opera*. No less than five versions of "Moritat (A Theme from *Three-Penny Opera*)" made the Top 40 in 1956, including a swinging vocal version called "Mack the Knife" by Louis Armstrong. Dick Hyman and his trio had the biggest hit (#8) featuring a beguiling harpsichord, while Richard Hayman and Jan August weighed in with an harmonica and piano arrangement. Lawrence Welk gave it the accordion treatment, which blessedly was never heard by the composer, who died in 1950.

SPACE AGE GUITAR

While the early fifties' pop charts were dominated by solo vocalists, successful instrumental artists were usually part of an orchestra or a smaller ensemble. An exception was guitarist Les Paul, who, more than any other instrumentalist in the post-war decade, led the search for new sounds in pop music. Like a Werner von Braun of the guitar, Paul combined a restless curiosity with a technical expertise to blaze a trail where none had gone before.

A tireless experimenter, Les Paul transformed the electric guitar into a versatile instrument capable of astonishing sounds. Here he is at work in his famed home studio, while wife and musical partner Mary Ford looks on approvingly. (Photo courtesy of Showtime Archives, Toronto/Colin Escott)

Born in Waukeska, Wisconsin, the year before the United States entered World War I, Lester William Polfus exhibited a penchant for musical gadgetry at a tender age. At age 12, the precocious redhead made what he called the "first digital recording," by punching holes in the piano rolls on his mother's player piano. Soon after, he fashioned a primitive electric guitar by jabbing a phonograph needle and arm into the body of his acoustic guitar to amplify its sound. On an early gig as a singing guitarist he discovered audiences at a local drive-in couldn't hear him, so he hooked up his parents' radio and used it as an amplifier.

The music Paul played in these early years was mostly bluegrass and country, with a little jazz thrown in, befitting a musician whose stage name was Red Hot Red and later Rhubarb Red. He discarded the hayseed act when he moved to Chicago in 1932, and was a featured player on some of the first radio soap operas while moonlighting as a disc jockey. For the next decade Paul paid his dues, playing swing music on an electric guitar with Fred Waring's Orchestra and then in his own trio.

In 1941 he built the first solid state body electric guitar, a square slab of wood with strings and a pickup. He called it "The Log" and took it to the venerable Gibson Guitar company, asking the firm to make a guitar from his prototype. Gibson was not impressed. The company president referred to Paul as "the character with the broomstick that had a pickup on it." But Paul persisted with the conviction of a true believer and Gibson finally relented, although it insisted that its name not be associated with the new-fangled instrument. Thus was born the Les Paul guitar. After sales of the new guitar took off, Gibson changed its mind and in 1952 agreed to put its name on it.

Decca Records was more supportive of Paul's invention and he found steady work backing the label's top performers in the early 1940s. In 1945 he backed Bing Crosby on the #1 home-from-the war hit, "It's Been a Long, Long Time." Now a successful commercial artist, Paul forsook the antiquated recording studios where his precise guitar work always came out "muddied," and built his own experimental studio in a garage in Hollywood. "I was trying to make myself different," he said in one interview, and vowed not to come out of the studio until he had created an entirely unique sound.

Like a mad scientist in his laboratory, Paul worked secretly for months, developing a multi-track sound system that allowed him to lay one track of himself over another, so his guitar sounded like two guitars, and then three. Experimenting tirelessly on tape, he was able to speed up the sound of his guitar, slow it down, stretch it like a piece of taffy and make it echo and quiver with reverb. The final result of months of experimentation was a new version of the Rodgers and Hart standard "Lover" that sounded like it had been recorded in outer space by a band of fun-loving Martians. Paul had signed with Capitol Records and "Lover" was his first single release, proudly described on the label of the 78-rpm recording as "the new sound of Les Paul," which hardly began to describe the sonic assault on listeners' ears back in 1947.

Paul's space age instrumentals sold extremely well ("Nola," another rein-vented chestnut, went to #1 in 1949), while his modest garage studio became a mecca for recording artists from W. C. Fields to the Andrew Sisters who want-ed to enhance their records with the "new sound" of multi-track recording. One pretty singer, Colleen Summer, a former vocalist with the Gene Autry Band, was invited by Paul to stop by and sing with his group. She ended up becom-ing his girlfriend, lead vocalist and wife. Under the name Mary Ford, she and Paul formed what would become the top musical duo of the pre-rock Hit Parade. With an uncanny knack for turning out hits, Paul relegated his guitar to backing Mary's seductive vocals. Her voice became just another instrument he could tinker with. He laid down multi-tracks so she sounded like a female cho-rus—a technical feat that would quickly be picked up by Patti Page and other rival songbirds.

While some of the Les Paul-Mary Ford hits were as saccharine and turgid as that of other Hit Parade artists, an amazing number ("How High the Moon," "Tiger Rag," "I'm Sitting on Top of the World") remain fresh and exciting today, due in large part to Paul's rhythmic arrangements and always inventive guitar work. The downside was that he produced precious few instrumentals, like 1952's sweet and engaging "Meet Mr. Callaghan."

With the advent of rock 'n' roll the duo's fortunes fell and shifting labels from Capitol to Columbia in the early sixties didn't improve things. The couple divorced in 1963 and Paul went into semi-retirement for twelve years, although he continued to invent new studio effects, including synthesizing and sound-on-sound.

He came back with a bang in 1976, teaming up with another guitar master and skillful sonic man, Chet Atkins, on the *Chester and Lester* album, which won a Grammy for Best Country Instrumental Performance. Since then, Paul has been garnering the fame and recognition that has eluded him since his glory days in the early fifties. His induction into the Rock and Roll Hall of Fame in 1988 as a predecessor of rock is well deserved. Without Paul there would have been no Duane Eddy, Link Wray, or Ventures. To say nothing of hard rockers from Eddie Cochran to Eddie Van Halen who have benefited from his inven-tion. What Edison was to the light bulb, Les Paul is to the electric guitar.

MILLION DOLLAR KEYBOARDS

In the summer of 1955, a classically trained pianist named Louis Weertz from Omaha, Nebraska, burst into the limelight with his florid version of a French song, "Les Feuilles Mortes," literally translated "The Dead Leaves." Actually, "Autumn Leaves," as it was called, with new English lyrics by Johnny Mercer, had been recorded by numerous artists including Bing Crosby. But it was not until the instrumental version by Weertz, rechristened all-American Roger

One of the first successful solo instrumentalists of the rock era, Roger Williams conceived of the famous arpeggios of "Autumn Leaves" when he misread the title of the French composition as "Falling Leaves." When asked about his florid technique, Williams admitted, "I milk it." (Photo courtesy of Showtime Archives, Toronto)

Williams by record producer Dave Kapp, that it became a hit.

What made Williams' piano version stand out from the pack were his endlessly cascading arpeggios, the perfect aural equivalent of the leaves tumbling from the trees in the sweeping wind of accompanying strings. With an orchestral opening and closing worthy of a Beethoven symphony, "Autumn Leaves" was pop music gussied up in Chopinesque chintz. But both orchestra and pianist played with such conviction that somehow the whole thing worked and "Autumn Leaves," to the distress of rock chroniclers everywhere, remains the #1 instrumental of the rock era to date.

It also lifted Roger Williams into the stratosphere of pop instrumentalists, making him, among other things, the "Pianist of Presidents." (He has performed for every one of them since Truman.) While Liberace may have had the candelabra and the flashy clothes, Williams sold the records—twenty-two *Billboard* hit singles in the fourteen years after his debut and thirty-eight bestselling albums. Williams remains a skillful and versatile performer, as adept at ragging old standards like "Near You," a Top 10 hit in 1958, as pounding out grandiose movie themes like "Born Free" (#7), his last major hit in 1966.

....

IF ONE CLASSY PIANO was pleasing to the ear, how much more would two be? Such was the thinking of two precocious graduates of the Juilliard School for

Music in New York. For those of us who remember Arthur Ferrante and Louis Teicher from the sixties as the Smith Brothers of easy listening with their identical goatees and plastic smiles, it may come as something of a shock to learn that this duo started their recording careers as wild-eyed avant gardists, closer in spirit to John Cage than Mitch Miller.

In an intriguing string of albums for ABC-Paramount in the fifties Ferrante and Teicher played "prepared pianos," stuffed with everything from rubber stops to sandpaper. More genuinely adventurous in their search for new sounds than most of the makers of what has come to be called "space age bachelor pad music," they were not above hyperbole, as these liner notes from Blast Off! their third ABC album confirms:

> The concert grand pianos belonging to these keyboard stylists could easily take a musical place in the space age alongside their scientific counterparts, the nuclear reactor and the moon rocket, even though they are the ordinary instruments available in any piano store. Because of the duo-pianists' innovations, sounds emanating from their twin 88's are far from identifiable with the music made by your living room piano.

What was possible in the recording studio became more difficult in other venues. On one occasion a nosey stagehand removed all the "junk" from their pianos only moments before a live TV broadcast.

Despite their lofty aspirations, Ferrante and Teicher's careers remained largely earthbound until they signed a recording contract with United Artists in

Before they grew beards and became the leading purveyors of middle-brow movie music at United Artists, Ferrante and Teicher were sonic experimenters, as suggested by this outrageous album cover. The album's liner notes compared their innovative "prepared" pianos to "the nuclear reactor and the moon rocket."

1960, a label that saw as its mission to capitalize on the soundtracks of its parent company's movies. The duo went from making inventive novelties to recording lush, overbaked movie themes without missing a beat. Their first single, and one of their best, was the "Theme from *The Apartment*" (#10), from Billy Wilder's comedy-drama, which won the Best Picture Oscar in 1960. This was quickly followed by the main theme from *Exodus* (#2), Otto Preminger's overstuffed epic on the creation of modern Israel. The movie's music composer, Ernest Gold, had conceived of the piece as a militaristic march, and the duo managed to wring every heroic ounce out of it with pounding chords and sweeping arpeggios, while never losing the thread of its folk-like melody.

Adult listeners who shunned Lawrence Welk and his accordions could rest assured they were in good cultured company with Ferrante and Teicher. The liner notes from *The World's Great Themes* boasted about the album's collection of "all-time favorites taken from the repertory of such immortal composers as Tchaikovsky, Rachmoninoff, Chopin and Beethoven. This music is old, like good wine, but it has been presented with an evergreen freshness."

By 1964, Ferrante and Teicher had become such moneymakers for United Artists that the label signed them to an unprecedented long-term contract, "in the area of $1 million," according to *Billboard*, paid out over twenty years at $50,000 annually. Although much of their music is like the sugary icing on a wedding cake, the duo did not completely abandon their experimental roots. In their 1969 version of the theme from *Midnight Cowboy* (#10) they featured the unique "water sound" guitar played by Vincent Bell, former lead guitarist for the rock instrumental group the Ramrods. It sounded like Duane Eddy's twangy guitar played underwater.

....

TWO OTHER MULTI-TALENTED pianists who made contributions to the pop keyboard craze were Eddie Heywood and Don Robertson. Heywood was the son of a jazz musician and played with Billie Holiday in the 1940s. He moved to California in 1947 and had two huge instrumental hits on the charts in the summer of 1956. "Soft Summer Breeze" (#11) was a beguiling tune played with a refreshing simplicity by Heywood's trio and just the right touch of jazzy improvisation. "Canadian Sunset" (#2), by contrast, was a gorgeous pop tone poem with Heywood's sturdy solo beautifully supported by Hugh Winterhalter's orchestra. Although he continued to make fine music into the 1970s, Heywood, unlike Williams, was unable to parlay his two hits into a successful recording career.

Robertson fared somewhat better, although his piano playing is almost lost in the infectious whistling and snappy handclapping beat of his lone hit, "The Happy Whistler" (#6). A gifted country songwriter, Robertson created the much-imitated "slip note" Nashville piano style, usually credited to Floyd Cramer. Cramer and producer Chet Atkins heard Robertson's performance on his demo for his song "Please Help Me I'm Falling" and applied the same technique to Cramer's "Last Date." Cramer got a million seller, Hank Locklin scored a hit with "Please Help Me I'm Falling" and all Don Robertson got were a lot of royalty checks.

....

NOT EVERY POP PIANIST in the mid-fifties played lush love ballads, inspirational movie themes and mood pieces. Ragtime, the classically influenced popular piano music composed by Scott Joplin and others in pre-World War I America, made something of a comeback at the time in a spate of best-selling albums. It was a questionable comeback because the performers played the delicate ragtime with the heavy hand of honky tonk performers and largely vulgarized the work of Joplin and his peers.

Some of the artists who played this tinkly piano music wisely used pseudonyms—Knuckles O'Toole was jazz pianist Dick Hyman, who is today Woody Allen's favorite film composer, and Joe "Fingers" Carr was respected orchestra leader and arranger Lou Busch. Hyman's alter ego produced no hit singles, but Carr/Busch had several, the last being "Portuguese Washerwoman" (#19) in 1956. (Portugal held an inexplicable attraction for fifties' instrumentalists.) Carr's nimble fingers, a zippy xylophone and a deliriously surreal male chorus, make this one of the more memorable exotic instrumentals of 1956.

Carr's competitors included former child prodigy Johnny Maddox, who had the good fortune to get a part-time job working at Randy Wood's record store in his hometown of Gallatin, Tennessee. Impressed by Maddox's piano playing, Wood took him to a local radio station and cut some singles. "The Crazy Otto," Maddox's rinky-tink rendition of eight German popular songs was released on Wood's new label Dot. Maddox's good-time medley peaked at #2 in early 1955.

A few weeks after "The Crazy Otto" hit the Top 40, German pianist Fritz Schulz-Reichel adopted the title as *his* alter ego and as Crazy Otto scored a doubled-sided honky-tonk hit with "Glad Rag Doll" (#19) and "Smiles" (#21) on Decca.

Within a year the rage for "ragtime" piano died down and Scott Joplin fans would have to wait until Marvin Hamlisch arranged his rags on the soundtrack of the movie *The Sting* (1973) for a real ragtime revival.

....

IF PIANOS WERE alternately grandiose and good-time in fifties' pop, organs were mysterious, a bit creepy, and something of a novelty.

Earl Grant, who started playing the organ in church in Kansas City, Missouri, studied to be a music teacher at the University of Southern California after Army service in World War II. But he found a more lucrative career in the nightclubs of southern California where he was a triple threat as a pianist, organist and singer. In 1957 Grant signed with Decca Records and had his biggest hit a year later with the vocal "The End" (#7), which wins the Nat King Cole soundalike contest. Grant revealed a more swinging side to his playing in the early sixties with such modest instrumental hits as "Swingin' Gently" (#44) and "Sweet Sixteen Bars" (#55).

More innovative and influential was another Decca artist, Lenny Dee, who pulled out all the stops on his electric organ in his sole hit from 1955, "Plantation Boogie" (#19). This bouncy number, named for the Plantation Club in Nashville where Dee was discovered by country singer Red Foley, was based on "Pine Top's Boogie Woogie." Dee used it to showcase the versatility of the electric organ and its uncanny ability to imitate other instruments. He took the organ out of the church loft and the cocktail lounge and, although hardly a rocker himself, pointed the way to its future as a mainstay of rock bands in the sixties and beyond.

....

THE EASY-LISTENING INSTRUMENTAL was not to disappear with the emergence of rock 'n' roll. In truth, it thrived right through the sixties, and found a new lease on life with the appearance of Herb Alpert and the Tijuana Brass, whose musical rise will be documented in a later chapter.

A *Billboard* headline in April 1960 proclaimed that "'60 Could Be That Band Revival Year," giving new hope to all the over-thirty crowd eager for the demise of rock 'n' roll and the return of the "good music" they grew up with. Nostalgia for the big band era seemed particularly strong that year: TV specials like *The Swingin' Years* drew large ratings, sixteen orchestra albums were on *Billboard*'s Top 30 stereo album list and United Artists, home of Ferrante and Teicher, were grooming a squeaky clean white rock band, Dickey Doo and the Don'ts, as a "new teen-style dance band attraction." And let no one forget that the perennial theme song for *American Bandstand* was not "Rock around the Clock" but "Bandstand Boogie," an unabashed big band jitterbug performed by Les Elgart and his orchestra.

But back in 1956, the year before *Bandstand* went nationwide, the supremacy of pop instrumentalists was being challenged by the alien sounds of raucous sax and beating drums. The rock instrumental was about to be born.

Chapter Two

Wailing Sax and Pounding Drums

> *. . . there is not a bass instrument to compare with it.*
> HECTOR BERLIOZ on first hearing a saxophone (1842)

> *We played for two hours before taking a break and the*
> *people just didn't respond...they just sat there like a bad*
> *spell, couldn't reach them at all. During the intermission,*
> *I was too worried to change clothes, I just sat there*
> *thinking "What can I do?" I thought, "I'll get on my*
> *knees," and during the second show that's just what I did.*
> *Still no reaction. . . . I laid down . . . and that did it. That*
> *broke the spell and people began screamin' and hollerin'.*
> BIG JAY MCNEELY

When Belgian instrument maker Adolphe Sax invented the saxophone around 1840 he could not have conceived of the raucous music that one day would issue forth from his creation—any more than the first big bands of the mid-thirties had any idea that the smooth swing jazz they played would evolve over a decade into wild rhythm and blues.

By the mid-forties, the big bands had become tame, appealing more to adults than to the teenagers who first helped make them popular. "Jazz had got so cool, we lost the kids who wanted to dance," band leader Lionel Hampton has said. "So we started playing this real gutty jazz, and people called it rhythm and blues."

TWO TENORS, ONE ALTO

Hampton's West Coast band included a young tenor saxophone player named Illinois Jacquet. Born in Broussard, Illinois, but raised in Houston, Texas, Jacquet had a loose and wild style of playing that melded perfectly with the dirty dance floors of the Texas joints where he first played in the early forties. Illinois liked the floor a lot. In fact, he was fond of lying down on it, flat on his back, and playing his horn while kicking his legs in the air.

Every big band had a theme song to identify it and Hampton's was a swinging number he wrote with Benny Goodman called "Flying Home." Jacquet's tenor sax solo on "Flying Home" broke all the rules. He didn't blow the sax; he honked it, sounding at times like a lost goose and at others like a braying moose in heat. He would persistently repeat one note like some crazy mantra until it threatened to break every window in the joint.

Despite the seeming recklessness of his playing, there was a deliberateness and technical expertise to Jacquet's performance, as if he were creating a whole new vocabulary for his instrument. Which he was. His sax, as Robert Palmer notes, "preached as passionately as a sanctified deacon on revival night."

Jacquet was indeed reviving jazz, returning it to its wild and woolly New Orleans roots, but in the process he also established something new: A fast tempo, heavy beat kind of music that was danceable, raw and wild—the music of choice in roadhouses and juke joints across the South and the West.

"Flying Home" made the Texas tenor saxophonist famous overnight and he soon flew from Hampton's nest, settled down with the Cab Calloway band and then joined up with Count Basie. Each of these bands were popular with the new generation of post-war teens, both black and white, offering a kind of jazz that appealed more to them than the cooler, intellectual bebop jazz being created by Charlie Parker and Dizzy Gillespie on the East coast.

Jacquet soon formed his own band and continues to tour in the nineties with undiminished popularity. Yet he never bolted from the fold for rhythm and blues and remains a jazz musician of sorts. Others of his followers made the leap, forming the first line of r & b instrumentalists.

....

IF ILLINOIS JACQUET CAME ACROSS on stage as wild, Big Jay McNeely's antics qualified him as certifiable. Born Cecil James McNeely on April 29, 1927, in Watts, Los Angeles, McNeely's father was a porter on a floating casino who played the piano. The young man took up the tenor sax after his older brother Bob left the instrument behind when he entered the Army. Herman Lubinsky of Savoy Records, who released McNeely's signature tune and biggest seller, "Deacon's Hop," in 1949, gave him his stage name, although Big Jay has mused that "I wasn't really big at all!"

But everything else about him was big—from the way he blew to the outrageous stage act he developed while touring with his trio in the late forties. His favorite ploy was to march off the stage, out into the audience, through the front door and into the street, playing his sax all the while and exchanging honks with passing motorists. Once in San Diego he was arrested for disturbing the peace. Brother Bob, a member of the combo, bailed him out of jail, at which point Big Jay returned to the club and rejoined the group on stage.

Of the fifties honkers, none was as irrepressible as Big Jay McNeely, seen here in a characteristically buoyant mood. While some headliners wouldn't dare share a stage with him, Little Richard told the saxophonist, "You're the only cat who can warm 'em up for something like me." (Photo courtesy of Showtime Archives, Toronto)

When other tenor saxmen began copying his act, McNeely found a new gimmick. After seeing a stripper in an after-hours club wearing fluorescent panties that glowed when the lights went out, McNeely painted his sax similarly so it would glow in the dark while he played. Big Jay's act became such an attention-grabber that many headliners, including Nat King Cole, refused to tour with him.

But it was the music that lay at the center of his riveting performance. The titles of his tunes, nearly all of them self-composed and recorded on a handful of small, pioneering r & b labels, make clear the frenetic nature of his music—"Blow Big Jay," "Ice Water," "Cherry Smash," "Wild Wig," "Man Eater," "Just Crazy," "Deac's Blowout," "Psycho Serenade." The madness reached a fine peak in the "Jaysfrantic" and "Real Crazy Cool" disk, which was recorded for Aladdin in 1950 and was actually one performance divided into two cuts. The exhilarating opening of "Jaysfrantic" is thirty seconds of searing, unmitigated honking that is exhausting just to listen to. From the low bass notes struck in the chorus of this number, McNeely reaches for the stratosphere in "Real Crazy Cool," his horn shrieking like a madwoman.

Ironically, his sole pop hit was the soulful 1959 ballad "There Is Something on Your Mind" (#44), sung by Little Sonny Warner. Written by Rocky Wilson of the Rivingtons, a group that figures large in the history of the rock instrumental (see Chapter 3), it gave McNeely little room to cut loose and became a bigger hit the following year for Bobby Marchan.

By the early sixties the "Deacon of the Tenor Sax" had stopped recording. He got a steady job with the postal system in 1971 and limited his sanctifying to the Jehovah's Witnesses, which he joined. But once a honker, always a honker. Big Jay returned to the club scene in the early eighties and is blowing still.

....

THE ALTO SAX OF EARL BOSTIC may seem almost sedate after Big Jay's horn, but his more sophisticated style was tremendously influential in the formative years of rhythm and blues. His signature hit, "Flamingo," and its swinging follow-up, "Sleep," helped cement the saxophone's importance as the premier instrument in both r & b and rock 'n' roll.

Bostic was born in Tulsa, Oklahoma, in 1920 and worked as an elementary school teacher before turning full time to music. After grounding himself in harmony and composition at Xavier University in New Orleans, he worked as an arranger for Lionel Hampton and later took up the alto sax, developing his own free and improvisational style. Bostic signed with New York's pioneering r & b King label in the early fifties. His ravishing "Flamingo" went to #1 on the r & b charts in early 1951 and stayed there for an amazing twenty weeks. Although he could honk with the best of them on such hits as "8:45 Stomp," Bostic's tastes were more commercial than McNeely's and he turned to re-energizing old standards from "Blue Moon" to "Blue Skies," lending them a rich, erotic tone that Arnold Shaw has described as "full of sand and sex." Earl Bostic died on October 28, 1965, at age 45.

Although he was the most commercially successful of the honkers, Bostic's appeal through the fifties remained largely limited to black record buyers. Like the other pioneering r & b saxmen, his career peaked too early to have much impact on the pop charts. "The saxophone was a little too black for most white kids," Big Jay McNeely has said. That situation would change radically with the rise of rock 'n' roll in 1956.

SLOW SAX

Among Earl Bostic's labelmates at King was a 40-year-old jazz organist, pianist and arranger, Bill Doggett. Doggett, who hailed from Philadelphia, had played with nearly every big name in jazz and jump from Louis Jordan to Louis Armstrong. He formed his own band in 1938 but found the strain too much and sold it to Lucky Millinder, claimed Doggett, "for the price of a coke."

Another Hampton alumnus, Doggett became the band leader's chief arranger after relocating to Los Angeles in 1947. He formed his own small combo in 1952 and the same year signed with King. The Doggett Combo played small venues,

"Honky Tonk" by Bill Doggett was the first hit rock instrumental and remained in the Top 40 for a total of twnty-two weeks in 1956. Doggett's organ was relegated to the rhythm section of his combo, but shone in the spotlight on such subsequent hits as the jazzy "Soft."

mostly rough, rowdy road houses where the group was free to improvise.

While Illinois Jacquet was "flying home," Doggett and other jazz veterans playing this new dance music walked the beat home. In 1955, Doggett and his combo (Billy Butler on bass guitar, Shep Shepperd on drums and Cliff Scott on tenor sax) wrote a twelve-bar bluesy boogie called "Honky Tonk" which featured a handclapping shuffle and a down-and-dirty sax solo by Scott, who adapted some of the flourishes of the honkers of the early fifties but kept more in step with the beat. Doggett's electric organ blended in with the guitar and drums to form the "bottom" of the heavy beat.

The success of "Honky Tonk" in the summer of 1956 was truly phenomenal. It rose to #2 on the pop charts and remained a fixture in the Top 40 for twenty-two weeks. On the r & b charts it went to #1. By 1979 it is reported to have sold three million copies. This granddaddy of rock instrumentals is distinguished for two more reasons. First, the spontaneous shouts of the musicians in the background give it the raw feel of a live performance, as if it were recorded in a real honky tonk and not a recording studio. Second, the one performance is broken into two parts, one on each side of the disk. Unlike Big Jay McNeely's two-parter, it was not given two titles but one—one of the first times this was done on a rock record. The device is well suited to instrumentals and gives the musicians a chance to expand and improvise on a melody or riff. It also provides them with two chances to score a hit. If part 1 doesn't catch a disk jockey's fancy, maybe part 2 will. Interestingly, in most two-part hit instrumentals ("Honky Tonk," "Topsy" and "You Can't Sit Down" are good examples), the second part was the hit side, as if the first part were just a warm-up for the main event. A few artists, Cozy Cole among them, managed to chart with both sides.

Although "Honky Tonk" would remain Doggett's signature tune, his later singles showed a surprising versatility and highlight his skill as an arranger. In the delightfully sparkling "Soft" (#35), a 1952 hit for King artist Tiny Bradshaw, he added flutes to the ensemble and came out from behind the big sax to show his dexterity at the keyboard. The cool jazz sound of "Soft" was in sharp contrast to the big band rhythms of "Blip Blop" (#82) or the more contemporary stinging guitar sound of "Hold It" (#92).

In 1959 the old master of rhythm and blues instros was "bottomed out" by an upstart white group from Memphis, Bill Black and his Combo. Doggett good humoredly referred to Black as his "heir" and showed how seriously he took him by releasing his own version of Black's first big hit "Smokie (Part 2)" in 1960. The same year he left King for Warner Brothers, where he had his last charting single, a slightly more contemporary version of "Honky Tonk" . . . Part 2, of course (#57).

A stalwart performer who toured and played his archetypal rhythm and blues for more than four decades, Bill Doggett died on November 13, 1996, at age 80.

··

"HONKY TONK" UNLEASHED A FLURRY of sax instrumentals with a slow beat. The first and biggest was "Slow Walk" (#17) by tenor saxman Sil Austin, which hit the charts in November 1956. Thirteen years younger than Doggett, Austin, born Sylvester, hailed from Donella, Florida, and moved to New York at age 17, where he played at Harlem's Apollo Theater talent show. He won performing "Danny Boy," which would later become a hit single for him in a lushly orchestrated arrangement. A two-week engagement at the Apollo stretched to six months and led Austin to find steady work with jazz bands through the mid-fifties. Ella Fitzgerald, whom he worked with, gave him the nickname "Sil."

In 1955 Austin formed his own combo and recorded a number of obscure sides for Jubilee Records. A year and a half later, he switched to Mercury and almost immediately scored with "Slow Walk," which sounds suspiciously like "Son of Honky Tonk" (or vice versa) right down to the sax solos. Austin's composition featured a heavier beat accented by louder handclapping and a wonderful tinkly piano played by George Stubbs. His guitarist was Mickey "Guitar" Baker, who later palled up with Sylvia Vanderpool to form one of rock's first singing male-female duos.

When Bill Doggett covered "Slow Walk" less than a month after Austin's record hit the charts, Norbay Music, the song's publisher, filed suit against King Records for failing to pay royalties on the tune. King argued that Norbay had failed to file a "Notice of Use," required by the copyright law. The judge decided in King's favor, stating that Norbay failed to comply with the law. It was a landmark case in the music industry.

....

WHILE DOGGETT AND AUSTIN AMBLED, Lee Allen strolled along at a brisker pace in "Walkin' with Mr. Lee" (#54). Allen started out playing tenor sax in the pioneering rhythm and blues band of Paul Gayten. By 1956 he was playing behind Fats Domino in Dave Bartholomew's classic Crescent City band and went on to play powerhouse sax on hit sides by Little Richard, Shirley and Lee and Sam Cooke among others.

Allen's 1958 entry in the slow-sax wars benefited from some national exposure on Dick Clark's *American Bandstand*, not that it needed it. "Walkin' with Mr. Lee" remains an eminent example of classic New Orleans rocking rhythm and blues that has lost none of its infectious charm. The pace is nimbly set by a great

Few fifties' instrumentals have retained their appeal as well as "Walkin' with Mr. Lee." One of the top tenor saxmen of New Orleans, Lee Allen can be heard to good effect on many hits by Fats Domino, Little Richard and Sam Cooke. (Photo courtesy of Showtime Archives, Toronto)

thumping drum beat and Allen's sax, which stays out in front all the way home. After a decade of playing on some of the most exciting rhythm and blues singles ever, Allen hung up his horn in the early sixties, only to be tempted out of retirement in 1982 to tour with the Blasters.

BIG BAND MEETS BIG BEAT

It must have been a strange moment for Tommy and Jimmy Dorsey as they watched a 21-year-old Elvis Presley sing "Heartbreak Hotel" on their musical variety television show the evening of January 28, 1956. It would be another seven months before Presley's first appearance on *The Ed Sullivan Show*, but he was already literally shaking up the musical establishment. The Dorsey Brothers probably didn't think much of rock 'n' roll, but they knew a star when they saw one. Presley was brought back on the program five times over the next two months.

The Dorseys may have had good reason to believe their kind of big band music had gone the way of the dinosaurs that year. But in fact, rock breathed, however briefly, new life into the big bands, creating a curious hybrid instrumental in the process. The Dorsey Brothers were, at the time, already enjoying a revival of their music. Having split up back in 1935 over personal differences, they reunited their two bands in 1953 and the following year got their own television show on CBS, *Stage Show*, originally a summer replacement for Jackie Gleason, who was himself an orchestra leader and a leading fifties' purveyor of mood-drenched music.

Around this time, Jimmy Dorsey signed with the small Cincinnati-based Fraternity label, owned by Harry Carlson, who ran a portrait photography studio and had a soft spot for big band music. In November 1956, Dorsey's band recorded "So Rare," which had been a big hit for Guy Lombardo two decades earlier. Featuring a lyrical alto sax solo by Dorsey, the only concession the single made to contemporary tastes was a large mixed chorus that sang the lyrics.

Fraternity released the single in January 1957, the year that rock 'n' roll would reach the peak of popularity. "To our great disappointment, we could not get the song accepted anywhere," recalled Carlson a few years later. "Our hopes had been so high, for we were sure all we needed was the record and success would be instantaneous. . . ." Carlson called in favors owed him by every disk jockey in Cincinnati to get airplay for a couple of weeks "and if it did not go over I would never ask another favor of them."

It went over. Big. The adult crowd, yearning for the "good old days," made this delicious slice of nostalgia a million seller, Dorsey's fifth. Unfortunately, he didn't live long to enjoy his new-found success. With his record peaking at #2 on the *Billboard* charts, Jimmy Dorsey died of cancer at age 53. Five days later, his orchestra was back in the studio recording the follow-up hit, "June Night" (#21). The prevalent beat of rock 'n' roll seeped into the orchestra's style with a

Relics of the big band era, Tommy (upper left) and Jimmy Dorsey returned to the pop charts with a vengeance in the midst of the rock revolution. Unfortunately, Jimmy died as his last hit was peaking and Tommy passed away nearly two years before his orchestra took "Tea for Two Cha Cha" into the Top 40. (Archive Photos/American Stock)

third single, "Jay-Dee's Boogie Woogie," which went to #77 late the same year.

Meanwhile, Tommy Dorsey's Orchestra followed up on Jimmy's success with its own revamp of a standard. Actually, Tommy had predeceased his brother in November 1956, choking to death during a meal at his Greenwich, Connecticut, home. But the orchestra continued under the baton of Warren Covington, who in the summer of 1958 dished up a crazy Latin rendition of Vincent Youmans's "Tea for Two." "Tea for Two Cha Cha" (#7) was a clever novelty with a choppy cha cha rhythm, heavy on the percussion and cow bell. Lightning didn't strike twice, however, when the band released "I Want To Be Happy Cha Cha." One cha cha big band instrumental was enough.

....

WHILE THE DORSEY BANDS FLIRTED with the new music, their contemporaries Ralph Marterie and Ernie Fields jumped in with both feet. Marterie, who was a native of Naples, Italy, grew up in Chicago, where his father played with the Civic Opera Orchestra. In the forties, Marterie played trumpet in a number of big bands and was later dubbed "The Caruso of the Trumpet." When he formed his own band in the late forties and signed with Mercury Records, he proved to be one of the most eclectic of orchestra leaders. His hits included big band exotica ("Caravan," "Skish-Kebab"), South African folk music ("Skokiaan"), Woody Guthrie's "So Long (It's Been Good to Know Ya)," and even a cover of Bill Haley's "Crazy Man, Crazy" in 1953 that went to #13. In 1957 Marterie gave the big beat another shot with the rocker "Tricky" (#25) with its slippery horn riff and boogie woogie piano.

Originally a revamp pianist for Glen Miller, Ernie Fields had played the big band circuit, then settled in Los Angeles in the mid-fifties to become an arranger for pop and rock artists. In late 1959, with the rock instrumental firmly established as a genre, Fields recorded a rock version of the classic Glen Miller tune, "In the Mood." The band included the cream of L.A. rock session musicians— Plas Johnson on tenor sax, Rene Hall on guitar and the indomitable Earl Palmer on drums.

Fields played the big band standard at a surprisingly slower tempo than the original. It didn't swing, but it sure rocked. Johnson's sax set a punchy, strutting riff that was rhythmically mated with Hall's electric bass, some strong supportive brass and Palmer's riveting drumwork that got a great thumping coda off at the end of each chorus. It may be the finest melding of two musical genres that, in some ways, weren't all that apart in spirit and energy.

With his instrumental peaking at #4, Fields was on a roll. He followed "In the Mood" with rocking versions of "Chattanooga Choo-Choo," "Twelve Street Rag," "Castle Rock" and even "The Charleston." None of these did all that well, but in 1959, a year where the raw energy of rock seemed to be seriously flagging with the rise of the teen idols, many vocal as well as instrumental artists were turning to older music for new hits.

PERHAPS THE MOST UNINSPIRED of the retro-instros was "Mexican Hat Rock" (#16) by the Applejacks, a studio band named after their leader Dave Appell, a Philadelphia arranger and producer at Cameo Parkway Records. The word "rock" in the title is used loosely: the group sounds about as hip as a local band at an ethnic wedding, which is where this tune has become a mainstay for nigh forty years. Appell based his little dance march on a Mexican folk dance and even had the chutzpah to throw in choruses from "O, Dem Golden Slippers" and "Mary's Little Lamb" in the breaks. Appell, by the way, was the producer of Chubby Checker's "The Twist," which inevitably led the Applejacks to release "Mexican Hat Twist."

WHILE THE SOURCE MATERIAL for these instrumentals were certainly eclectic, none was as strange as Cozy Cole's blockbuster "Topsy, Part 2" (also known as "Topsy II"). Another big band alumnus, drummer Cole played with Cab Calloway, Benny Goodman and Artie Shaw. When he formed his own group, he stuck with the big band sound he had played for years. "Topsy" was adapted from a 1939 production of *Uncle Tom's Cabin*, hence the title, and sounds like a hip version of Benny Goodman's "Sing, Sing, Sing," with Cole's drum set piece standing in for Gene Krupa's classic solo.

The exuberant single featured an electric organ playing the slinky main

Jazz drummer Cozy Cole burst onto the pop charts in the summer of 1958 with the big band-influenced "Topsy II." Although his chart career lasted less than six months, he had a profound influence on the pioneer rock 'n' roll drummer Sandy Nelson, who patterned his "Teen Beat" in part on Cole's tasty drum solos. (Archive Photos/Metronome Collection)

theme and Cole's kinetic drumming that, despite the big band trappings, surely appealed to the teen market. It all helped to make "Topsy, Part 2" one big band instrumental with something for everyone. After scoring twice more with "Topsy Part 1" and "Turvy II" in the Top 40, Cozy disappeared from sight, eventually playing drums with jazz ensembles like Jonah Jones in the seventies. He died of cancer in January 1981.

Despite his short chart career, Cozy Cole's thundering drums had a profound influence on many a budding rock drummer, including a young Sandy Nelson, who would model his own breakthrough hit on Cole's dynamic style.

After laying the groundwork for the rock instrumental, the big band veterans of the forties and the rhythm and blues wild men of the early fifties would see a new generation of musicians, many of them white, take up the drumsticks and sax.

ONE INTOXICATING INSTRO

Gene Autry, one of the richest men in America by the fifties, dabbled in a number of media after his initial success in films as America's foremost "singing cowboy." Having sold millions of records with hits like "Rudolph the Red-Nose Reindeer," a song his wife had to convince him to record, Autry started his own recording label, Challenge, in Southern California in 1957.

Challenge's Artists & Repertoire (A & R) director and one of its first recording artists was guitarist Dave Burgess. In late 1957, Burgess went into the studio to record his fifth single for the label, an instrumental with the unfortunate title "Train to Nowhere." Among the experienced musicians on the session was saxophonist Danny Flores, who had written a catchy Latin number while on a recent trip to Tijuana. Burgess liked the tune and decided to record it on the spot as the single's B side. They knocked off the number in short order and left before even hearing it in playback. Before the single could be released, the group needed a name. They settled on the Champs, in honor of their boss's horse Champion and, at Autry's insistence, songwriter Flores changed his name to Chuck Rio, because it sounded less Mexican.

Deejays across the country, unimpressed with "Train to Nowhere," started playing the flip side, "Tequila." By March 1958, the sax-driven instrumental was starting to percolate up the charts, helped along by a quickie cover by Cleveland saxophonist Eddie Platt. Platt's version made it to #20 on the charts, but it was a pale imitation of the juicy original and it disappeared after only a month in the Top 40. The Champs' "Tequila" went all the way to #1—the first rock instrumental to reach the top of the charts. It remained there for five weeks.

That "Tequila" was originally a B-side throwaway is remarkable. Everything about it has the sound and feel of a carefully crafted rock classic. It opens simply with strumming acoustical guitars and hand claps, joined a few bars later by drums and tapping cymbals. Then Rio's seductive sax makes its grand

*The Champs were the first popular white rock instrumental group. After their classic
"Tequila," their line-up was constantly changing and at one time Jimmy Seals, Dash Crofts
(Seals and Crofts) and Glen Campbell were all band members. (Photo courtesy of Showtime
Archives, Toronto)*

entrance, blowing out the tantalizing, Latin-tinged melody. The release is a
jazzy throwback to swing, breaking the Latin mood momentarily. After the second chorus, Rio opens up with some startling improvising, shifting into a cool
jazz mode. After another release, the party goers drift off one by one—first the
sax, then the lead guitar, the percussion, until we're left with that lone strum-
mer and those clapping hands. And you have as perfect and inevitable a rock
instrumental as has ever been put on wax. "Honky Tonk" and its down-and-

dirty imitators were great r & b, but this was real rock 'n' roll, played not by seasoned black musicians, but a bunch of West Coast white boys.

An added fillip that helped the number to the top was Burgess's clever idea of having Rio growl the song's title in a deep, mean-hombre voice twice during the musical breaks. At the end, the entire band joined in, giving "Tequila" a great finale. Spoken intros would become standard for many rock instrumentals, from Cozy Cole's "Topsy" later the same year through the Surfaris' "Wipe Out."

The power of "Tequila" on the public consciousness was intoxicating. Worries about parental boycotts over an alcoholic drink in the title proved groundless. In fact, tequila sales went up nearly 100% thanks to the record. The Champs' triumph was complete when "Tequila" was named, ironically, the best r & b performance at the first Grammy Awards in May 1959. (It was #1 on the r & b charts for four weeks.)

By then the group had an almost completely new line-up. Guitarist Buddy Bruce and bass player Chris Hils left quickly and were replaced by Dave Norris and Joe Burnas, who in turn was replaced by Van Norman. The talented Chuck Rio left after the group's second hit for a solo career that went nowhere, as did drummer Gene Alden. They were replaced by Jimmy Seals and Dash Crofts, who would go on to make very different music in the mellower seventies as the singing duo, Seals and Crofts. Another budding star who would pass through the Champs briefly in 1960 was guitarist Glen Campbell. Despite all the changes in personnel, Dave Burgess would remain in creative control of the group for its eight-year life span.

"El Rancho Rock" (#30), the much anticipated follow-up to "Tequila," was an energetic revamping of the 1934 Mexican song, "El Grande Rancho." Burgess's guitar and Alden's drums provide a pulsating background that Rio's easy sax floats above. Burgess adds some neat Chuck Berry-like licks in the bridge, while Rio's jazzy improv at the fade-out is even wilder than his work in "Tequila" and makes one wish he had stuck around longer. The flip side, "Midnighter" (#94), was a solid, hard-driving rocker without the salsa that should have been one of the group's biggest hits. It remains a favorite with instrumental aficionados.

The Champs' third hit single, "Chariot Rock" (#59), was a rather coy rock version of the Negro spiritual "Swing Low, Sweet Chariot," sparking a subgenre that would bring fame and fortune to Johnny and the Hurricanes a year later. The number ends with a totally gratuitous reprise of "Tequila."

Unfortunately, the Champs rarely strayed far from the shadow of their monster hit and their brand of "South of the Border" rock quickly wore thin. There are charms in the syncopated "Caramba!" (1959) and "Jumping Bean" (1961), a B side without the signature sax but with great Fireballs-style guitar work from the underrated Dave Burgess. But far more successful was 1960's "Too Much Tequila" (#30), an uninspired novelty with lots of drunken hiccups. The

Mexican stereotypes became more distasteful in such numbers as "Sombrero," where a Mexican hombre discovers by the song's end that his missing sombrero is on his head.

When the Champs did break from the formula, as in another intriguing B side, "Beatnik" (1959), the results were great progressive rock. With its slinky sax riff and haunting plunky guitar line, "Beatnik" shows that the Champs were far from a one-hit wonder.

The group's last Top 40 hit in 1962 was the unremarkable "Limbo Rock" (#40), based on the latest dance-craze-of-the-week. It was basically the instrumental track of the Chubby Checker vocal version that went to #2.

Burgess stuck with his ever-changing lineup until 1965, when he finally called it quits. He made one comeback using all new members of the group in the mid-seventies with—what else?—"Tequila '76," the Bicentennial version, which was followed the next year by "Tequila '77." But by now the bottle was empty.

The Champs were the first, and one of the most successful, white rock instrumental groups of the fifties. Despite the musical rut they found themselves in, they were a class act. The irresistable sound of "Tequila" would have a profound influence on rock's newest and brightest genre.

YOU GOTTA HAVE A GIMMICK

The Champs opened the floodgates for sax-driven white instrumental groups, and those groups poured out onto the airwaves in 1958 and 1959. "Cerveza" (#23) by Boots Brown and his Blockbusters sounded like a slick cousin of "Tequila," from its opening strumming guitar to the syncopated, rhythmic sax. The riff was trickier and more ingenuous than "Tequila" and proved a tour de force for West Coast jazz trumpeter Milton "Shorty" Rogers, who was moonlighting as Boots Brown. This fine instrumental deserves to be better known.

The Gone All Stars' "7-11" charted the same day as "Tequila"; like so many of these groups, the band was made up of session musicians. Under the direction of Buddy Lucas, its members were brought together by Gone Records' head George Goldner; hence the name. The tune features a strong bass guitar riff and an insistent, rough-hewn sax line.

....

FAR LESS THREATENING was "Ruby Duby Du" (#30) by Illinois guitarist Tobin Matthews and Co., with its straightforward, child-like melody line and strong supporting sax. Interestingly, the song appeared in the teen crime film *Key Witness* (1960) where it accompanied a vicious switchblade killing.

Matthews speaks the title at the record's start, while a bass voice intones the title of 1958's "Got a Match?" (#39) by the Daddy-O's twice during this perky little piano and guitar instrumental. He finally gives up at the end with a "Never mind." More bizarre was "Nu Nee Nu Na Na Na Na Na Nu Nu" by Dicky

Dickey Doo and the Don'ts started out as a vocal group, but their zany "Nee Nee Na Na Na Na Nu Nu" was among the plethora of novelty instrumentals that flooded the airwaves in the late fifties.

Doo and the Don'ts. The group was formed in Brooklyn by Gerry Granahan, who had his own vocal hit the same year with the rock novelty "No Chemise— Please." Granahan named the group after Dick Clark's son, Dicky Doo, probably a wise career move. Its first hit was the vocal "Click Clack," dreamed up by Granahan and vocalist Jerry Grant while on a train ride in Brooklyn.

The group's instrumental follow-up, which reached #40 for one week in the spring of 1958, was an easy, swinging sax rocker with the nonsense title spoken during the musical breaks in a high-pitched voice that sounded like a little man from outer space. Not a bad ploy in the year of the Purple People Eater, the Witch Doctor and the Chipmunks.

THE FINE LINE BETWEEN novelty records and instrumentals was further blurred by the fact that three of the year's biggest novelties were quasi-instrumentals with sung or spoken interludes. "Short Shorts" (#3) by the Royal Teens featured a good wailing sax that squeaked every time the male chorus sang "Who wears short shorts?" "Dinner with Drac" (#6), a most unappetizing recitation by late-night TV horror host John Zacherle, featured a bluesy guitar riff and gutsy sax breaks that punctuated Zacherle's gruesome punchlines. Most intriguing of all was "The Blob" (#33), the unlikely theme from the sci-fi movie of the same name, and written by a then-unknown Burt Bacharach. Performed by the Five Blobs (another studio band) with vocals credited to one "Bernie Nee," the instrumental interludes had a snappy, syncopated, sax riff that owed more to "Tequila" than to any ectoplasmic monster.

OTHER INSTRUMENTAL ARTISTS relied on weird sound effects to grab the jaded ears of disk jockeys and their audiences. A good example was "The Rockin' Crickets" (#57) by the Hot Toddies (aka Big John Little and the Rockers), who turned their electric guitars into rather creepy chirping insects under an otherwise not very exciting sax solo. The single would be resurrected by producer/deejay Tom Shannon four years later and attributed to the Rockin' Rebels (see Chapter 4.)

A more ingenious insect instro was "The Green Mosquito" (#42) by the Tune Rockers, a group about which virtually nothing is known. Each time the pesky mosquito, brought to life by a twitchy guitar, interrupts the bluesy chorus, the drummer tries to bash it. Finally, at the number's finale, the drummer hits his target and the poor bloodsucker expires.

Other groups combined human voices with animal sounds. A good, if obscure, example is "Wolf Call" by Lord Dent and His Invaders which combines a menacing counterpoint of tenor and bass sax with wolf cries, an eerie girl chorus (the company president's daughter and a friend) singing the title and, to make sure nobody missed the point, a couple of high-pitched wolf whistles. All that effort and the record didn't even chart!

MOST OF THESE SAX-LED teen groups came and went quickly, but two of them had considerably more in them than one hit and with better handling might have had far more fruitful careers.

The Royaltones hailed from Dearborn, Michigan, and started out playing in Detroit clubs and for local dances. The group's kinetic act, which featured not one, but two saxophones, attracted the attention of an executive from Jubilee records, who promptly signed them. "Poor Boy," their first release and a Top 20 hit, is a rollicking merry-go-round of a rocker with an infectious syncopated beat that stops and starts with all the boisterous humor of a drunken elephant. A wonderfully twitchy guitar plucks out the main melody and is joined by the powerhouse saxs. In the tune's most memorable chorus, the tenor sax breaks into raucous laughter that sounds almost human.

The Wailers, one of the first rock instrumental groups from the Northwest to hit the charts in the fifties, evolved into one of the region's best garage bands of the sixties. They recorded "Louie, Louie" in 1961 on Liberty, only to have the Kingsmen lift their arrangement a year later and turn it into a huge hit. (Buck Ormsby)

While making their own recordings, the Royaltones provided top-notch backing to bigger stars, most prominently another Detroit native, Del Shannon. But their own promising career never took off. They didn't have another charting record until 1961 with the more somber but hard-rocking "Flamingo Express" (#82).

The Royaltones continued to record on the local Goldisc label into the mid-sixties, but without much success. What many connoisseurs consider one of the best rock instrumental groups ever is long overdue for a reassessment in the age of compact disks, particularly since the dozen or so singles the band released were never collected on an album.

The second unjustly neglected group is the Wailers (not to be confused with Bob Marley's reggae band of the seventies). The first of many instrumental groups to come out of the Northwest, the Tacoma, Washington, quintet was discovered by musician Art Mineo, actor Sal's uncle, who introduced the band to the Golden Crest label out of New York.

The Wailers' second release for Golden Crest, recorded at 2 a.m. after a gig at a Knights of Columbus Hall, was "Tall Cool One" (#36), whose carefully crafted opening is one of the most memorable of any rock instrumental. The bass guitar plays some sparse chords backed by tapping cymbals. Then a jangly piano joins the jazzy ensemble, playing an Oriental-sounding riff. Finally a wailing tenor sax enters, raising the temperature considerably.

The Wailers followed one of the finest rock instrumentals of the fifties with one of the strangest—"Mau-Mau" (#68), whose hypnotic, minor mid-Eastern rhythm propels an equally strange sax solo, more woodwind than brass. Unfortunately the title, which conjured up marauding African cultists, proved too controversial, even for the liberal-minded Alan Freed, who refused to play it on his program.

The group left Golden Crest soon after the release of its first album, the strikingly original *Wail*, and founded its own label, Etiquette, in 1961. It now became one of the first garage bands in the Northwest, recording "Louie, Louie" for Liberty. Two years later the Kingsmen had a monster hit with the song using the Wailers' arrangement. When Golden Crest reissued "Tall Cool One" in 1964, it became a Top 40 hit all over again—a rare phenomenon for any single, vocal or instrumental. The Wailers, with new members, signed with Imperial, but the instrumental wave was receding by then and the group never regained its momentum. The band returned to producing its own recordings, now mostly vocals, but unlike the Kingsmen and Paul Revere and the Raiders, they remained a regional phenomenon, albeit a popular one, into the late sixties. Three of the band's original members re-formed in the nineties and put out an excellent CD collection of their vintage material, *The Boys from Tacoma*.

....

THE WAILING SAX WAS INDEED king of the fifties' rock instrumental. It would, however, be challenged and eventually superceded by a supporting instrument, played by a young man who would become rock 'n' roll's first and most successful superstar—all in that landmark year of 1958.

Chapter Three

Twangy Guitars

*. . . [that's] the raunchiest damn thing you've
ever done. You'll miss a hit if you don't release it.*
Session player to BILL JUSTIS

*I wanted to get out of that high range, and on the
few sessions I'd done, fooling around in the studio
I knew that the low strings recorded better. . . .*
DUANE EDDY

I've always looked for the sounds.
LINK WRAY

It was a little Southern tune that Bill Justis just couldn't get out of his head. The 31-year-old studio musician at Sun Records in Memphis recalled the tune, which he titled "Backwoods," from his childhood in Birmingham, Alabama. Thinking it might make a good instrumental, he wrote it down with the help of guitarist Sid Manker, who also worked at Sun, and played it for their boss, Sam Phillips.

Phillips, the man who had launched the careers of Elvis Presley, Carl Perkins, Johnny Cash, Roy Orbison and his latest discovery, Jerry Lee Lewis, was not known for producing instrumentals. But he was taken with Justis's little riff, and agreed to release it on his new Phillips International label, which he reserved for so-called "sophisticated talent."

There was nothing very sophisticated about "Backwoods," retitled "Raunchy"—teenage slang for dirty or messy—which came out in November 1957. It consisted of Manker playing the short guitar riff over and over, alternating with Justis on tenor sax leading the Sun house band. Although Justis played a mean sax, the only remarkable thing about the recording was the riff and the unorthodox way Manker played it. Rather than play in the high to middle string range, as most rock and country guitarists would, Manker used the bass strings, further exaggerated in the studio by echo. It gave the riff a sound that was deep, resonant and a little creepy. Thrust stage center, the riff took on a life of its own. Although repetitive in the extreme, it didn't bore, but was strangely hypnotic. It grew on you.

"Raunchy" shot up the *Billboard* charts, just missing becoming #1 and spending fourteen weeks in the Top 40. It was covered by band leader Billy Vaughn and West Coast producer-arranger Ernie Freeman, who both had Top 10 hits with their versions. The record became a classic, one of the first true rock instrumentals, but Bill Justis enjoyed only one other charting record, "College Man" (#42), before returning to relative obscurity at Sun Records, where he was soon promoted to musical director.

Justis eventually left Sun after a spat with Phillips and for a brief time produced for his own label, Play Me Records. He moved to Nashville in 1961 and became a successful arranger and producer for everyone from Ronnie Dove to the Dixiebelles. Neither he nor Sid Manker, who remained a session man at Sun, capitalized on the uniquely original guitar sound they had created. That job would fall to an enterprising deejay and part-time record producer in far-off Phoenix, Arizona, and his 19-year-old protégé.

Looking decidedly "un-raunchy" in this publicity shot, Bill Justis had created the sound of the twangy guitar in his classic "Raunchy" in 1957. One of his last assignments before dying of cancer in 1982 was arranging and scoring the two Smokey and the Bandit films. (Photo courtesy of Showtime Archives, Toronto)

THE INSTRUMENTAL GETS ITS ELVIS

The electric guitar had been a vital ingredient in the development of rock 'n' roll, as it had been for its progenitors—black rhythm and blues and white country music. But the guitar wasn't seen as a solo instrument in mainstream rock the way the saxophone was until "Raunchy" opened up new and tantalizing possibilities.

The guitarist who would first realize those possibilities was born in Corning, New York, on April 26, 1938. Duane Eddy was given his first guitar when he was age 5 by his father, a grocery store manager and amateur musician. Young Duane came under the spell of the country and western music he listened to on the local radio and those singing, guitar-toting

Duane Eddy was a perfect guitar hero for the fifties— shy, good-looking and vaguely rebellious. His much-imitated twangy guitar sound was largely the studio creation of his producer Lee Hazlewood.

cowboys, Gene Autry and Roy Rogers, whom he watched during innumerable Saturday matinees.

Duane made his public debut as a performer at age 10, playing the "Missouri Waltz" on a lap steel guitar at a local radio station. When he was 13, his family moved to Tucson, Arizona, then to Coolidge, a small city nearly halfway between Phoenix and Tucson. An indifferent student, Duane dropped out of Coolidge High at 15 and started playing guitar with country and western bands in clubs around Phoenix. He teamed up with another aspiring guitarist, Jimmy Delbridge, professionally known as Jimmy Dell, and the two formed a duo. One day, disk jockey Lee Hazlewood heard them on a tape and put them on an amateur show he produced at Phoenix's Madison Square Garden.

Hazlewood was also a record producer with one hit under his belt, his own composition "The Fool," recorded by rockabilly singer Sanford Clark, that reached #7 on the *Billboard* charts in 1956. He had been working with local guitarist Al Casey, who had provided the gritty guitar riff on "The Fool." Hazlewood amplified the sound of Casey's guitar with echo in the studio, creating an arresting new sound.

In his early forties, Casey was a seasoned rock musician who had come out of jazz. He began his career playing in Fats Waller's sextet, the Rhythm, and in 1943 went solo, winning honors as top session man in *Esquire*'s jazz poll in 1945-46. He was a first-rate musician, but what Hazlewood needed was a young, good-looking musician who would appeal to the young rock 'n' roll audience. Handsome six-footer Duane Eddy fit the bill.

Hazlewood got Eddy and Jimmy Dell some local television appearances and produced a demo of them singing and playing two songs he had written that went nowhere. As Eddy told rock critic Dan Forte years later, "I figure one of my bigger contributions to the music business was not singing."

Remembering the success of "Raunchy," Hazlewood suggested Eddy try playing his Gretsch 6120 on the bass strings for a different sound on their next demo, an instrumental penned by Eddy with some help from Hazlewood. The two also decided to feature a saxophone, as Justis had done, for a more rock 'n' roll sound. The sax would complement the deep, bassy sound of the guitar. Unable to find a good rock saxman in Phoenix, Hazlewood got hold of Plas Johnson on the West Coast, took the master of the demo, "Moovin' 'N' Groovin'," to Los Angeles and overdubbed Johnson's playing on the tape. Overdubbing was still a little-used technique in 1957, but Hazlewood would soon prove to be a master of it.

"Moovin' 'N' Groovin'" is a pleasant enough guitar instrumental, in which Eddy's rambling guitar melody is overshadowed by a twirling opening riff by Casey and his wife Corki on backup guitars. It was later lifted note for note by the Beach Boys on their first Top 10 hit, "Surfin' USA."[1]

"Moovin' 'N' Groovin'" was picked up by Jamie, an independent label in Philadelphia. Among the small group of investors who owned Jamie was a man who would perhaps do as much for Duane Eddy's career as Lee Hazlewood—disc jockey Dick Clark. Clark's *American Bandstand* was a proving ground for many new artists who went on to successful careers after their records were played on the Philadelphia-based teen dance show. With its wide exposure on *Bandstand*, "Moovin' 'N' Groovin'" reached #72 on the *Billboard* charts and moved no further. It was encouraging enough to send Hazlewood back to the studio to perfect the distinctive sound from Eddy's guitar, which his business partner, Lester Sill, had christened "twang."

The twangy guitar in "Moovin' 'N' Groovin'" was just not big enough for

---

[1] Duane Eddy isn't the only one who was ripped off on "Surfin' USA." The main melody is a direct steal from Chuck Berry's "Sweet Little Sixteen." Berry sued the Beach Boys and won. When the song was re-released in 1974, Berry was given writing credit.

Hazlewood and for Eddy's next single he decided to create an echo chamber. Together with Floyd Ramsey, who owned the studio where they recorded on North Seventh Street in Phoenix, Hazlewood went shopping for a water tank. "Lee and Floyd Ramsey went to a water tank yard and yelled into tanks until they found one they liked at a price they could pay," engineer Jack Miller explained in a 1993 interview. "It was big—probably 15 feet long and six feet high." The tank was dumped in the studio's parking lot, since it was too big to fit inside. "We put a speaker in one end and a mike in the other and piped the sound through there," Eddy told *Rolling Stone* in 1985. Employees had to periodically go out and chase nesting birds from the tank. To further distort the sound of Eddy's guitar, Hazlewood fitted a basic Bigsby vibrato unit to his Gretsch.

Hazlewood decided to augment the new record even more with background vocals. He hired a black doo-wop group, the Sharps, who had backed Thurston Harris on his big 1957 hit, "Little Bitty Pretty One," humming and moaning one of the longest and most striking openings on any rock single. The Sharps would later emerge from the studio shadows as the Rivingtons with their classic 1962 novelty hit, "Papa-Oom-Mow-Mow." In the meantime, they would provide endless rebel yells, cries, moans, desultory comments, hand claps and foot stomps on nearly every Eddy single for Jamie. One wonders what Eddy's redneck fans in the Deep South of the late fifties would have thought if they knew all those rebel yells came from the throats of four young black men.

The new single, carefully crafted by Hazlewood, was a moody, atmospheric instrumental called "Stalkin'," which featured a sinuous melody line by Eddy backed effectively by the Sharps' moaning chorus, a bluesy sax solo by Gil Bernal, replacing Plas Johnson, and Al Casey, switching from bass guitar to a tinkling piano. Casey, Bernal, Bob Taylor on drums and the other musicians who backed Eddy on his recordings would collectively be known as "the Rebels."

"Stalkin'" got the obligatory *Bandstand* play from Clark, but failed to strike a chord with the studio and TV audience. More downbeat than "Moovin' 'N' Groovin'," it didn't have much of a dance beat, a major sin for the *Bandstand* bobbysoxers. Eddy himself claims he wanted Hazlewood to push the flip side, "Rebel-'Rouser," a more upbeat number, which, legend has it, Clark played only when he ran out of A sides at a record hop. When the kids at the hop asked Clark to keep playing it, he knew he was on to something.

The elements of "Rebel-'Rouser," which went all the way to #6, are so perfectly meshed, that it seems incredible in retrospect that the savvy Hazlewood did not recognize its potential earlier. With its infectious musical hook, studio-enhanced sound and emphasis on novelty, "Rebel-'Rouser" established the twangy guitar sound and made Duane Eddy a major rock artist.

Perhaps the most original and daring idea that Hazlewood struck upon was the premise that less is more. In "Rebel-'Rouser," Eddy plays one simple, unadorned sixteen-bar melody that, like "Raunchy's" riff, is repeated over and over. But unlike "Raunchy," Hazlewood builds on the melody line, each time adding another layer of sound to it. The effect by the end is not one of boring repetition, but of mounting excitement. It was, admittedly, a gimmick, but one that Hazlewood and Eddy, with their overdubbing, sound mixing delay and masterful arrangements, made work like a charm. Here is the way the main theme is repeated in "Rebel-'Rouser":

1. Solo guitar
2. Guitar joined by drums and hand claps
3. Saxophone enters in response to guitar
4. Sax is joined by the Sharps' chorus
5. Sax takes off in improv with rebel yells
6. Guitar solo with chorus (sotto)
7. Sax returns under guitar
8. Fade-out with sax taking off again

Eddy himself was at once the most important and least important factor in this winning equation. Surrounded by wailing sax, rebel yells, hand claps and pounding percussion, he and his twangy guitar remained solid, aloof and a little stiff. As Charlie Gillett observed wryly in his seminal study *The Sound of the City: The Rise of Rock and Roll*, "If Duane Eddy was any kind of guitar virtuoso, he displayed admirable restraint on his records."

But virtuosity was not what Hazlewood and Sill were looking for. The simple riffs of Eddy's records were not only catchy and great listening, but were the kinds of tunes young guitarists could aspire to play themselves. Getting that ultimate "twang" outside the studio would be another matter.

Another critical ingredient in Duane Eddy's success was his image. Young, good-looking, and just the right combination of misunderstood, shy teen and lonely rebel, Eddy was a second-generation Elvis, who strummed instead of sang. Before him, rock instrumentals had been the province of aging jazz musicians like Cozy Cole, balding session men like Bill Justis and faceless groups like the Champs. In Eddy, the rock instrumental found its first teen idol, a guitar hero whose sound was big and macho with a nice Western flavor. It had sex appeal, but was also good clean fun. As Dan Forte perceptively noted, "No longer was the guitarist the goofy guy standing behind the sexy-looking singer [à la Scotty Moore and Elvis]; suddenly, he was the moody frontman with the chiselled cheekbones who . . . all but put singers out of work."

This last part might be a bit of hyperbole, but over the next five years, Duane Eddy placed fifteen singles in the Top 40, six of them in the Top 20 and three in the Top 10, making him the number one rock instrumentalist to date. In 1959, Eddy placed second after Elvis in England's *New Musical Express* reader's poll as the Number One World Musical Personality. The next year he topped the King.

"Ramrod" (#27), the follow-up to "Rebel-'Rouser," had a stronger rocking beat than its predecessor, a little less twang and a lot more layered sound from the Rebels and the Sharps. Eddy's playing gave a glimpse of what he was capable of if he hadn't been restricted by Hazlewood's formula. The single's genesis is a tribute to the resourcefulness of Lee Hazlewood and the hit-making power of Clark's *American Bandstand*. Eddy and the Rebels played the song at Clark's suggestion as filler during a Saturday night *Bandstand* appearance. Monday morning Jamie was flooded with 150,000 orders for the single, an Al Casey original, recorded by Eddy back in 1957. Hazlewood rushed to L.A., where he dubbed in Plas Johnson and the Sharps, and had the finished record in the stores by the end of the week.

"Cannonball" (#15), the next single, was back on more familiar ground with

Duane Eddy and his Rebels make an appearance on American Bandstand. Eddy's label Jamie was partly owned by Dick Clark and the TV host made sure the young guitarist got plenty of exposure on his program. (Archive Photos)

an infectious square dance-type melody and a honking sax this time by Steve Douglas, who would alternate with Plas Johnson and Jim Horn on all Eddy's remaining Jamie hits. Hazlewood added castanets and maracas that responded to Eddy's guitar call.

Eddy and Hazlewood tried their hand at a ballad next, "The Lonely One," sans saxophone, but with tom-toms and lots of "ahhing" from the ever-faithful Sharps. The suggestive title and Eddy's looks were enough to put "The Lonely One" in the Top 40 for eight weeks in early 1959.

Shortly before this, Eddy's first album, one of the first rock LPs in stereo— *Have "Twangy" Guitar Will Travel*—was released. The title was a take-off from *Have Gun, Will Travel*, one of the most popular Westerns on television at the time. Eddy's affinity for the West and Americana was a strong one. He recorded an album of old American songs, had hit singles of "Dixie" and "The Ballad of Paladin" and even recorded his own twangy version of "The Battle Hymn of the Republic."

The "twang" in his first album's title became Eddy's trademark, and he and Hazlewood managed to squeeze it into no less than eleven subsequent albums:

> *The "Twangs" The "Thang"*
> *$1,000,000.00 Worth of Twang* (Vols. 1 and 2)
> *Twistin' 'N' Twangin'*
> *Twangy Guitar, Silky Strings*
> *"Twang" a Country Song*
> *"Twangin'" Up a Storm!*
> *Twangin' the Golden Hits*
> *Twangsville*
> *The Biggest Twang of Them All*
> *The Roaring Twangies*

Eddy's next single, "Yep!" (#30), was one of his most rollicking with an opening riff that sounds like a slowed-down version of "Wipe Out," an influence that Surfari Jim Pash, in an interview with the author, readily admitted. But the best gimmick in the song is Steve Douglas's yakety sax sliding around like a drunken cowboy on a horse, with the Sharps' "yepping" and hooting all over the place. Those rebel yells, so critical in establishing the "Duane Eddy sound," were becoming increasingly extraneous. But Hazlewood clung to them like a talisman.

"Forty Miles of Bad Road" (#9), which came out in mid-1959, was cast in the "Rebel-'Rouser" mode, and the title and leisurely, cruising guitar line suggest a truck or car cruising down a rough road. Eddy claimed, however, that the title was actually inspired by a conversation he and Hazlewood overheard in a movie line where a Texan referred to his buddy's girlfriend as having "a face like forty miles of bad road."

The deceptively titled "Some Kind-A Earthquake" (#37) was a catchy Texan two-step. It demonstrated the guitarist's love for country picking that would result a few years later in his *"Twang" a Country Song* album, one of his best. The single's main claim to fame is its length—1:18 minutes—making it the shortest record to reach the Top 40.

Like Elvis, Eddy had been bitten by the acting bug and in 1960 he played his most ambitious movie role as a high school student in the Dick Clark vehicle, *Because They're Young*. Clark himself played an understanding guidance coun-sellor whom the kids could actually talk to. The best that can be said for the film is that its theme song gave Eddy his biggest hit. Hazlewood finally abandoned both sax and Sharps and pitted Eddy's guitar against a full live orchestra in a Hollywood studio. The result was a pleasing ballad that reached #4. Several critics have ridiculed the melody, comparing it to TV's *Jeopardy* theme song. In truth, "Because They're Young," slight though it might be, is expertly orches-trated, with Eddy's rambling guitar perfectly complemented by a soaring string section. His signature twang undercuts the sentimentality and gives what oth-erwise might have been a dreamy ballad some laconic bite.

It is not surprising that Eddy was reluctant to record the title theme from Craig Stevens' hit TV detective show *Peter Gunn*. The guitarist told Steve Douglas that there was "nothing for me to do in it" except play the driving opening riff that runs through the jazzy Henry Mancini music. In actuality, "Peter Gunn" (#27) gave the guitarist little less to do than he had on most of his hits. As Douglas told Dan Forte, "I always considered Duane's music my music, too, and lot of these songs . . . are saxophone instrumentals." None perhaps more so than "Peter Gunn," which is highlighted by Douglas's blistering solo, while poor Duane is stuck picking that endless riff.

About this time Eddy parted ways with Hazlewood, probably more over a payola scandal at Jamie than artistic differences. He realized his mistake after the rather dismal "Pepe" (#18), another theme song from a bad movie that, by his own admission, lacked the big, distinctive sound of his earlier hits. Ready to expand his horizons, Eddy tried his hand at film scoring next, although his sole effort, *Ring of Fire* (1961), a disaster movie starring David Janssen, consists almost entirely of the tepid title number, not to be confused with the 1963 Johnny Cash hit of the same name.

Discouraged with the way his career was floundering at Jamie, Eddy signed with RCA in 1962 and rejoined forces with Hazlewood. After a couple of false starts, they regained momentum with the rousing "The Ballad of Paladin" (#33), which replaced the supportive saxophone with a whole brass section. For their next outing, Hazlewood shrewdly replaced the Sharps with a girl chorus of "Rebelettes," capitalizing on the girl group sound then at its peak. The Rebelettes were in reality the Blossoms led by Darlene Love, one of the great voices of the early sixties.

For all practical purposes "(Dance With The) Guitar Man" (#12) and its follow-up, "Boss Guitar" (#28), were girl group records with Duane twanging between choruses. I have a special affection for these two singles because they were the first Duane Eddy songs I remember hearing on my tinny little Zenith transistor. "Boss Guitar," which gave Eddy more rocking room than he had on most of his hits, was his last Top 40 single.

Like other rock legends who were losing their bearings in the shifting sands of the sixties, Eddy and Hazlewood tried to regain their momentum by latching onto every new musical trend to come along. But albums like *Surfin' with Duane Eddy*, *Duane A-Go-Go* and *Duane Eddy Does Bob Dylan* did not rejuvenate a fading career.

Although his hits ended in the early sixties, Eddy, like many another early rocker, continued to enjoy unabated popularity in England, where he remained the top instrumental artist in music polls throughout the decade. In 1975 he issued a new album, *Guitar Man*, exclusively in England. It produced a single, "Play Me Like You Play Your Guitar," that again featured the Rebelettes. A contemporary soul-tinged ballad with strings, written for the New Seekers, it was a monster hit in England and elsewhere, although contractual red tape prevented its release in the United States.

Reunited yet again with Lee Hazlewood, Eddy finally had a comeback single in the States, "You Are My Sunshine" in 1977, that boasted Willie Nelson and Waylon Jennings on vocals. Despite excellent airplay on several stations, Asylum Records withdrew the single before it could make any impact on the charts. More comebacks followed. In 1983 Eddy began a series of club jam sessions in California with such younger admirers as Ry Cooder, Eric Clapton and Jeff Beck. The most bizarre collaboration came three years later when the British techno-pop trio, The Art of Noise, joined him for a weird but memorable revisionist "Peter Gunn." The electronic squeals and squiggles of the eighties' rock band filled the sound space around Eddy's twangy guitar as successfully as the Sharps' hand claps and hollering. In this context, Eddy's endless guitar riff begins to sound like another techno-trick of electronic wizardry, proving that his sound really hasn't dated all that much in thirty years.

The world popularity of this version of "Peter Gunn,", which reached #9 in England, did not translate stateside and it only reached #50 on the *Billboard* charts. It did, however, win a Grammy for best rock instrumental of 1986, Eddy's first. It also gave him enough clout to record a new album for Capitol the next year, called simply *Duane Eddy* (no twang in the title this time). The album featured such guitar luminaries as Steve Cropper and James Burton, along with such Eddy enthusiasts as George Harrison and Paul McCartney and John Fogerty of Credence Clearwater Revival. One cut, "The Trembler," in which Eddy puts his twang to a sitar figure by Ravi Shanker, is a tour de force with George Harrison on slide guitar and old Rebel pal Jim Horn on sax.

Produced by Jeff Lynne, who plays a creepy synthesizer, "The Trembler" is a moody, atmospheric number with echoes going all the way back to "Stalkin.'" It sums up the best of Duane Eddy's talents, past and present.

Today, Eddy, who lives near Nashville with his third wife, a guitarist, may be tired of comebacks that lead nowhere. For a rock idol, packaged and sold by a studio mentor, the guitar man has aged well. Whatever one thinks about his early career, his influence on the rock instrumental is incalculable. This fact was acknowledged in 1994 when Duane Eddy was inducted into the Rock and Roll Hall of Fame—the first solo rock instrumental artist to be so honored.

He and Hazlewood made the rock instrumental a viable genre of rock, not just a one-shot novelty but a genre that artists could grow and mature in. The layered, studio-controlled sound of his hits had a far wider effect on rock music. When Leonard Sill broke up with Hazlewood in the early sixties, he began Philles Records with Phil Spector, whose celebrated "wall of sound" was a logical extension of what Hazlewood and Eddy pioneered in that water tank in a Phoenix parking lot. Hazlewood himself created another, albeit lesser, pop star in 1966—Nancy Sinatra. The memorable hook on their first and biggest hit together, "These Boots Are Made For Walkin,'" is a descending bass guitar line that reaches rock bottom with that unmistakable Duane Eddy twang.

Perhaps Eddy himself best sums up his achievement when he tells the story of first meeting his idol Chet Atkins in 1959. The king of country guitar asked the young upstart, "How'd you get so damn commercial, boy?" "By not playing over their heads, Chet," Eddy replied.

Duane Eddy rarely played over the heads—or ears—of his listeners, but his twangy guitar brought a lot of rollicking fun and energy to rock 'n' roll when they were much needed. Maybe that's not such a bad legacy, after all, for a guitar hero.

WRAY THE RIPPER

In May 1958, the same month "Rebel-'Rouser" was released, another strikingly original guitar instrumental entered the charts. "Rumble" had none of the studio sheen of Duane Eddy's single and didn't need it. A growling lead guitar, bass and drums were enough to convey its mood of impending menace. If Eddy's twangy Gretsch was macho, Link Wray's fuzztone Gibson came on like gangbusters. As one reviewer put it, "Wray unleashed more destructo power with three chords than Godzilla wreaked on Tokyo."

Although it has lost a little of its shock value today, hearing "Rumble" on the radio back in the summer of 1958 must have been quite an experience. Deejays must have checked their turntables or the record to see if it was warped. Nobody would *deliberately* try to distort their guitar that way. Nobody but Link Wray. "I've always looked for the sounds," he once said in an interview. In "Rumble" he found a sound that would ring down through the next three

Looking very much the rebel, Link Wray has spent much of his recording career out of the mainstream by choice. His refusal to compromise his music may have condemned him to relative obscurity in the sixties, but today his sizzletone and power chords are seen as a seminal influence on generations of rock guitarists. (Photo courtesy of Showtime Archives, Toronto)

decades, giving birth to psychedelic, heavy metal, grunge and punk.

Fred Lincoln Wray, Jr., was born in Dunn, North Carolina, on May 2, 1935. His great grandfather was a full-blooded Shawnee and his father was a preacher ("I'm not religious, but I'm very spiritual," Wray says today.) Like Eddy, he grew up listening to and playing country and western music. When he was age 16, the family moved to Portsmouth, Virginia, where his Dad went to work in the post-World War II shipyards. Link was soon drafted into the Army and sent to Germany where he served as a medic; there he contracted tuberculosis, a disease that would plague him for years.

Link and his brother Doug joined older brother Vernon's country and western band, the Lazy Pine Wranglers (later Lucky Wray and the Palomino Ranch Gang). He cut quite a dashing figure as a singing cowboy, complete with six-shooters. The family moved again to Washington, D.C., and Wray recorded under the name Lucky Wray on the local Starday label in 1956. His TB grew worse, he was hospitalized and lost one lung. The doctors suggested he give up singing and concentrate on playing the guitar. Sound medical advice that changed the course of rock history.

Vern, under the name Ray Vernon, had a brief fling as a teen idol (his local hit on Cameo Parkway, "Remember You're Mine," was quickly covered by the Prince of Covers, Pat Boone), then joined Doug and Link in a new rockabilly band, the Raymen, that played record hops and local honky-tonks around Fredericksburg, Virginia. This time Link was the leader.

Legend has it that "Rumble" was born in a Fredericksburg dive, inspired by a barroom brawl that broke out while the band was playing. Wray's own version of the instrumental's genesis is less dramatic. The combo was playing a record hop with local celebrity deejay Milt Grant and backing the white doo-wop group the Diamonds. When the Diamonds started to sing their big hit "The Stroll," Grant asked Wray to play a stroll beat. Link had no idea what that was, so Brother Doug filled in with the drums and told Link to just play "something." Out came "Rumble," which has the slow downbeat of the stroll, a stroll past a graveyard perhaps. Wray attributed the "fuzztone" sound of his guitar to overload on a pair of Sears and Roebuck amplifiers that Vern had put a microphone in front of.

Unfortunately, when the Raymen went to record the number in a studio, the distortion was missing. "I had a Premier amplifier with a big speaker on the bottom and two tweeters on each amp. . . . I got me a pen and started punching holes in the tweeters," Wray explained in a 1993 interview in *Guitar Player*. "Ray said, `You're just screwing up your amplifier.' I said, `Who cares as long as we get a fuckin' sound, man!'"

He got the sound he wanted in just three takes on one track. Vern, aka Ray Vernon, now took over as the Raymen's manager and played the demo for Cadence Records' chief Archie Bleyer. Bleyer wasn't crazy about "Rumble" but was persuaded by his enthusiastic teen-age daughter, who said the tune reminded her of a rumble from the musical *West Side Story*. Cadence signed the group and released the single.

Link's sizzling guitar, combined with the controversial title, gave many radio station managers reason to pause. Three decades before rock lyrics brought forth the wrath of Tipper Gore, Link Wray found himself banned on New York City stations and in other markets for "promoting juvenile delinquency." A rare achievement for a rock instrumental! The controversy only inspired higher record sales. "Rumble" remained in the Top 40 for ten weeks and reputedly has sold four million copies to date.

Wray's fuzztone was as great a breakthrough in rock 'n' roll as Duane Eddy's twang. But in 1958 the world wasn't ready for heavy metal. Neither was Archie Bleyer, whose taste in instrumentals ran more to orchestral versions of "The Naughty Lady of Shady Lane," a hit of his own back in 1954. He wanted the Raymen to return to their country and western roots and the boys quickly departed for Epic Records.

Here they hit pay dirt again with their first release, a slightly more conventional rockabilly number, "Rawhide," that had nothing to do with the TV Western of the same name but everything to do with raw riffs. To his lean ensemble Wray added a tinkling piano, played by brother Vern. The number's hard-edged, six-note guitar riff is echoed to great effect by Shorty Horton, Vern's replacement, on bass, while Doug Wray pummels the drums mercilessly. "Rawhide" reached #23 on the *Billboard* charts. It was Link Wray's last excursion into the Top 40.

Follow-up singles like "Comanche" and "Slinky" failed to chart at all and Epic tried to make Wray into another Duane Eddy with such Western fare as "Trail of the Lonesome Pine," backed by a full orchestra. When they suggested he record "Claire de Lune" next, Link had had enough. Vern had opened his own recording studio in Washington, D.C., and the brothers formed their own small independent label, Rumble Records. They recorded a new Wray original, "Jack the Ripper," which became a local hit and two years later helped them land a contract with the Philadelphia-based Swan label.

At Swan, Link Wray finally found the artistic freedom he had been looking for. The label gave him carte blanche to record whatever he wanted and wherever he wanted (mostly in a three-track studio in an abandoned chicken coop in Vern's new home in Accokuk, Maryland). "Jack the Ripper" became his first Swan single in 1963 and served as my introduction, at age 14, to the world of Link Wray.

I had never heard an instrumental quite like it before. It was a kind of tone poem, vividly describing in two minutes and twenty-three seconds a night on the town with the world's most infamous serial killer. "Jack the Ripper" was a big hit in the Hartford, Connecticut, area, rising to #13 on WDRC's Swinging

Sixty Survey. Nationally, it peaked at #64. My copy of the single, won in a WDRC request contest, was later shattered to pieces by a drunken pal of my little brother's during a beer bash, along with a good portion of the rest of my cherished collection of 45s. I still haven't quite forgiven him for that.

After listening vainly for the song on numerous oldies stations (they never play the ones you really want to hear), I finally met up again with "Jack the Ripper" on a compilation CD. Three decades have not dimmed the power of what may be Link Wray's finest moment. The record opens with two resounding powerhouse chords, the leitmotif of Jack, to put it in Wagnerian terms. Next come the drums, beating out an ominous tattoo with a tinge of tambourines. Then three muted chords from the big Gibson that seem to rise out of the murky subconscious of a psychopath. The growling opening chords are repeated and followed by a snatch of an Eastern-sounding melody that conjures up the garish environs of Whitechapel and its painted ladies. Next the guitar picks out a more conventional run, the musical equivalent of the killer making his way quickly through fog-shrouded, narrow streets. The chords grow in intensity, the drumbeat picks up a notch. Then comes the payoff. Jagged chords cut through the air like shards of glass as the knife finds its victim. His work finished, Jack sheathes his blade and moves on. The tip-toeing guitar run is repeated. The drum beat grows faster, faster, faster—a pounding heartbeat. Then suddenly . . . silence. Jack is gone without a trace.

If the censors thought "Rumble" was dangerous in 1958, lord knows what they would have said about *this* one. But then it was 1963 and nobody, to my knowledge, accused the Raymen of promoting serial killing.

The *Jack the Ripper* album featured some other fine tracks, such as the muted, mysterious "Cross Ties," which sounded like an aboveground "Pipeline," and "Big Ben," another vivid slice of London town, this one more upscale. "Run Chicken Run," which became Wray's third Swan single, had a fatback riff worthy of "Rawhide" and featured some chicken-scratching guitar runs that have to be heard to be believed (although a group called the Atmospheres had pulled off the same trick four years earlier in their forgotten "The Fickle Chicken").

The LP should have been Link Wray's big comeback. But poor marketing and cut-rate graphics on the cover quickly consigned it to the bargain bin. There would be no further Swan albums. Wray continued undaunted, releasing a string of singles over the next four years that were bold and adventurous, with a raw power unmatched by any other rock instrumentalist of the period. Barely heard at the time, they have been lovingly reissued on Norton Records' double CD *Mr. Guitar*, along with the rest of Wray's Swan catalogue.

"Deuces Wild" (1964) and "I'm Branded" (1965) with their wild tremolo and outrageous "wah wah" were early forays into what would later become heavy metal, while Wray's stinging version of the "Batman Theme" (1966) should have given the Marketts's version a run for their money, despite the corny opening and closing dialogue between Batman Link and a weirdly funky Robin.

Wray's last single for Swan in 1967 was fittingly a remake of "Jack the Ripper." Shortly after, the company closed shop and Wray retreated to the chicken shack in Maryland, better known as "Wray's Shack Three Track," where he continued to record his more and more daring sonic experiments for his own pleasure and that of his friends. He would encourage the Raymen to beat out the rhythm with their feet and bang pots and pans on the table, as much to get "new sounds" as to stay within a tight budget.

The group continued to play live gigs in the same low-life bars and dives it was playing in during the fifties. A chance meeting in one of these with independent producer Steve Verroca led to Wray's first LP in eight years, *Link Wray*, on Polydor, which included some of the "shed session" numbers. This and several subsequent albums on Polydor and other labels were ignored by the public, despite general acclaim from the critics.

With the resurgence of rockabilly in the mid-seventies, Wray's time seemed to have come at last. He recorded a well-heralded album, *Fresh Fish Special* (1978), with new wave rockabilly artist Robert Gordon. From the interest this generated, he came out with the solo album *Bullshot* (1979), which again failed to find an audience.

In the early eighties he moved to Denmark with his new wife, Olive Julie, where he was appreciated for the pioneer rocker he is. Later in the decade, he put out two albums on his own, *Apache* and *Wild Side of the City*,[2] which showed that age had not diminished his fiery vision.

In the summer of 1994 Wray released his first "commercial" album in more than ten years, *Indian Child*, recorded in his kitchen with the Danish band Shaky Ground. The album is a surprise—all vocals—with Wray's well-worn voice bringing life to a collection of rockabilly rave-ups and melancholy ballads.

The Raymen—Shorty, Doug and Vernon—are all gone now, but at age 62, Link Wray continues to go his own way, listening to the sound of his own growling guitar beat. This gifted artist, who has been called everything from a wide-eyed primitivist to a repetitive three-chord guitar picker, has had as great an influence on rock music as any musician of his generation. His uncompromising vision, artistic integrity and unique style mark him as one of rock's great originals. As he once told his brother when he called Link crazy for deliberately burning up his amplifiers with his sizzletone, "I'm not crazy. I just want to hear myself." We have not heard the last of Link Wray.

A PROFITABLE VENTURE

Bob Reisdorff listened to the demo from the four, eager fresh-faced young men and shook his head. The song, a guitar instrumental, didn't impress him. The

---

[2] Both of these albums have been reissued together on an Ace CD.

sound quality was poor and the group's members were obviously amateurs just starting out in the business. Reisdorff was an executive at Seattle's Dolton Records and manager of the Fleetwoods, a vocal trio whose first release, "Come Softly To Me," had topped the charts for four weeks in 1959. What he needed were more vocal groups like the Fleetwoods, not four guys who played electric guitars and drums. Besides, he already had an instrumental group, the Frantics, signed to his label and one instrumental group was enough for any record company.

Twenty-three-year-olds Bob Bogle and Don Wilson, the leaders of the nascent group, the Versatones, were discouraged, but they weren't about to give up. With some financial help from Wilson's mother, they decided to form their own record company, optimistically named Blue Horizons. They bought time in Seattle's Boles Studio, located in John Boles's basement, and recorded their first demo. Perhaps feeling Reisdorff was right about the instrumental, they recorded a couple of original vocal numbers—"Cookies and Coke" and "The Real McCoy." When these went nowhere they recorded the rejected instrumental, which Bogle and Wilson had picked off a Chet Atkins album, *Hi-Fi in Focus*.

They took the demo to a deejay friend, Pat O'Day, who worked at Seattle's biggest rock 'n' roll station, KJR. O'Day liked the boys and as a favor agreed to play the instrumental in the dead space each hour before the newscast. KJR's

The Ventures perfected a guitar group sound that is still admired today. Their marketing skills were easily the equal of their musicianship and they survived every change in musical style from surf to psychedelic by adapting it as their own.

switchboard was soon lit up with calls from curious listeners wanting to know the name of the catchy guitar instrumental and saying how much they liked it. Among the callers was Bob Reisdorff, who didn't recognize the song he had turned down months earlier. He also didn't recognize the group he had rejected, which had changed its name. Since the band members were venturing into a new business (Bogle and Wilson's previous "day" jobs had been carrying wet cement to bricklayers), they had decided to call themselves the Ventures.

Reisdorff was so taken with the Ventures and their record that he sent off a copy to Dolton's distributor, Liberty Records. When the president of Liberty failed to share his enthusiasm, Reisdorff offered to cover all the costs of releasing the single if it failed to sell. He needn't have worried. The Ventures' version of "Walk—Don't Run," a little-known instrumental by jazz guitarist Johnny Smith, went on to become a national hit, peaking at #2 on the charts for four weeks in the summer of 1960, right behind Chubby Checker's "The Twist." The career of the most successful and longest-running instrumental group in rock history was off and running.

Unlike Duane Eddy and Link Wray, the Ventures created no new, startling sound. Instead they consolidated what other musicians had done before them, from Les Paul to Rick Nelson's gifted guitarist James Burton, and put it all together into a four-man band that was to become the quintessential rock 'n' roll guitar group. Stripped of the excesses of Eddy's heavy accompaniment and Wray's all-enveloping fuzztone, the Ventures' sound was clean and easy, rhythmic and yet lyrical. "Walk—Don't Run" (the title came from a sign composer Smith had seen in a New York subway) had a weaving melodic line that allowed for intricate interplay between Bogle's lead guitar and Wilson's rhythm guitar. The sweet metallic twang at the end of a phase from Bogle's Fender sounded almost like a Hawaiian steel guitar and would become as much a Ventures' signature as Eddy's bass twang or Wray's growl.

Within three months of the release of their first hit, the Ventures came out with another classic, "Perfidia" (#15), an old chestnut that had been a big hit for several vocal groups back in the forties. Howie Johnston's driving drums and Nokie Edward's rhythmic bass gave the old song a fresh rock beat while Wilson's and Bogle's lilting guitars wrung the last drop of romance out of the melody.

Their third hit, a less imaginative remake of Bill Dogett's "Ram-Bunk-Shush" (#29), was something of a letdown, but by then the Ventures had firmly established themselves as the premier instrumental group of the early sixties. Although technically sophisticated, their sound could be more easily imitated than Eddy's elaborate studio product, and legions of teens rushed out to buy electric guitars and form their own group "venture."

About this time the group put out its first album, which became a best-seller, even without a picture of the Ventures themselves on the cover. The group

WALK—DON'T RUN / THE McCOY / HONKY TONK / RAUNCHY
CARAVAN / HOME / SLEEP WALK / MORGEN / NO TRESPASSING
NIGHT TRAIN / THE SWITCH / MY OWN TRUE LOVE (Tara's Theme)

The Ventures were off touring when it came time to shoot the cover of this, their first album. The boys in the band are actually stockroom workers at Liberty Records and wore dark glasses to make themselves unrecognizable. When Walk Don't Run, Vol. 2 *came out, the real Ventures took their places in an almost identical pose.*

was on tour and unable to make the photo session, so four guys wearing dark glasses were recruited from the Dolton stock room as stand-ins. "They put some pretty model walking by in the forefront so no one would notice their faces," Wilson recalled in an interview with rock writer Steve Kolanjian.

If the Ventures had a definite gift for making music, they were true geniuses when it came to marketing that music. Don Wilson's experience working as a used car salesman for his father back in Tacoma helped him appreciate the importance of a good marketing strategy. Bob Bogle's business acumen was no less developed. As he told an interviewer during an Armed Forces Radio program in 1961, "When anyone asks me what my ultimate achievement in show business is I just say it's the six-figure bracket." Over the next three decades, the Ventures would more than achieve that goal.

Their first album's mix of proven hits and Ventures' originals set a pattern they would not stray from. "[We'd] cut vocals that were coming up on the charts at the time," explained Wilson, "do them instrumentally, and put about six or seven of them on the album for title strength. Then we'd write songs that had the same feel for the rest of the LP. We'd release maybe four or five albums a year doing that."

The formula worked extremely well. Each album released in 1961 and 1962 sold 10,000 copies. *Walk Don't Run* was followed quickly by *The Ventures*, *The Ventures Another Smash* and *The Colorful Ventures*, their first "concept album," another innovation they pioneered. Every cut on the album had a color in the title ("Blue Moon," "Greenfields," "White Silver Sands").

The group was also quick to capitalize on new musical trends. It put out two twist albums in 1962 and the same year took on a bewildering array of other teen dances of the day from the limbo to the hully-gully in *Going to the Ventures Dance Party!* and *Mashed Potatoes and Gravy*. When sales declined on an album, Dolton would recycle it later by merely changing the title. So *Twist with the Ventures* became *Dance!* and *The Ventures' Twist Party, Vol. 2* resurfaced as *Dance with the Ventures*. If fans were disappointed to discover they'd bought the same album twice, they didn't say so.

The group even put out a play-by-the-numbers instructional album, *Play Guitar with the Ventures*, that included a sixteen-page booklet with diagrams. According to a full-page ad in *Billboard*, the record featured "slow-speed and normal-speed solo parts plus complete recordings with solo part missing."

For their ninth album, the Ventures felt confident enough to make a complete "cover" album, *The Ventures Play Telstar* (1963), which featured many of the biggest rock instrumentals of 1960-62. To compensate for the fact that the music had all been done first by other artists, the liner notes took pains to assure the consumer that the sounds were all Venture-originated:

> When male voices are required on one of the numbers, the Ventures sing the parts themselves. In this latest of their efforts, they play electric guitars, round-hole guitars, mandolins, and harpsichord. They handclap, finger-pop, and foot-stomp their way through what may be the most exciting album of their exciting careers.

But there was much more excitement to come. *Surfing, I Walk the Line* and *Let's Go*, the latter two shameless steals of hit titles by other artists, all came out in 1963. The following year saw *The Fabulous Ventures* and *Walk Don't Run, Vol. 2*. After recycling everybody else's hits, it was inevitable the Ventures would start cannibalizing their own. "Walk—Don't Run '64" was a technically expert and original reinterpretation of their first hit done à la surf guitar. It went all the way to #8, their first Top 40 single since "Ram-Bunk-Skush," three and a half years earlier. The band became the first rock group to score twice in the Top 10 with two versions of the same song.

The Ventures' popularity spread far beyond the United States. They first toured Japan in 1962 with teen idol Bobby Vee. The timing was serendipitous. Liberty had just sold the masters of their records to the entertainment conglomerate Toshiba, which released them to coincide with the tour. The Ventures were an overnight sensation in the country. The sale of electric guitars there boomed, as thousands of Japanese youths formed their own bands in their garages and basements. By the time the group returned a few years later its members were national heroes. "There were about 10,000 people at the airport waiting for us," recalled Don Wilson. "It was just pandemonium. They called it Venturemania!"

Thirty years later, the Ventures are still a major draw in Japan. They claim to have sold forty million records there, including the two domestic albums *Live in Japan* (1977) and *Pops in Japan '81*. In 1972 they were the first foreign inductees into the Music Conservatory of Japan. What has made this rather low-keyed instrumental group the Beatles of Japan? Perhaps it is the band members' very lack of charisma and their strong dependence on teamwork that the Japanese admire, along with their technical skill and cool professionalism. Whatever the reasons, the Ventures will never have to worry about losing their popularity back home—they will always have Japan.

As the sixties unfolded, the Ventures, like musical chameleons, proved their ability to change with the times. *The Ventures A-Go-Go* (1965), *Wild Things* (1966), *Super Psychedelics* (1967) and the inevitable *Christmas with the Ventures* (1965) kept them in the public eye and ear. In 1968 they took on acid rock in an album titled *Underground Fire*, which was heralded by this murky radio ad spot:

A heavy liquid sheet of heat weaving patterns into the ghost of the earth . . . quicksilver burns bearing the weight of change. . . . The Ventures . . . Underground Fire . . . the harbinger of the flames yet to come. . . .

The Ventures' attempt to become Cream did not please many of their loyal fans, but by then, who cared?

The following year the group would have one more shot at the Top 10. On September 26, 1968, a new TV crime show entered the CBS lineup. Filmed entirely on location in the fiftieth state, *Hawaii Five-O* got off to a rocky start, pitted against the incredibly popular *Rowan and Martin's Laugh-In*. The Ventures had been asked to do a record of the title music before the show's debut. Digressing from their usual style, they entered the studio with a total of twenty-eight musicians, including a full brass section. The rather standard theme song, played with lots of brio and blare, was catchy. The only problem was you could barely hear the Ventures over all the din. Both show and single seemed destined to bomb, until nearly a year after the record's release when an enterprising Hawaiian deejay played it under a radio ad spot for the show. "Thousands called wanting to know who it was by and where they could buy it—it was "Walk—Don't Run" all over again," recalled drummer Mel Taylor, who had replaced Howie Johnston in 1963. "Hawaii Five-O" took off, peaking at #4. The TV series went on for thirteen seasons, to become the longest-running crime show in television history.

Interestingly, the Ventures' last sixties' single to land in the Hot One Hundred was their version of "Theme from *A Summer Place*," the instrumental that had topped the charts in 1960, the same year "Walk—Don't Run" debuted. The decade had come full circle.

Now the Ventures ventured boldly forth into the seventies, where no vintage instrumental group had gone before. With unabated enthusiasm they took on the classics and country and western. The albums, now issued on their own label, Tri-Dex, slowed down by the mid-seventies, but the group continued to tour on the club circuit and in the eighties even had a minor hit single with the all-girl group the Go-Gos called "Surfin' and Spyin'." In 1985 the band matched guitars with heavy metal guitarist Paul Warren on a new version of "Wipe Out" that has unfortunately never been released. Today the indestructible Bob Bogle and Don Wilson continue to perform and record with Mel Taylor and Gerry McGee, who replaced Nokie Edwards in 1985. Howie Johnston, who rejoined the group several times, died in 1988.

One anticipates with mixed feelings the release of such future efforts as *The Ventures Go Grunge* and *Come Rap with the Ventures*. But you just can't keep a good band down.

From the perspective of thirty-five years in the business, it is hard to separate the Ventures the group from the Ventures the marketing phenomenon. However, under all the commercial hype and the skillful but often empty covers of other people's songs, they produced a remarkably consistent level of good music. Listening to some of their early singles, such as the drum-driven "Lullaby of the Leaves" (#69), the rockers "Yellow Jacket" and "Pedal Pusher," and the playful "Flight of the 2,000 Pound Bee, Part 2" (#91; their first venture into fuzztone, which was played at Killer Bee John Belushi's funeral), makes one wish they had done more original material. And a high percentage of their re-makes, especially in the early years, were skillfully arranged for their guitar sound, perhaps none more so than their nifty hit interpretation of the Richard Rodgers' classic, "Slaughter on Tenth Avenue" (#35). It featured old Duane Eddy standby Steve Douglas playing his saxophone over a Leslie speaker, making it sound like a circus calliope.

The Ventures firmly established the four-man guitar group as the prototype rock band, setting the stage for John, Paul, George and Ringo and all those other self-contained sixties' bands on both sides of the Atlantic. As the man said in one of those overheated radio ad spots for their *Hawaii Five-O* album: "The Ventures created a universal instrumental institution and when they do a hit you know it's been done!" Amen, brother.

SONS OF TWANG

The combined allure of the rebel image of Duane Eddy and Link Wray, the production wizardry of Lee Hazlewood and the phenomenal success of the Ventures launched the careers of hundreds of guitar instrumental groups in the late fifties and early sixties. Like the Ventures, they started out playing in church basements and Sons of Italy dance halls, and the vast majority of them never left these modest venues. However, some of them were persistent, ambitious or lucky enough to cut a record, which sometimes led to a local or regional hit. A very lucky few broke into the national charts when their single caught the attention of a national distributor. Most of these groups were one-hit wonders, quickly fading back into the obscurity from whence they came. But in their brief moment of fame, they left their mark, providing some ingenuous permutations on the guitar instrumental.

....

THE WESTERN THEME that runs through Eddy's work was taken to its logical conclusion by the Ramrods, who out-twanged the master himself in their novel 1961 rendition of Vaughn Monroe's cowboy classic, "(Ghost) Riders in the Sky" (#30). The Ramrods, who hailed from wild and wooly Connecticut, got together in 1956 and were one of the few groups of the early rock era to feature a female drummer, Claire Lee, who also did their arrangements. The rolling twangy guitars of "Ghost Riders," complemented by a blaring sax, didn't really need the added weight of a full cattle drive, but one wonders if this tasty rock Western would have caught the fickle ear of the record-buying public without its heavy-duty sound effects. Lead guitarist Vincent Bell Lee returned to the limelight eight years later, playing the striking "water sound" guitar in Ferrante and Teicher's Top 10 version of the theme from *Midnight Cowboy*.

....

SOUND EFFECTS WERE USED to better advantage a few months later in one of the first and most successful car instrumentals, "Stick Shift" (#25), by the Duals. This Los Angeles-based group consisted of black guitarists Henry Bellinger and Johnny Lageman, whose driving guitars were the perfect complement to the revving car engine that starts off the record. The rhythmic road riff accelerates as the car picks up speed, only to be brought to a final halt by a wailing police siren. Fifteen years before Kraftwerk brought the German freeway to vivid life in "Autobahn," the Duals recreated a wild ride down the L.A. freeway in their hit single.

....

THE APTLY NAMED Rock-a-Teens used an insistent falsetto crooning "Woo-hoo-hoo-hoo-hoo-hoo" to juice up their sole hit (what else?) "Woo-Hoo" (#16) in the fall of 1959. The Rock-a-Teens played their acoustic guitars (more strum than twang) with joyful abandon, and threw in a snappy drum solo that Cozy Cole might have envied. No melody, no method, the only real hook that crazy "woo-hoo," but in their two minutes and five seconds of glory the Rock-a-Teens captured the irrepressible energy of a thousand late fifties' garage bands.

....

ANOTHER TEEN GUITAR GROUP with brio to spare were the Rockin' R's, who scored a hit on Tempus Records with their first release, "The Beat" (#57), in the spring of 1959. Their follow-up single, "Heat," had a relentless, blistering guitar riff backed by an equally mean sax.

....

MORE MELLOW THAN MEAN were the String-A-Longs, a sextet from Clovis, New

Mexico. How their "Wheels" rose to the #3 single in the country is one of the mysteries of pop music in 1961. The best that can be said for this wisp of an instrumental is that it rolls along pleasantly enough with a vaguely Spanish flavor that betrays the heritage of lead guitarist Jimmy Torres. Local producer Norman Petty, the man who had discovered Buddy Holly four years earlier, had a keen interest in instrumentals and once fronted his own group, the Norman Petty Trio, that had a few minor hits in the fifties. Petty wrote "Wheels" for the String-A-Longs and sold the record to Warwick Records, where the group had a couple of modest follow-ups before it rolled into oblivion. When last heard from, in the late sixties, the band was playing psychedelic music as the Strings of Fortune.

A MUCH MORE INTERESTING group from Petty's stable were the Fireballs. This quartet from Raton, New Mexico, was the era's most influential guitar group after the Ventures and one of the very few instrumental groups to achieve greater chart success as a vocal group.

Petty placed the Fireballs, who took their name from Jerry Lee Lewis's "Great Balls of Fire," with Kapp Records, but their first release, "Fireball," was too derivative of Duane Eddy to get much airplay. Moving to the Top Rank label, the Fireballs found their own original style with a catchy number written by lead guitarist George Tomsco. The head of Top Rank liked the tune, but insisted on changing its name from "Curious" to "Torquay," an English resort he had recently visited which he claimed the song reminded him of. One wonders if the man was tone deaf or simply an egomaniac, since "Torquay's" Tex-Mex sound is a far cry from the English seaside. But despite the misleading title, "Torquay," which went to #39, established the Fireballs' style. Their stripped-down, rhythmic guitar sound, partly created by tuning their guitars down one full step, was a refreshing change from the heavy-layered studio work of Duane Eddy and Lee Hazlewood.

"Bulldog" (#24), their next single, featured a fast guitar riff that prefigured the rapid-fire reverb of Dick Dale. It may explain why the Fireballs' tunes were favorites with the emerging surf bands. "Quite a Party" (#27) in 1961 was a full-out rocker with an opening thumping drum solo that was admired and imitated by countless drummers. The flip side, "Gunshot," was equally fine, and was adapted by the Swedish guitar group, the Spotniks, who updated the title to the spacey "Moonshot."

Like many instrumental groups, the Fireballs performed vocals to give their act variety and wider appeal. Chuck Tharp, their vocalist and co-composer of some of their best songs, left the group in 1960 and Petty suggested they replace him with singer and guitarist Jimmy Gilmer from Amarillo, Texas.

The group was given a song by Keithe McCormack, a member of the String-A-Longs, about a guy who falls in love with a waitress at a beatnik coffeehouse.

The Fireballs never achieved the fame of the Ventures, but their guitar sound was highly original. They were one of the few instrumental bands to have greater success as a vocal act with "Sugar Shack," the #1 record of 1963, sung by Jimmy Gilmer (lower right).

McCormack was surely writing from his imagination. Southwestern Texas in the early sixties was the last place you'd find a beatnik or a cup of Expresso. Yet the very innocence of his lyrics made "Sugar Shack" a crowd-pleaser wherever the Fireballs played. They finally recorded the song with Gilmer on vocals in early 1963. It might have disappeared without a trace except for the persistence of Gilmer's father, a salesman for Phillips 66, who played it at every radio station along his route. Airplay made "Sugar Shack" a local hit and then a national one; it remained in the #1 spot for five weeks. By the end of the year, *Billboard* ranked "Sugar Shack" as the #1 song of 1963.

Although the sweet lyrics and Gilmer's quiet, understated delivery helped put the song across, they were well supported by the rhythmic, economic playing of the other Fireballs. Most arresting was an infectious bass guitar riff and a neat hook on the Solovax, a small keyboard instrument played by Norman Petty himself. The Fireballs originally thought the funny flute-sounding organ would ruin their record, but Petty knew better.

Although they continued to record instrumentals, including an updated "Torquay 2" in 1965, the Fireballs' remaining hits would all be vocals. "Daisy Petal Pickin'," with its catchy "She loves me, she loves me not" lyrics set against

The Viscounts from New Jersey strike a joyful pose that belies their moody, melancholy version of "Harlem Nocturne." It resurfaced on the charts in 1966, actually scoring higher than the first time around.

another strong organ riff, went to #15 in early 1964. Four years later they took a Tom Paxton folk song, "Bottle of Wine," into the Top 10. Gilmer's sweet tenor had roughened into a Barry McGuire-like baritone by then, with all the Fireballs singing backup. The group broke up soon after, but Tomsco and Tharp revived the band in 1989 on the oldies circuit. Today Jimmy Gilmer is a vice president of CBS Sony's southern operations.

Never achieving the fame of the Ventures, the Fireballs nevertheless staked out a unique Tex-Mex guitar sound that is still admired today by musicians and rock music connoisseurs alike.

THE VIRTUES' "Guitar Boogie Shuffle" had a different kind of rhythm, one derived from "Guitar Boogie," written by group leader Frank Virtuoso's (aka Virtue) friend and ex-Navy buddy Arthur Smith. The shuffle beat enlivens Smith's original tune and turned it into a #5 hit in 1959. Virtuoso formed the group in Philadelphia in 1946 and played locally for thirteen years before striking gold. After three more hitless years, Virtue tried to update the tune again with the "Guitar Boogie Twist," which spent one week on the Hot One Hundred. After that he devoted his energies to producing and was responsible for such diverse fare as the rhythm and blues' hit "That's Life" by Gabriel and the Angels and the polka novelty "Who Stole the Keeshka?" by the Matys Brothers.

Virtue does indeed have its own rewards.

PERHAPS THE GROUP to get the most dramatic mileage out of a twangy guitar were the Viscounts, whose soulful interpretation of the Sid Robin-Earle Hagen standard "Harlem Nocturne" is itself something of a classic. It is a rare example of a record that not only charted twice in seven years but actually charted *higher* the second time around (#52 in 1959 and #39 in 1966).

The number opens powerfully with the ominous jangling chords of lead guitarist Bobby Spievak, sounding like distant thunder breaking the stillness of a Harlem night. Then Henry Haller's mournful sax breaks through with the main melody, while the electric guitars trail menacingly behind. With its strong bluesy jazz flavor, "Harlem Nocturne" had a surprisingly adult, contemporary sound for a late-fifties' instrumental, which may explain its resurfacing in the more sophisticated sixties.

IF "HARLEM NOCTURNE" WAS dark and moody, "Sleep Walk" by the guitar duo of Santo and Johnny was sheer heaven on a slow dance floor. The strength of this hauntingly beautiful ballad is due in no small part to the enticing ring of Santo Farina's steel guitar, an instrument previously associated almost exclusively with Hawaiian and country and western music. The sweetness of the steel guitar is nicely underpinned by brother Johnny's rhythm guitar and the soft swell of an organ.

The Farina brothers were raised in Brooklyn and Santo took up the steel guitar at age 9. They wrote "Sleep Walk," one of the great instrumental titles, with

Santo (left) and Johnny (right) Farina wrote "Sleepwalk" with their sister Ann. The steel guitar had rarely been featured before in rock 'n' roll, but it brought a sublime beauty to their guitar instrumental, the only one of its kind to go all the way to #1.

their sister Ann. The loveliness of the song and the unique blending of the guitars took "Sleep Walk" all the way to #1 on the *Billboard* charts, the only guitar instrumental ever to achieve that distinction.

On the strength of their monster hit, Santo and Johnny toured North America for the next three years, logging over 100,000 miles. Their version of "Sleep Walk" was a hit in Europe as well, and led to at least twenty cover versions, including one by the less-than-original Sleepwalkers in England.

The duo's follow-up, "Tear Drop," cracked the Top 30 and they continued to chart sporadically until 1964 when their last hit was a version of the Five Satins' "In the Still of the Night," a song they seemed destined to record. Their oddest charting single, however, is 1962's "Twistin' Bells" (#49), a wild rocking version of "Jingle Bells." That the most lyrical guitar group of the fifties was cashing in on the twist says something about American pop music of the early sixties. Yet the dance craze that swept the pop world ended up giving new life and vitality to the still evolving rock instrumental.

Chapter Four

Let's Dance!

The heavy influx of hot instrumental sides has record execs searching small night clubs and dance halls across the nation for tomorrow's hit makers. Jazz, rock and hotel orks are all being surveyed for unusual material and sounds. Disk talent scouts also have looked with a friendly eye at the society and dance band leader rosters for potential stars.
BILLBOARD, August 1961

I think it would have been nice to have shared a room with Beethoven and when someone remarked, upon hearing one of his compositions, "Isn't that great!" I could say, "Yep, my roommate wrote it."
MASON WILLIAMS

LAND OF A 1,000 DANCES

In his original recording of "Land of a 1,000 Dances," New Orleans' rhythm and blues artist Chris Kenner actually mentions only a dozen or so early sixties' teen dances, ranging from the well-known twist, mashed potatoes and watusi, to the intriguingly esoteric "sweet peas" and "the chicken in the pot." Yet at the time this strangely hypnotic song was released in June 1963, young America was indeed the land of a 1,000 dances, or so it seemed to anyone who watched *American Bandstand* or tuned in an AM radio.

It all began in March 1959 when Hank Ballard, long-time lead singer of the famed r & b group the Midnighters, released a self-penned dance record that was supposed to be the B side of a ballad "Teardrops on Your Letter." But it was the catchy upbeat "The Twist" that became the bigger hit, reaching #28 on the *Billboard* Hot One Hundred.

Ballard's "The Twist" quickly faded from the charts but the dance itself was picked up by the premier arbitrators of teen taste in this period, the regulars who danced on Dick Clark's *American Bandstand*. Kal Mann and Bernie Lowe of Cameo/Parkway records in Philadelphia, *Bandstand*'s home base, took note and assigned the tune to their latest discovery, a former chicken plucker Ernest

Evans (aka Chubby Checker) whose only previous hit was a novelty number, "The Class." Checker's note-for-note transcription of Ballard's version of "The Twist" was so convincing that when its author first heard it on the radio he thought it was *his* record.

In the intervening year and a half, rock's creative energy was beginning to flag. Doo-wop was as antiquated as Gregorian chant, rockabilly had faded and many of the original pioneers of rock had died, were in jail, or going soft. At the start of a new decade, rock 'n' roll was at a crossroads, looking back on a rich past and ahead to an uncertain future.

The twist at once revitalized rock 'n' roll and all but completed its assimilation into mainstream pop culture. A simple, really quite silly dance, compared to the stroll, the continental and other teen dances of the fifties, the twist was non-threatening enough to be favored by the older generation anxious to join the youth cult that accompanied John F. Kennedy's ascendancy to the White House. This bulletin from the Philadelphia bureau of *Billboard* in August 1961 makes the transition clear:

> Rock and roll may finally be getting through to adults. At least it has here, where after-hours spots and regular night clubs report that their middle-aged clientele is doing "The Twist" between cha chas. . . . The suburban Philly line of the Sinantrama Clubs is also featuring "Twist" dance competitions, and other nitery ork [orchestra] leaders are hastily putting the rock and roll novelty into their books, sandwiched between "Tea for Two" and "Night and Day."

What was a novelty in summer had by late autumn blossomed into a full-fledged national craze. Twist dance classes, twist movies (three were in production by late November) and a Twister shoe from Thom McAn were all vying for the public's attention.

This twist craze was a boon to the rock instrumental. Here was a genre that seemed perfectly matched for dancing. Instrumental groups sprouted up like mushrooms to meet the burgeoning demand at dances and sock hops for live, unadorned dance music. They didn't need a singer out front, just a strong beat and a catchy riff to start feet moving. It was a good opportunity for kids still in high school to make some extra money, gain local fame, impress the girls and maybe get a chance to record their best original tune at the nearest recording studio.

Established instrumental groups who already had a hit or two tried to regain the momentum of their flagging careers by latching on to the twist. Some even used the title of a previous hit for name recognition. The Champs weighed in with the "Tequila Twist," the Applejacks with "Mexican Hat Twist" and the Virtues with the "Guitar Boogie Twist." The Mambo King Pérez Prado abandoned his Latin beat for "The Patricia Twist" and the venerable Count Basie vainly pursued the teen crowd with "The Basie Twist." While some of these efforts charted, it was only in the lower echelons.

Ironically, the Ventures, who plowed every farrow of pop music in their long careers, never came out with a twist single, although they did release "Instant Mashed" (as in mashed potatoes) in 1962, "Skip To M'Limbo" the following year and an intriguing medley of "Walk—Don't Run" with "Land of 1,000 Dances" as late as 1968.

Some groups actually released old hits with the word "twist" simply inserted into the title. Bill Black's Combo did so well with "Twist-Her" (#26), one of the few twist instrumentals to break into the Top 40, that his label, Hi Records, re-released the group's biggest hit from two years earlier, "White Silver Sands," as "Twistin' White Silver Sands" and then its first hit "Smokie—Part 2" as "Smoky—Part 2 (Twist)." The first of these actually charted for a couple of weeks in the spring of 1962.

But the biggest twist instrumental, and the only one to reach the Top 10, was "Percolator (Twist)" (#10) by Billy Joe and the Checkmates. It was a bright and bouncy little novelty that ingeniously, if repetitively, recreated the sound of coffee perking on a xylophone played by that ubiquitous pianist and arranger Ernie Freeman. Legend has it that Dore Records was set to release it as "Percolator" when at the last minute producer Louis Bideu had the word "Twist" added in parentheses after the title. Whether "Percolator" would have been as big a hit as "Percolator (Twist)" is debatable, but adding the twist to the title certainly didn't hurt sales. Bideu (aka Louis Bedell and Billy Joe Hunter), a one-time comic and New York local TV show host, wrote the tune with Freeman, who probably did most of the work. The Checkmates were just one of several phantom groups made up of Freeman and his top-notch session men—Rene Hall (guitar), Earl Palmer (drums), Red Callender (bass) and Plas Johnson (sax).

The idea was so good that Maxwell House Coffee later bought the rights to the number and used it in its television commercials, making "Percolator (Twist)" the first of a long line of rock instrumentals to have a profitable afterlife on Madison Avenue. Freeman and Bideu continued trying to mine the novelty market with items like "One More Cup," but it all sold like yesterday's coffee grounds.

....

FREEMAN AND HIS ALL-STAR SESSION MEN scored again with another parenthetical dance number later the same year, "Let's Go (Pony)" (#19), this time as the Routers. The pony was the first of a long line of animal-inspired dances.[1] "Let's Go" had an infectious guitar hook played by Rene Hall, backed by Plas Johnson's raspy sax, syncopated handclaps and the repeated group cry of "Let's

---

[1]These included the monkey, the fly, the turkey trot and the dog. There was even a slow-stepping dance called "The Turtle," recorded for posterity by a group called Ichabod and the Cranes.

Go!" that sounded like something you'd hear at a school pep rally. (Which is where this catchy instrumental has had a long afterlife.)

The group was assembled and produced by Joe Saraceno, the king of studio groups. He hired Mike Gordon and other white musicians to tour as the Routers and they may well have made the group's subsequent singles, including the similarly snappy "Sting Ray" (#50). The Gordon Routers continued to tour and record for Warners into 1967 and briefly reappeared in 1973 to little effect on Mercury.

IN AN AUGUST 1962 ISSUE of *Billboard*, deejay George Lorenz announced that the latest dance craze among his listening audience was the wobble. "This new dance has been picked up by the record companies and in the next three months look for a rash of wobble releases," predicted Lorenz.

While there may have been many wobble records, only one wobbled very high up the charts—"Wiggle Wobble" (#22) by Les Cooper and the Soul Rockers. Cooper's previous claim to fame was managing the New York doo-wop group the Charts, who had a hit with the dreamy ballad "Desire" in 1957. Joe Grier, the lead singer of the Charts, played the pounding tenor sax solo on "Wiggle Wobble." The other distinctive sound on this highly danceable record was a bottomed-out bass line that sounded like the vibrations of a mammoth rubber band.

"HOT PASTRAMI" WASN'T EXACTLY a dance, but it was the offspring of the mashed potatoes, a sloppy dance first celebrated by James Brown and his band moon-lighting under the name Nat Kendrick and the Swans. Their two-part instrumental, "(Do the) Mashed Potatoes," disappeared quickly in 1960, but was resurrected a year later by twist king Joey Dee and the Starliters, who accelerated Brown's slow, heavy beat. Their live, noisy version, recorded at New York's Peppermint Lounge, was released as "Hot Pastrami (with Mashed Potatoes)."

The Dartells, a six-man band from Oxnard, California, covered the Starliters version for Arlen Records, dropped the mashed potatoes from the title and condensed the long, loose instro into a tight two minutes and change. Dominated by a piping hot organ and bass player Doug Phillips' strangled cries of "Yeah!" "Hot Pastrami" was a minimalist instro, to be sure, but the boys' hearts were in it and you could sure dance to it. It went all the way to #11, and the flip side, "The Dartell Stomp," got some airplay too, while the Starliters' version stalled at #36. The follow-up, "Dance, Everybody, Dance," lasted one week at #99 and after that the Dartells were out to lunch.

ANOTHER DANCE INSTRUMENTAL that dominated the airwaves in late 1962 started life as the theme song for a Buffalo, New York, deejay. The genesis of "Wild Weekend" and the Rockin' Rebels is so convoluted that you would need a scorecard to follow it. The feel-good tune was co-written by WKBW deejay Tom Shannon and his business partner Phil Todaro and recorded by a local vocal group, the Russ Hollet Trio, to introduce Shannon's weekend show.

The jingle became so popular that when a local Buffalo band, the Rebels, played their instrumental version for Shannon, he saw a potential hit record on the horizon. The Rebels' version was recorded on Shannon and Todaro's Mar-Lee label in 1959. It became a big hit locally and did well in several other markets, including Philadelphia, where the Rebels appeared on *American Bandstand*. At Dick Clark's suggestion, the group changed its name to the "Buffalo Rebels" to avoid confusion with Duane Eddy's backup band.

Two further singles fizzled and the Rebels and Shannon went their separate ways. Fast forward three years. Tom Shannon was a private in the Army now, stationed at Fort Dix, New Jersey, but his famous theme song was still on the air, appropriated by a friend, Jerry O'Brien, on his radio show in Syracuse, New York. Bernie Binnick, head of Swan Records, heard the show on a visit to Syracuse and wanted to record the song for his label. He tracked down Shannon at Fort Dix, who gladly leased him the original recording. Binnick rechristened the group the Rockin' Rebels.

This time around "Wild Weekend" clicked in a climate more friendly to instrumentals and peaked nationally at #8. Its classic opening riff, strummed on a bass-string guitar made way for a warm, raspy sax line that was not so much wild as an invitation to a mellow good time.

TOM SHANNON PRESENTS...
THE ROCKIN' REBELS

The Rockin' Rebels of Buffalo, New York, look pleased as punch about their 1962 hit, "Wild Weekend." The only trouble was they had recorded it four years earlier and were long gone when Swan Records brought out their instrumental. Deejay Tom Shannon, who owned the master, enlisted several other groups to put out follow-ups, but none recaptured the magic.

Such a big hit deserved a quick follow-up, but Shannon had a problem. The Rockin' Rebels now existed only on a record label. Rather than find a new group to take over as the Rebels, Shannon and Todaro scrutinized their catalog and found another 1959 release that sounded amazingly close to the Rockin' Rebels guitar-sax sound. "Rockin' Crickets" by the Hot Toddies (see Chapter 2), now credited to the Rockin' Rebels, only went to #87 in early 1963.

There was still money to be made on the Rockin' Rebels, however, and Shannon's thoughts turned to an album. For this chore he chose a third group, the Jesters, who had recorded the flip side of the new "Rockin' Crickets." They did a creditable job of sounding like the Rebels on the album and put out two more singles on Swan under that name. One of these, "Happy Popcorn," carried the cricket gimmick into the kitchen, using wooden blocks to recreate the sound of popping corn.[2]

In 1966 Swan reissued "Wild Weekend" with a new flip side by still another group, Kathy Lyn and the Playboys. They adapted another track by the Buffalo Rebels, "Donkey Walk," renaming it "Donkey Twine." And what happened to the original group that started it all? According to Dave Burke and Alan Taylor of England's *Pipeline* magazine, the Rockin' Rebels forsook rock for jazz and played for some years under the name "The Sophistikats." Considering the fate of the hit they never had, who can blame them?

....

IN CONTRAST TO "WILD WEEKEND," "You Can't Sit Down" (#29) started life as an instrumental and later went to greater fame as a vocal number. Bass guitarist Philip Upchurch was leading Dee Clark's touring band when organist Cornell Muldrow came to him with an exhilarating dance number he had penned. "You Can't Sit Down" became the band's opening number. In 1961 Upchurch formed his own combo and recorded the instrumental on the small Oklahoma label Boyd.

"You Can't Sit Down, Parts 1 & 2" remains one of the finest dance instrumentals of a dance-crazed era. It is a joyous jam session in which each musician gets to strut his stuff—from Muldrow's screeching organ to Upchurch's slippery bass to David Brooks' wailing sax that dominates part 2, the hit side. But anyone who loves get-down dance party music should hear the tune in its entirety as reissued on Ace's excellent compilation *Teen Beat, Vol. 3*.

In early 1963 Parkway's Kal Mann added lyrics to the number and had the Dovells, the label's premier dance/vocal group, record it. It became the Dovells' second-biggest hit, with Len Barry's piping tenor replacing the Upchurch Combo's brass section on the hard-driving hook, "you can't sit down." Few listeners could.

---

[2]The same idea was attempted more successfully in 1972 with a Moog synthesizer on "Popcorn" (#9) by Hot Butter (aka Stan Free).

As for Philip Upchurch, he went on to become one of the most in-demand bass guitarists in sixties' rhythm and blues. That's him playing the famous opening guitar riff on Fontella Bass's soul classic "Rescue Me."

ANOTHER TWO-PART DANCE HIT of 1962 was "The Jam" (#29) by Bobby Gregg and His Friends. Gregg, born Robert Grego, was a jazz drummer from Philadelphia and a strong jazz flavor runs through his rocking jam session. One of the "friends" is top guitarist and crazy man, the late Roy Buchanan, who turns in one of his most noteworthy performances on a Top 40 record here. For what it's worth, "The Jam" is one of the few two-part instrumentals where part 1 was the hit side.

SIMILARLY FORGOTTEN IS "Bust Out" (#25) by (who else?) the Busters from western Massachusetts. This mean rocker has a feverish beat that lives up to its original title, "Typhoid." Tribal drums backed by some frantic twangy guitar work and a barking sax create a jungle-like orgy of sound that threatens to bust out of the record's grooves. Regrettably, the Busters left only one follow-up single and no album in their wake.

PERHAPS THE STRANGEST of the dance instrumentals of the period was "El Watusi" (#17) by Latin band leader and percussionist Ray Barretto. The watusi, as the Orlons seductively sang in their hit dance record, was "the dance made for romance."

There was nothing romantic, however, about "El Watusi," an unusual hybrid—part novelty, part instrumental, part foreign language record. It began with a percussive piano riff punctuated by drums and handclaps. Then a lively conversation in Spanish ensues about a mean, huge hombre named El Watusi of whom everyone but the central speaker is afraid. This leads into the catchy but repetitive Latin dance beat, run through with a perky flute solo. It ends with the return of the piano riff and the two hombres continuing their animated discussion about El Watusi into the fade-out. Kooky, but somehow memorable.

MONGO SANTAMARIA WAS another Latin percussionist with a knack for novelty. His "Watermelon Man" (#10) was written by jazz flutist Herbie Hancock, who recorded it on his first album, *Takin' Off*, in 1962. Santamaria, who played drums for Pérez Prado and other Latin band leaders before striking out on his own in 1961, gave the tune a heavy brass and conga beat with some colorful vocalizing scattered through. An early practitioner of Latin soul, Santamaria parlayed his hit into a string of funky, rhythmic dance albums for Columbia and a few more charting singles.

BEFORE WE SAY FAREWELL to the land of 1,000 dances, we must take note of the biggest dance instrumental of 1962, which was, oddly enough, a striptease. We're talking, of course, about "The Stripper" by David Rose. A highly regarded conductor, arranger and composer of numerous film and TV series' scores (he wrote the theme for *Bonanza*, among others), Rose was best-known for the pizzicato-crazy "Holiday for Strings" way back in 1943, which established what Joseph Lanza calls the "holiday shopper's jubilee style" of pop music.

"The Stripper," which might be retitled "Holiday for the Tired Businessman," was originally recorded in 1958 as background music for a television drama called "Burlesque." Rose later recorded it as a joke during an album session, scandalizing the top brass at MGM, his label, who refused to release it. Four years later, a subversive at MGM slapped it on the flip of his latest single, "Ebbtide." Los Angeles disk jockey Robert Q. Lewis was so taken with Rose's musical caricature, that he played it nonstop for forty-five minutes. "The Stripper" bumped and grinded its way to #1 in Los Angeles and, soon after, across the country.

Rose enjoyed his ill-reputed hit to the hilt and it remained his signature song until his death from heart disease in August 1990.

ORGANS—HAPPY AND PIPING

The value of the electric organ to rock had been aptly demonstrated by Bill Doggett in 1956 with "Honky Tonk." Doggett, however, often played second fiddle to the showier sax and guitar in his combo. It took a 21-year-old former doo-wop singer in 1959 to show that the rock organ had star power.

Dave "Baby" Cortez will be forever linked to the rock 'n' roll organ, although he was a far better piano player than organist, and not a bad rhythm and blues singer, either. This versatile entertainer was born David Cortez Clowney in Detroit in August 1938. His father and two brothers were musicians and Cortez studied piano for several years before joining a local doo-wop group, the Five Pearls, as second tenor. The group moved to New York City where they recorded for several small labels and Cortez also sang briefly with the Valentines.

One of Cortez's first solo efforts on the Ember label was a piano instrumental called "Movin' 'N' Groovin,'" the same title as Duane Eddy's first instrumental release. This and another single flopped, at which point Cortez signed with the small Clock label, run by the father and son team of Wally and Doug Moody, whose ad slogan was "Clock rings in the hits."

For his second Clock single, Cortez was set to record a vocal number, "The Cat and the Dog," but he lost his voice at the recording session. Instead, he started improvising on the piano and came up with a catchy riff that sounded like a rocking variation of "Shortnin' Bread." The engineer was intrigued and suggested Cortez try the same tune on a Hammond B-3 organ stuck off in a corner. The organ was pulled out and, although Cortez had never played one before, he sat down and started pounding away at the keyboard.

Dave "Baby" Cortez was a far better pianist and singer than organist, but his boundless energy, as depicted on this sheet music for his #1 hit, "The Happy Organ," made him, and the electric organ, rock stars. (Photo courtesy of Showtime Archives, Toronto)

Cortez's bouncy riff was simplicity itself and the primitive recording conditions make the single sound, as Cub Koda has written, "like it was cut at a roller rink." However, the novelty of the electric organ playing lead, the energy of Cortez's performance, and some great guitar work by legendary session man Jimmy Spruill, turned "The Happy Organ" into a monster hit, eventually reaching #1 on the charts for one week in March 1959. The novelty wore off with the weak follow-up, "The Whistling Organ," which deserved to languish at #61. Further Clock releases failed to do even that well, although some of these sides were surprisingly good. There's the sly, jazzy "Cat Nip" with its neat sliding guitar imitation of a cat's purr, the hard rocking "Dave's Special" and the foot-tapping "Piano Shuffle," which showed Cortez's skillful touch on the ivories.

Clock eventually ran down and out of business and Cortez began recording on his own label. In 1962 he came up with an intriguing tune with an Oriental lilt set to a heavy cha-cha beat called "Rinky Dink." Eminently more listenable today than "The Happy Organ," "Rinky Dink" was picked up by Chess and went all the way to #10. It was Cortez's last Top 40 record, but he continued to chart regularly on Chess for a couple of years with a string of upbeat tunes with such typical titles as "Happy Weekend" and "Organ Shout." He ended his recording career on a variety of labels in the late sixties, moving into funk and soul. Today he is retired from the music business and works a day job in Jamaica, New York.

Less than a major figure in the history of rock instrumentals, Dave "Baby" Cortez was still more than a two-hit wonder. His showmanship, if not his organ playing, helped promote the organ into a central position in sixties' rock for both instrumental and vocal groups.

....

ANOTHER PIONEERING ROCK organist who preferred the piano was New Orleans' legendary session man James Booker, whose sole hit "Gonzo" reached #43 on the pop charts in 1960. Despite the wild title (Gonzo was Booker's nickname), the tune is a tame, easy-going rocker in a jazz vein with a feathery flute accompaniment. Booker cut his first record at age 14 with Dave Bartholomew and in the mid-fifties toured with Joe Tex, Shirley and Lee and Huey Smith's Clowns. A minister's son whose sister was a gospel singer, Booker's erratic temperament and drug problems landed him in Angola State Penitentiary in the mid-sixties. After his release, he returned to touring with Fats Domino, Dr. John, whom he helped get started, and other top acts. Booker toured Europe in 1977 after another spell in prison and recorded the excellent album *New Orleans Piano Wizard: Live!* The first well-known New Orleans' musician to play the electric organ, Booker died under mysterious circumstances in November 1983.

....

THE GROUP THAT MOST capitalized on the electric organ's unique sound was Johnny and the Hurricanes of Toledo, Ohio. The group's founder and guiding light for over thirty years was Johnny Paris (originally Pocisk), who formed his first group, the Orbits, while still at Rossford Catholic High School. After graduation, the group found a modicum of fame backing a local rockabilly singer before moving to Detroit in 1959. Here, they signed with Talent Artists, Inc., a management agency run by two shrewd businessmen, Irving Micahnik and Harry Balk, who also had the Royaltones under contract. In early 1959, the group recorded its first single for Micahnik and Balk's Twirl label at an old Detroit movie house.

"We'd record upstairs," Paris recalled years later to Bill Millar. "They'd pipe the sound downstairs, where it would slap around inside this monstrous auditorium. They had microphones to pick it up and feed it back to the tape machine upstairs. That was the only way we could get a reverb. . . . We took 32 takes to get it right but we still got a lively, exciting feel."

"Crossfire" was both lively and exciting, a hard-rocking instrumental dominated by Paris's gritty, gut-bucket sax. It was an impressive debut for the group that now called itself Johnny and the Hurricanes. Leased to Warwick Records, which was home to several hit instrumental groups, "Crossfire" climbed to #23.

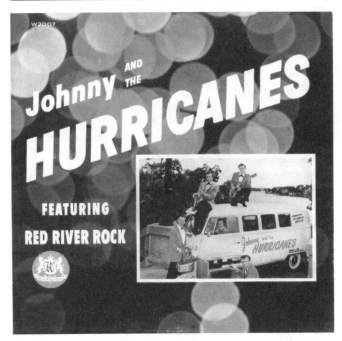

Johnny and the Hurricanes created one of the most recognizable instrumental sounds of the early sixties with their endlessly piping organ. Their string of hit "folk instros," starting with "Red River Rock," was an ingenious way for their managers to collect composer royalties.

With the group's next Warwick release, Micahnik and Balk hit upon a formula that would become the Hurricanes' signature sound. Taking the old Western folk song, "Red River Valley," and rearranging it with a rock beat, the managers gave the melody line to Hurricane Paul Tesluk and his piping electric organ. Paris's sax was relegated to a supporting role along with Dave Yorko's and Lionel "Butch" Mattice's driving guitars. "Red River Rock's" high-piping organ was a wild and woolly novelty that had real teen appeal. It went to #5 in the United States and to #2 in Britain, where the Hurricanes were far bigger stars than at home.

The best thing about "Red River Rock," as far as Micahnik and Balk were concerned, was that the tune was in the public domain and there was no composer to pay royalties to. Instead, the two managers took the composer's royalties for themselves, under the names Tom King and Ira Mack. Encouraged by the success of "Red River Rock," they ransacked the catalog of folk songs, old pop standards and even hymns, to find similar free material for the Hurricanes to record.

In quick succession came "Reveille Rock" ("Reveille"), "Beatnik Fly" ("Blue Tail Fly"), "Down Yonder" ("Way Down Yonder in New Orleans"), "Revival" ("When the Saints Go Marching In"), "You Are My Sunshine," "Ja-Da," and "Old Smokie" ("On Top of Old Smokie"). Nearly all of these placed in the Hot One Hundred and "Beatnik Fly" topped at #15. Today most of these instrumentals sound contrived and gimmicky. A contemporary listener may well cringe at the sound of that endlessly piping organ, only relieved by Paris's exuberant sax solos. Not all of these "rocked-up" oldies were bad, however. "Reveille Rock" (#25), a rocking version of the old Army bugle call, gave Paris a field day and he blew that horn like a literal hurricane. The interjections by a gruff sergeant ("All right you guys, rise and shine!") added a nice novel touch.

As with the Champs, the B sides of the Hurricanes' big hits were often far more interesting than the A sides, showing just how extraordinary a group it could have been if freed from the commercial and creative restraints of its managers. "Buckeye" and "Time Bomb" (the flip sides of "Red River Rock" and "Reveille Rock") were fine rockers, showcasing Paris's considerate talents with not an organ pipe in ear range. "Time Bomb" had a cool, hand-clapping opening, strongly reminiscent of the Wailers' "Tall Cool One." "Sand Storm" (flip of "Beatnik Fly") and "Sheba" (flip of "Down Yonder") were atmospheric mood pieces, highlighting the polished lead guitar of Dave Yorko playing strange middle-Eastern flavored melodies with fine support from a for once subdued and powerfully haunting Tesluk on organ.

Unable to dump Micahnik and Balk, the Hurricanes were at least able to cut loose from Warwick and move to Big Top Records, which offered them a better financial deal. Warwick head Morty Craft's cavalier reaction to losing the Hurricanes is all too typical of the money men in the rock business. "Let's face it," Craft told *Billboard* in an April 1960 interview, "we're dealing with a sound, not specific individuals. The people who make that same sound from one record to the next may be entirely different. It's a specific sound and I can make it all over again with a new group I have, the Craftsmen. We already have their first record 'Rock-Along' released."

To the great satisfaction of Johnny Paris, the Craftsmen disappeared without a trace. However, the Hurricanes had their troubles, too. By the end of 1961, Paris was the only original member of the group left. By then the Micahnik-Balk formula had about played itself out with less than enthralling versions of "Stack-O-Lee" ("High Voltage"), "There's a Tavern in the Town" ("Rockin' T"), and, worst of all, "Bringing in the Sheaves" ("Salvation").

Paris took the new Hurricanes abroad to tour Germany and the United Kingdom, where they continued to be stars for years to come. In Germany, the Hurricanes often appeared with the then unknown Beatles, who idolized them. Paris, his streak of hits long over, tried to jump on the Beatlemania bandwagon in 1964 with a dreadful single, "The Saga of the Beatles," and an album *Live at the Star Club*. To this day, Paris continues to play with hired Hurricanes, making regular tours of Britain from his home base in Hamburg, Germany.

A dedicated musician, Johnny Paris was always better than his "greatest hits" would indicate. He and his band have earned their honorable mention in the Kinks' song from *Preservation Act I*. Johnny and the Hurricanes are truly "one of the survivors."

DRUMS WERE HIS BEAT

The drummer, the primal keeper of what Fats Domino called in a 1958 hit song "The Big Beat," is the heart throb of rock 'n' roll. But while sax players, guitarists and organists were able to break away from vocal rock and glow in the instrumental spotlight, drummers remained at the back of the bandstand, pivotal but unheralded members of their groups. Cozy Cole changed that briefly with his monster hit, "Topsy II." But Cole was a jazz drummer and "Topsy" was a crossover hit.

The calypso craze of 1957 and the appearance of the beatniks brought a new and novel percussion instrument to the coffeehouses and bars of New York and San Francisco—the bongos. Preston Epps, from Oakland, California, didn't learn to play the bongos in a beatnik coffeehouse but halfway around the world in Okinawa, where he was stationed during the Korean War. On his return to California, Epps took odd jobs as a waiter, gas attendant and night club manager. But his real love was beating those skins in a Hollywood coffeehouse.

He may look like Harry Belfonte in this publicity shot, but Preston Epps from Oakland, California, played rock, not calypso. While his "Bongo Rock" was a big hit, the novelty quickly wore off and he soon departed for the Hall of One-Hit Wonders. (Photo courtesy of Showtime Archives, Toronto)

L.A. disc jockey and record producer Art Laboe, the West Coast's answer to Alan Freed, caught Epps's act and saw potential for a rock record. He signed the bongo player to his Original Sound label and crafted a nifty little instrumental that backed Epps's frenzied beating with an equally frenzied guitar riff. "Bongo Rock" had a raw if unfocused energy that took it to #14 on the national charts in mid-1959. Some critics hear the prototype for "Wipe Out" in Epps's drumming, although the Surfaris took the idea to another dimension. The novelty of the bongo sound quickly wore off and Epps's follow-up single, "Bongo, Bongo, Bongo" (#78), was probably three bongos too many. He persevered, however, taking his bongos onto the dance floor ("Hully Gully Bongos") and then to the beach in his *Surfin' Bongos* album that featured the (please!) Bongo Teens.

....

LABOE REMAINED ON the lookout for the rhythmic beat of drums to ignite another hit and only a few months after "Bongo Rock's" success he found what he was looking for.

Sandy Nelson was born on December 1, 1938, in Santa Monica, California, and grew up in the midst of Hollywood's last glory days and the birth of West Coast rock 'n' roll. His Hungarian-born father was a film projectionist at 20th Century Fox studios and Sandy himself worked briefly at Fox in his teens as a laborer. He got his first drum kit as a Christmas present when he was age 7 and by 12 was playing percussion in the school orchestra. His classmates in high school were Nancy Sinatra, Jan Berry and Dean Torrence (Jan and Dean), and a strange kid named Phil Spector. His first band, the Barons, was led by Jan and Dean, until Dean left to serve in the Army and Jan teamed up with friend Arnie Ginsberg on their first hit, "Jennie Lee." After quitting high school, Nelson joined Kip Tyler and the Flips with his friend pianist Bruce Johnston, who would go on to fame as one of the Beach Boys.

The Flips played back-up for Art Laboe's Rock and Roll shows in the L.A. area with Phil Spector on guitar. Spector had larger ambitions and hired Nelson to play drums on a demo of his song, "To Know Him is to Love Him," for his group the Teddy Bears. "To Know Him" went to #1, but Nelson would later be dropped by Spector on future sessions for a more experienced drummer, Hal Blaine.

Nelson found a friend, however, in Richie Podolor who played guitar for Spector and had his own recording studio. Podolor had tasted fame the previous year as a member of the studio group the Pets who had a dance instrumental hit, "Cha-Hua-Hua" (#34). He encouraged Nelson to try a solo drum record, similar to Cozy Cole's "Topsy."

Nelson took a demo tape of his composition "Teen Beat" to Laboe, who was intrigued by the instrumental, but knew it needed work to become a hit. If Lee Hazlewood can take a large share of credit for Duane Eddy's "twangy" guitar, then Laboe was at least partially responsible for Nelson's "bouncy" drums. He

After his striking debut with "Teen Beat," Sandy Nelson had the good sense to surround himself with top session musicians to enrich and vary the sound of his drum instrumentals. A serious motorcycle accident in 1962 cost him his left foot but he soon returned to performing, hardly missing a beat. (Photo courtesy of Showtime Archives, Toronto)

knew Nelson's drumming, however dynamic, was not enough to sustain a record. Rather than simply throw in guitar accompaniment to provide a melody line as he did in "Bongo Rock," Laboe came up with an ingenious effect to enhance the big beat of Nelson's drums. He had guitarist Guybo Collins tune down his bass strings to the same pitch as the drums. The bass guitar line echoed the drum beat so perfectly that it was almost impossible to detect by the casual listener. But the reverberating bass line added juice and power to the drum beat, making the first 45 seconds of "Teen Beat" (#4) one of the most strikingly original openings of any rock instrumental. Only when the record is nearly half over do Podolor's and Barney Kessel's lead guitars come in with a more conventional, skittering guitar riff. The riff quickly fades as Nelson goes into a slow, infectious march-like beat that Laboe patterned after the year's second-biggest hit, Johnny Horton's "Battle of New Orleans." The tom-toms and the clip-clop sound of the wood block add color to the drum beats, while the bass keeps up its steady throb underneath. Syncopated cymbal crashes bring the record to a dazzling finale.

"Teen Beat's" pure kinetic energy sold 750,000 copies and put Sandy Nelson in the forefront of rock instrumentalists. He signed with Imperial records, the label of Fats Domino and Ricky Nelson, and wisely surrounded himself on subsequent singles with such master musicians as Rene Hall, Ernie Freeman, Red Callender and Jim Horn. But such promising follow-ups as "Big Noise from the Jungle" went nowhere and Nelson, who had signed away most of his royalties to his big hit, was soon back playing drums on other people's records—"Alley Oop" by friend Gary Paxton and his Hollywood Argyles and "A Thousand Stars" by Kathy Young and the Innocents. By late 1961 Imperial was ready to drop him and it looked like Sandy Nelson would be just another one-hit wonder in the Rock Instrumental Hall of Fame.

Then, with Podolor on guitar, Nelson recorded his own composition, the grandiosely titled "Let There Be Drums," on a tape recorder in his garage. The instro gets off to a faster start than "Teen Beat" and the guitar riff, raw and twangy, comes in much sooner. The guitar plays against the drums, raising the pitch periodically to create a wonderful tension against Nelson's steady drum pounding. It wasn't all that much different from "Teen Beat," but it worked like a charm and gave Nelson his second Top 10 hit and an accompanying album, *Let There Be Drums*, that sold 500,000 copies and stayed on the *Billboard* album charts for forty-six weeks, an incredible feat for an instrumental album. The album included a ten-minute drum solo, "Birth of the Beat," the first of many extended albums cuts to showcase Nelson's skill with a bewildering array of percussion instruments.

The year 1962 got off to a thumping start for Nelson with his third Top 40 hit, the low-keyed "Drums Are My Beat" (#29), which, for the first time, saw Sandy's drums take a back seat to a jangly piano figure, played by Nelson himself via the magic of overdubbing. Rock's number one drummer had seven more charting singles that year, including the big band-influenced "All Night Long" (#75) and the Eastern-flavored "And Then There Were Drums" (#65).

But 1963 saw a promising career begin to unravel. In April, Nelson was cruising down Mulholland Drive on a new motorcycle, when he crashed into a school bus rounding a corner. His right foot became entangled in the bus's wheels and had to be amputated. The 24-year-old drummer was devastated, but he refused to give up. He taught himself to play the bass drum with his left foot and rigged a board up to his artificial right foot to allow him to play the hi-hat.

Another disaster proved harder to adjust to. Imperial was sold to Liberty Records and the new regime took away Nelson's artistic freedom and forced him to crank out covers of current hits in album after album. Utter frustration, he admitted in a candid interview with Bob Cianci, drove him to drink, which only complicated his problems. Retreads of his hits, "Teen Beat '65" (#44) and "Let There Be Drums '66," were less than inspired, but Nelson was still capable of making sparks fly with his drumsticks as can be heard on the fine "Drums a Go Go," a single that should have charted much higher than #124.

It wasn't until the early seventies that Nelson broke out of his alcoholic haze and returned to his first love—jazz. He started playing with a small combo in a

Santa Monica bar and stayed with it for ten years. In 1982 he founded his own label, and cut the ill-named "A Drum Is a Woman," a cult favorite, that he later renamed "Drum Tunnel."

Always a very private person in a very public profession, Sandy Nelson today lives contentedly in a mobile home in the Mojave Desert where he continues to write music, but only plays the drums when the spirit moves him. Like other first-generation giants of the rock instrumental—Link Wray, Duane Eddy and the Ventures—he has survived the changing musical scene by the sheer force of his talent. Although many fine and some even more gifted drummers have kept the beat since the dazzling debut of "Teen Beat," none has been able to sustain a solo career. Sandy Nelson was the first, and to date, the last.

CLASSICAL GAS

In the seventies two seemingly divergent musical styles, rock and classical, intertwined in a trio of monster instrumentals—"Joy" by Apollo 100 (#6), "Also Sprach Zarathustra (2001)" by Deodato (#2), and "A Fifth of Beethoven" by Walter Murphy and the Big Apple Band, which reached #1 in the disco summer of 1976.

As influential as these records were, they were predated by more than a decade by three unheralded instrumental groups that first hit upon the idea of melding classical music and rock.

....

THE FIRST ARTIST TO TAP the commercial potential of this unlikely coupling was a classically trained jazz pianist from Philadelphia named Jimmy Wisner. Forming a trio with Chick Kinney on drums and Ace Tsome on bass in 1959, Wisner composed an instrumental based on a theme from one of his favorite piano concertos by Norwegian composer Edward Grieg. "We bought this upright piano for $50," Wisner told writer Wayne Jancik, "and painted the hammers with shellac to give it a sound between that of a tack piano and that of a hard harpsichord. . . ." Since the concerto was written in the key of A minor, the group came up with the clever title, "Asia Minor." Afraid that his pop instrumental, despite its classical roots, would damage his reputation in jazz circles, Wisner released the single on his own Future Records label under the pseudonym Kokomo. The novelty of the Grieg theme in a pop setting and the sound of that tacky piano put "Asia Minor" in the Top 10 in March 1961.

The Norwegians, who regarded Grieg as a national institution, were not amused. The Norwegian bureau of composers' copyright (TONO) claimed the "American-Turkish" pianist Kokomo had "insulted the memory of composer Edward Grieg by stealing the main theme from the Piano Concerto No. 1 in A-Major." Although the international arm of the Norwegian organization attempted to ban the record in Europe, it hardly put a dent in sales. After all, Grieg, like most good dead classical composers, was in the public domain.

Wisner only made a couple more singles and the obligatory album before retiring Kokomo. He soon abandoned jazz as well and became a successful arranger and producer for such mellow late sixties' artists as the Cowsills and Spanky and Our Gang. He also co-wrote one of the most hauntingly beautiful non-Beatle songs of the British Invasion, the Searchers' "Don't Throw Your Love Away."

....

BY 1961, THE EVERLY BROTHERS had established themselves as rock's biggest recording duo. Looking for new worlds to conquer, Don Everly formed his own record company, Calliope. His first release on the label was an upbeat marching band version of Edward Elgar's famous "Pomp and Circumstance March No. 1," complete with a chorus of cheerleaders. Elgar's estate argued that the instrumental, "The Graduation Song," produced by Everly under the pseudonym Adrian Kimberly, should be banned in England and elsewhere. Besides being one of the most famous compositions by an English composer, the song version of the march, "Land of Hope and Glory," was considered a second national anthem after "God Save the Queen." Whether the ban contributed to the single stalling at #34 stateside is difficult to say, but Calliope had no further hits.

....

WISNER AND EVERLY may have "jazzed up" classical themes, but the rock ensemble known as B. Bumble and the Stingers turned them upside down and shook the life out of them, or, more accurately, into them. In its first release on Rendezvous Records,

B. BUMBLE AND THE STINGERS NUT ROCKER and all the classics!

ace

B. BUMBLE AND THE STINGERS

NUT ROCKER, BUMBLE BOOGIE, APPLE KNOCKER and all the classics!

These three cool cats are not B. Bumble and the Stingers, although they may have played them on the road. The wonderful string of classical rock instros were created by the golden quartet of L.A. sessionmen—Ernie Freeman, Plas Johnson, Red Callender and Earl Palmer—and a few other unsung musicians.

"Bumble Boogie" (#21), written years earlier by jazz pianist Jack Fina, the group took Nicolai Rimsky-Kosakov's ever-popular "Flight of the Bumble Bee" and set it to a frantic boogie-woogie beat that wouldn't quit until that bee had buzzed its last. Two pianos were used in the recording—a grand, playing rhythm, and an upright with thumb tacks placed on the hammers for a tinny, nickelodeon sound. Both tracks were played by master keyboard man Ernie Freeman and then mixed together.

B. Bumble and the Stingers were actually another incarnation of L.A.'s super session group—Plas Johnson, Rene Hall, Earl Palmer, Red Callender and Freeman (later to be replaced by Lincoln Marjorga). In true commercial fashion, Rendezvous dug up a trio of good-looking, white musicians to tour as the Stingers.

In its Artists' Biography feature in a May 1961 issue, *Billboard* displayed a publicity photo of three virile, young white males in striped tops, one of them sporting a beatnik goatee. The accompanying text read:

> Bumble, whose real name is William Bumble, shortened to Bill, shortened to B., comes from Ada, Oklahoma. . . . Bumble's first introduction in music was in his brother's small band which played local school dances. One night he sat in for the guitar player. Although he had never picked up the instrument, Bumble managed to keep the rhythm, and even impressed a young girl so well she asked him for his autograph. As a result, Bumble decided on a musical career and began to take lessons.

The publicity mill did its work well, for as late as 1994 rock critic Greg Shaw identified B. Bumble as a real person, albeit black.

Rene Hall, the real guitarist of the Stingers, in an interview before his death in 1986, accepted the ruse as just another way to sell records to white, middle class teens and avoid the grueling road tours. "That's why I always kept it all simple," he explained, "so that whatever group we sent out could follow our records." Substitute economic and tight for "simple" and you have a good description for B. Bumble and the Stingers. Stripped down to the essentials—boogie woogie piano, thumping drums and a rhythm guitar—the Stingers were instrumental rock at its best: syncopated energy with a novel sound.

A second Bumble release, "Boogie Woogie" (#89), wasn't a classical take-off but a straight rendition of "Pine Top's Boogie Woogie" and lacked the uniqueness of the group's first hit. The band's fourth single, however, "Nut Rocker," released in early 1962, was a tiny masterpiece. It opens with the piano playing the familiar stately strains of the March of the Wooden Soldiers from Tchaikovsky's *Nutcracker Suite*. As the piano takes off, pounding out the chords in increasing speed, the drums and guitar kick in like clockwork. The number reaches a peak of excitement with the piano pounding out a boogie woogie riff with the left hand while the right hand brings back Tchaikovsky's theme. The whole thing speeds forward to a virtuoso finish worthy of Liszt himself. While "Nut Rocker" peaked at #23 stateside, it went all the way to #1 in England, where listeners had a deeper appreciation for this kind of musical parody.

With two sizable hits under the belt, Rendezvous and producer Kim Fowley ransacked the classical catalogue for more material, producing half a dozen singles, all to little avail. A few of these "rock classics" were nearly as good as "Nut Rocker" and deserved a better fate. "Rockin' On 'N' Off" was a bravado rendition of Rachmaninoff's Prelude in C Sharp Minor with Palmer doing double time on percussion and Freeman's piano battling for attention with a snappy electric organ. "Dawn Cracker" ("Morning" from Grieg's *Peer Gynt Suite*) was another winner with Palmer on the tom-toms and a piping organ subbing for Grieg's flute. In "The Moon and the Sea," the B side of "Apple Knocker," an uninspired replay of Rossini's *William Tell Overture*, the Stingers created their own sublime nocturne, showing they were capable of more than simply parodying the classics.

But with no further hits in sight, the session men moved on to other projects and Rendezvous soon closed. "Nut Rocker" was re-released in England in the summer of 1972 and went to #19 on the charts, proving the timelessness of their novel music that was too good to be merely a novelty.

WE CAN'T LEAVE THIS intriguing subgenre without mentioning Mason Williams, who while handling the duties of head writer for *The Smothers Brothers Comedy Hour* in 1968, found time to write and record his "Classical Gas" (#2), a nifty pop rendering of an intricate fugue for classical guitar. The solo guitar, expertly played by Williams, is backed by a symphony orchestra, somewhat in the manner of Jack Nietzsche's "The Lonely Surfer" (see Chapter 7). Although he had several mild chart follow-ups, Williams soon turned to writing books, the first of which was the pretentiously titled *The Mason Williams Reading Matter*, a self-indulgent collection of poems, photographs and incidental pieces that could only have been produced in the late sixties.

Chapter Five

The European Connection

It was partly the sound, I just liked the sound.
It was also the myth, the whole aura that surrounds it.
CHRIS BARBER on what first attracted
him to New Orleans jazz

In America, they needed a new craze—something
to revive interest in rock 'n' roll. The Twist filled
the bill, but over here you should remember
we've already got one new fad—It's Trad, Dad!
MR. ACKER BILK

oreigners have always taken pop and rock instrumental music more seriously than their American cousins. How else does one explain the fact that the Ventures were as popular in Japan in the sixties as the Beatles (and still are) or the incredible popularity of such American rock instrumentalists as Duane Eddy and Johnny and the Hurricanes in England long after they were has-beens in the United States? Two current British magazines, *Pipeline* and *New Gandy Dancer*, are devoted to rock instrumentals, while vintage European instro groups like Sweden's Spotnicks continue to tour and record in the nineties.

What has rarely been noted, however, is that the Europeans have given back nearly as good as they got, enriching the golden age of instrumentals in the United States with some of the oddest, most offbeat and memorable sounds heard on either side of the Atlantic.

THE THREE BS

"Here Comes . . . a Whole Platoon of Redcoats" announced the headline in *Billboard*. "British disk talent, agency representatives and disk executives are flocking to these shores in near record numbers . . . ," read the accompanying article. "The flow of Britons, which is taking on the character of a mass migration, highlights the importance of this country both as a vital sales medium for overseas disk talent and as reservoir of salable acts for British personal appearances."

Oddly enough, the dateline was not February 1964, but October 1962, and this "British Invasion" was not led by the Beatles, the Rolling Stones or the Dave Clark Five, but by Acker Bilk, Kenny Ball and Chris Barber. While the artists that followed them—Frank Ifield, Anthony Newley and Lonnie Donegan among others—were pop vocalists, the "Three Bs" were instrumentalists, purveyors of the biggest craze to hit Britain since rock 'n' roll—Dixieland jazz.

While American rock 'n' roll was taken up with a passion by British youth in the mid to late fifties, the homegrown product was, to be charitable, derivative. But another kind of American music took as firm a root in British soil, albeit twenty-five years after the fact. Jazz, the original New Orleans kind, first arrived on British shores with U.S. servicemen and their record collections during World War II. While big band jazz was hitting its stride in the states, the first British Dixieland band, George Webb's Dixielanders, was knocking them dead in London's clubs and dance halls.

By the early fifties, British traditional or "trad" bands (a more hip a term than the old-fashioned Dixieland) were sprouting up all over the Isles, but with a twist that gave pause to jazz purists. The trad bands had a most un-jazz-like rhythm section that included piano, guitar and banjo, along with the more traditional bass and drums. This gave the music more of a beat and a contemporary sound. "Britain has always been a dance-crazy nation," explained Harold Pendleton, executive secretary of the National Jazz Federation in an interview. "Trad appeals to people because of its simple, danceable rhythms."

Trad's attractions, however, went beyond the music itself. It became associated in Britain with a political radicalism and intellectual bohemianism that drew on the frustrations of the young much as rock 'n' roll did. American jazz would play a similarly subversive role in Czechoslovakia and other Eastern European countries in the seventies and eighties.

....

THE FIRST OF THE Three Bs to hit it big in America, and probably the least remembered here today, was Chris Barber. This is unfortunate, because his influence, both in Britain and subsequently in the United States, has gone far beyond jazz. Born in Hertfordshire on April 17, 1930, Barber planned to become an actuary "until he got bitten by the jazz bug," according to his official biography. In 1953, the 23-year-old trombonist founded a trad band with clarinetist Morty Sunshine and veteran band leader Ken Colyer, whose Crane River Jazz Band was the first true trad band in the late forties. Colyer, who had been to New Orleans, knew what real Dixieland was supposed to sound like and balked at the variety of music that Barber and the other members wanted to play. Colyer quit and the band replaced him with Scottish guitarist and banjo player Lonnie Donegan, whose musical interests were as eclectic as Barber's.

With Barber on bass, Donegan on guitar and Beryl Bryden on the washboard, they formed a new subunit of the jazz band that played a weird mix of American rhythm and blues and country that came to be called skiffle. Skiffle caught on locally partly because it was homegrown music and didn't require expensive instruments. (Every British household had a washboard.) One of the two skiffle numbers on the Barber Jazz Band's 1954 album was American blues-man Leadbelly's "Rock Island Line," sung with characteristic brio by Donegan. When Decca issued the tune as a single in 1956 it became a smash for Donegan and he promptly left the band for a successful solo career.

With Donegan's departure, Barber steered back toward pure jazz and later that same year produced the album *Chris Barber Plays* that included a moody, Slavic-sounding melody called "Petit Fleur" ("Little Flower") written by American jazz clarinetist Sidney Bechet. The number, which had already been a big hit in Paris where Bechet wrote it, was a last-minute choice to fill out the Barber album. Two years later he was surprised to hear it was the #1 single in Germany.

"Petit Fleur," with its melancholy clarinet solo by Morty Sunshine, is jazz in a minor key and light years away from the kinetic energy of skiffle and trad. Yet it struck a chord with American listeners as well as European ones, and went to #5 on the charts in early 1959. Barber became the second British band leader to land in the American Top 10. He was preceded there only a few months by Reg Owen, whose drum-thumping, hand-clapping, big band version of "Manhattan Spiritual" (#10) is one of the forgotten gems of fifties' instrumentals.

While Barber had no further hits in America, his far-ranging musical inter-ests would have a tremendous impact in Britain for years to come. A deep love of the blues led him to sponsor the first U.K. appearances of such top American blues performers as Muddy Waters and Sonny Boy Williamson, and he was instrumental in starting the annual British Folk and Blues Festival. Barber even dabbled in rhythm and blues (he brought Louis Jordan over on his first British tour) and helped to spark the musical explosion that would lead to the Beatles, the Mersey Beat and the second, far greater, British Invasion.

Today, Chris Barber teaches at Leeds Musical College and is working on a six-volume autobiography.

....

THE OTHER TWO-THIRDS of the trad triumvirate didn't arrive in America until 1962. Kenny Ball and his Jazzmen were the closest of the three to an authentic Dixieland band. In 1963, Ball, despite his fondness for the banjo, became the first British jazzman to be named an honorary citizen of New Orleans, no small honor. A salesman and advertising man before he turned to music full time, Ball and his band were seen on a television audition by Lonnie Donegan, who arranged an audition for them with Pye Records.

After an initial flop with "Teddy Bear's Parade," Ball's raucous Dixieland interpretations of pop standards hit it big. His fourth British hit was unlikely material even for a free-wheeling trad band. "Padmeskkoverya Vietchera" was a Russian tune and about as melancholy as any Russian folk song. Ball's rousing trumpet, backed by strumming banjo, bass, drums and a wicked trombone, turned the Russian song into a joyous revelry in a minor key. "Midnight in Moscow," a curious translation considering it was released at the height of the Cold War, became a huge hit in America, going to #2.

Although Ball had ten more hit singles in Britain, only two further releases in America made the charts. Dixieland jazz, no matter how well played, could not compete with the cooler new American jazz from the West Coast that was just beginning to make its own impact on the pop charts.

THE THIRD "B" WAS the most commercially successful in the states, due in no small part to smart marketing. Bernard Stanley Bilk was the son of a Methodist preacher and a church organist in Somerset, England. He claimed to have taken up the clarinet while serving three months in the brig for falling asleep on military guard duty in Egypt. After service, he worked as a blacksmith and tobacco factory worker before replacing Morty Sunshine in Ken Colyer's jazz band in 1954. Four years later, Bilk, who now went by the moniker "Acker," rural English for "pal," formed his own Paramount Jazz Band.

Band members dress nattily in bowler hats and striped waistcoats and their leader added affectation on top of artifice by billing himself as Mister Acker

With his bowler hat and striped vest, Acker Bilk was the best marketed of the British trad band-leaders. "Stranger on the Shore," the theme from an English children's television program, stayed on the British charts for fifty-five weeks and made Bilk the first British artist to have a #1 record on the Billboard charts.

Bilk. The cuteness spilled over to the liner notes on Bilk's debut American album on Atco Records, written by publicist Peter Leslie in tongue-in-cheek Shakespearese: "A taciturn Stalwart reared in the Welsh Border Country . . . Mr. Bilk, Doyen of interpretative Musicians under whose able Tutelage a whole new School of rhythmic Apostates has blossomed upon English Soil, performs upon the Clarionet."

The album featured Bilk and his clarinet without his band, backed by his friend Leon Young's String Chorale, whose lush arrangements were the epitome of easy listening before the term was invented. The album's hit single was a sad, introspective melody penned by Bilk and Young and originally titled "Jenny," after Bilk's daughter. When asked to contribute the title song for a BBC children's television series, Bilk changed the title to the name of the show, "Stranger on the Shore."

Pop fodder though it may be, there was nothing childish about "Stranger on the Shore." The bittersweet beauty of Bilk's playing still glows warmly more than thiry-five years later. The bright, lush strings only make his lonesome clarinet all the more forlorn and isolated. In a year of remarkable instrumentals, "Stranger on the Shore" led the pack, making Acker Bilk the first British recording artist to reach #1 on the American charts. The song logged in at #9 for the year and gave Bilk a soft berth for years as an easy-listening artist and radio personality when the trad jazz bubble burst shortly afterward.

Trad jazz had the slightest of influences on the American music scene, but gave us three memorable instrumentals. A fourth British import was about to take the nation by storm—literally arriving from out of this world.

MUSIC OF THE SPHERES—JOE MEEK AND THE TORNADOES

On July 12, 1962, Telstar, the world's first commercially sponsored Transatlantic communication satellite was launched. The lofty goal of Telstar was to relay television signals between the United States and Europe. Among the thousands of Britons who sat glued to their sets watching the first transoceanic transmission from America was a 33-year-old former sound engineer and independent record producer, Joe Meek. Meek went to sleep that night inspired by the satellite and determined to write a paean to its technological glories.

The next morning he sat down in his tiny home studio and vocally recorded the melody rolling around in his head. He quickly called back from a tour his house recording band, the Tornadoes (or the Tornados in England), and within two days had a finished recording. The general consensus of Meek's colleagues, including several of the Tornadoes, was that the instrumental "Telstar" was embarrassing fluff. Nonetheless it was released by Decca Records in August and went on to sell five million copies worldwide. "Telstar" went to #1 in the United States for three weeks at the end of 1962, making the Tornadoes the first English group to reach the top of the U.S. charts, beating the Beatles by over a year.

If he looks a little weird, Joe Meek was. The producing genius behind the Tornadoes and "Telstar," Meek's musical themes—extraterrestrial life, horror and dead rock stars—came out of a deeply troubled psyche. (Razor & Tie)

The Tornadoes, seen here in a British TV appearance, were never able to duplicate the success of "Telstar," although they continued to have hits for a few years in England. German-born bassist Heinz Burt (third from left) left the group and briefly became a British teen idol. (Clem Cattini)

Anyone who was within ear range of a transistor radio in the winter of 1962-63 remembers hearing this astonishing instrumental that sounded quite like nothing else on the airwaves. With its soaring clavioline—a small, battery-operated, electronic keyboard, cheesy sound effects (a Meek trademark), unrelenting rhythm, and ethereal voices "aahhing" away in the background, "Telstar" was at once immensely corny and strangely endearing. A spiritually uplifting and naively optimistic celebration of technology, it may be the closest rock has come to the "music of the spheres."

The Tornadoes recorded "Telstar," but it was Meek's unique vision that propelled it. Known in this country primarily for "Telstar" and the Honeycombs, a second-tier British Invasion group who hit these shores with "Have I the Right" two years later, Meek was a major force in pre-Beatle British rock who scored an impressive forty-five Top 50 singles in the early sixties.

But Joe Meek was also a deeply troubled man of bizarre tastes and strange obsessions. This would be of only peripheral interest, if his music didn't so strikingly reflect those obsessions. A clinical psychologist would have a field day going through the Meek catalogue, if one hasn't already done so.

Meek's first passion growing up on his family's Gloucestershire farm was for electronics. He served as a radar technician in the Royal Air Force in the forties, which may have aroused his lifelong interest in outer space and the possibility of extraterrestrial life. He moved to London in the early fifties and quickly earned a reputation as a crack sound studio engineer. Meek was a genius at dreaming up new and unconventional ways to improve the sound on British pop and jazz records, which was at the time notoriously poor. He was, for instance, the first engineer to put a microphone in or up against each component of a drum kit to get a stronger, cleaner rhythm beat.

One of his early successes was Chris Barber's "Petite Fleur," which he, for all practical purposes, produced, according to Dennis Diken in the accompanying booklet to Razor & Tie's excellent compilation, *It's Hard to Believe: The Amazing World of Joe Meek*. Meek eventually founded his own independent label, Triumph Records, and went on to even greater success as an independent producer, leasing masters to the major record companies. From his cluttered home studio on Holloway Road in North London, Meek, like some sound Svengali, turned out incredibly sophisticated recordings using homemade equipment and whatever else was at hand, from kitchen utensils to a flushing toilet (supposedly the opening Telstar rocket sounds).

Many of Meek's hits were vocal numbers, like the haunting "Johnny Remember Me" by Johnny Leyton and Mike Berry's "Tribute to Buddy Holly," a singer whom Meek not only idolized, but believed he could communicate with via seances. But Meek had a special fondness for instrumentals and, besides the Tornadoes, he nurtured several other successful instro groups.

The Outlaws, a guitar group that backed up several Meek acts, lent an authentic Western tang and Duane Eddy twang to such nifty charters as "Swingin' Low." The Moontrekkers, a group still hitting the oldies circuit in the nineties, were an outlet for Meek's penchant for horror and perversity.[1] The Moontrekkers biggest single, "Night of the Vampire," is an oddly jolly dance macabre led by a grotesquely twangy guitar and concludes with one of Meek's more outlandish sound effects, the flapping wings of a bat in flight.

But Meek's most innovative instrumentals were produced on a rare 1960 extended play (EP) recording *I Hear a New World*, performed by the Blue Men. For those who think "Telstar" sounds out of this world, these tracks truly sound like they were recorded on another planet. "Valley of the Saroos" and "The Bublight" are bold slabs of industrial technomusic that were a couple of decades ahead of their time. No further evidence need be given of Meek's visionary genius.

By 1966, Meek's own fragile world was starting to crumble around him. The Mersey Beat revolution suddenly made the once hip producer look like a relic of the past. The worldwide success of the Beat groups must have been a particularly bitter pill to swallow since Meek had years earlier turned down the Beatles for a session in his famed studio.

Like his American counterpart, Phil Spector, Meek was an eccentric loner with a colossal ego and a deep suspicion of others that bordered on the paranoiac. He was also homosexual. He had a long affair with Heinz Burt, German-born bass guitarist for the Tornadoes, and transformed him into a teen idol with another one of his tributes to dead rock stars, "Just Like Eddie" (Cochran), who died in an auto accident in England in 1960. The relationship with Heinz ended bitterly in early 1967 in a dispute over royalties.

Lawsuits from Heinz and other former music colleagues left Meek nearly destitute and he turned to barbiturates for solace. The voices and sounds he heard now didn't come from his tape recorder but from inside his head. His home studio had become a kind of private hell.

Following a sleepless night in his studio, a distressed Meek got into an argument with his landlady, who ran a leather shop downstairs. She turned away to leave and he seized a hunting rifle left behind by Heinz and shot her in the back. Moments later he turned the rifle on himself and blew out his brains. What seemed like two senseless acts of violence may have been premeditated. Meek died on February 3, 1967—eight years to the day after the death of his idol, Buddy Holly. In imitating a legend, Meek himself became a legend, one whose legacy is growing as more and more of the incredible music he created is rediscovered.

As for the Tornadoes, their moment in rock heaven was brief. "Jungle Fever," the B side of "Telstar," showcasing the skillful drumming of Clem Cattini, and the American follow-up single, "Ridin' the Wind" (#63), captured some of the excitement and innovative sound of "Telstar," but further singles proved only

---

[1] He also produced Screaming Lord Sutch and the Savages, England's answer to Screamin' Jay Hawkins.

pleasant pieces of easy listening, despite Meek's always excellent production values. An exception was "Hot Pot," another jungle rocker that featured some of Meek's wildest sound effects. Were those squealing sounds grunting pigs or noisy cannibals about to eat their captives? Unfortunately "Hot Pot" failed to chart even in Britain and a year later Cattini, the last original Tornado, left. A new lineup under Meek's tutelage failed to reverse the group's fortunes.

In 1975 most of the original members reunited and, as the "New Tornadoes," released a new version of their big hit. But without Joe Meek to guide it, this "Telstar" remained sadly earthbound.

FROM DENMARK WITH LOVE

For decades, Denmark's leading cultural export was comedian/pianist Victor Borge, whose hilarious parodies on the serious world of concert music have made him one of the world's most beloved entertainers.

In the early sixties, however, two other Danish musicians managed to crack the American pop charts with two highly unusual instrumentals.

....

IF VICTOR BORGE WAS the doyen of Danish music in the fifites, Bent Fabric (real name Bent Fabricius-Bjerre) was its wunderkind. A child prodigy, he was conducting his own jazz band while still in his teens. The Danes discovered

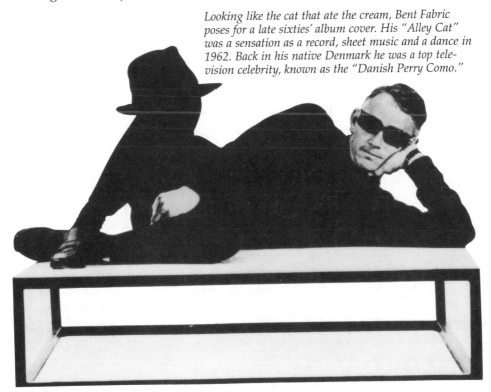

Looking like the cat that ate the cream, Bent Fabric poses for a late sixties' album cover. His "Alley Cat" was a sensation as a record, sheet music and a dance in 1962. Back in his native Denmark he was a top television celebrity, known as the "Danish Perry Como."

American jazz around the same time as the English, and Fabric made some of the first jazz recordings in his country in the late forties. At age 26, he formed what would become Denmark's most prestigious record company, Metronome.

But Fabric wore many hats, besides the bowler that sat jauntily on his head. He was a composer, pianist, A & R man, and, most successfully, a television personality. Like Acker Bilk in England, Fabric drifted effortlessly from jazz to pop and hosted Danish TV's *Around a Piano* show on Saturday nights for several years. With his relaxed playing, casual dress and a cigarette dangling from his lips, he earned the title "the Danish Perry Como."

In the early sixties, Fabric recorded "Alley Cat," a catchy little piano novelty, that sounded like a cat strutting over the keyboard. With a faint jazzy feel and a very danceable rhythm, "Alley Cat" scaled the charts in Denmark, then the rest of Europe, and finally America, where it peaked at #7. Its rhythmic beat made it the most popular group dance at weddings and parties since the Hokey-Pokey. The simplicity of the tune also made it a must-have piece for the family piano. Over 200,000 copies of the sheet music alone was sold in the United States by the end of 1962.

"Alley Cat" became an instrumental standard, arranged for marching bands and elevators. (Fabric was commissioned to write a special Muzak version.) There was even a vocal version, "The Alley Cat Song" (#76), crooned by David Thorne. Fabric's triumph was capped when "Alley Cat" was incongruously named Best Rock and Roll Record of 1962 at the Grammy Awards.

The popular Dane went through a musical menagerie to try to repeat his success in the states, but clever ditties like "The Happy Puppy," "The Drunken Penguin" and "The Pink Elephant" missed the mark. His only other charting American single was "Chickenfeed" (#62), a witty variation on chopsticks. Bent Fabric went back to being the Danish Perry Como, playing regularly for the king and queen at the Royal Palace in Copenhagen. He continues to compose songs, musicals and ballets today, most recently the music for a ballet version of *The Little Mermaid*.

....

A YEAR AND A HALF BEFORE "Alley Cat" became a hit, Fabric had helped another countryman to instrumental glory in the United States. Like him, Swedish-born Jorgen Ingmann was first drawn to American jazz and in his late teens formed a quintet in which he played jazz guitar in the style of Charlie Christian.

By 1953, Ingmann was under the spell of another American guitarist, Les Paul, whose multi-tracking techniques inspired the Dane to build his own home studio in Copenhagen. He even formed a duo with vocalist Grethe Clemmenson, whom he later married and who played Mary Ford to his Les Paul. Fabric, Ingmann's manager at Metronome, was intrigued by his experimenting with echo and other electronic effects, and arranged to release some singles in the United States.

Swedish-born Jorgen Ingmann looks more like a Comanche than an Apache on this album cover. With layered tracking, modeled after Les Paul's multi-tracking, he created intriguing sonic bursts and echoes on his guitar, taking "Apache" to #2 on the U.S. charts. (Photo courtesy of Showtime Archives, Toronto)

At about that time, "Apache," an evocative guitar instrumental by Jerry Lordan, was the #1 song in England. First recorded by British guitarist Bert Weedon, "Apache" was covered by teen idol Cliff Richards' back-up band, the Shadows. It was their first instrumental solo and reached the top of the charts in July 1960. The Shadows quickly established themselves as the number one British group, instrumental *or* vocal, and had an astonishing thirty-two chart entries over the next two decades, including four more #1 hits.

It is one of the mysteries of instrumental rock why the Shadows never made a dent in the American market. Perhaps it was the similarity of their sound to the Ventures, whose first hit, "Walk—Don't Run," came out the same summer as "Apache," that hurt them. Whatever the reason, when their "Apache" was released on ABC-Paramount in America, it disappeared without a trace.

Soon after, Jorgen Ingmann came out with his own version of "Apache," the B side of his "Echo Boogie," which he was certain would be a hit. The single was released in America on Atlantic, ironically the same label that the Shadows signed with after leaving ABC. "Apache" was the side the disk jockeys liked and played. And this time, with Ingmann's electronic gimmickry, it was a solid hit, rising to #2 in the winter of 1961.

The Shadows' "Apache" was straight-on rock, driven by the clean, metallic lead guitar of Hank Marvin and the percussive power of drummer Tony Meehan, beating a Cuban tom-tom he found gathering dust in a cupboard at the recording studio. The tom-tom lent the tune a Native American flavor, appropriate to the title. Ingmann's version, despite the silly album cover that showed him in a chief's bonnet wearing war paint, sounded like it came from outer space. Guitar strings exploded and ricocheted like electronic blips, pulsating through space. The Shadows' "Apache" may have been better rock, but Ingmann's had mystery and elegance.

Always more at home in his studio than on the concert stage, Ingmann never capitalized on his hit with a U.S. tour and hastened his exit from the scene as another one-hit wonder. By the mid-sixties he forsook performing entirely and became a head producer at Metronome Records.

THE MASTER OF GEMÜTLICH

One day in March 1961 German record producer Bert Kaempfert came to the Top Ten, a new club among many in Hamburg's burgeoning rock scene, to hear up-and-coming British singer Tony Sheridan. Kaempfert was impressed by Sheridan, whose neo-rockabilly style was knocking them dead at the Top Ten, and offered him a contract with Polydor Records. Sheridan's back-up band was another transplanted British act that had been playing the Hamburg clubs since their arrival the previous summer.

The recording session took place one June morning in the auditorium of a local school. Sheridan and the group lay down two rave-ups of old standards, "My Bonnie" and "When the Saints Go Marching In." Satisfied with the session, Kaempfert, in an expansive mood, offered to listen to some of the back-up group's original material. He wasn't impressed and advised the players to stick with established songs for the time being. He did, however, agree to record their version of "Ain't She Sweet" and their original instrumental "Cry for a Shadow," the title of which was a clever swipe at the biggest group in Britain, the Shadows.

Kaempfert paid each band member the equivalent of $125 for the session and sent them on their way with a new name, the Beat Brothers. He talked them out of calling themselves the Beatles because it sounded like "peedles," the German slang word for penis. Fortunately, they later changed their minds about that one.

Bert Kaempfert's brush with the Beatles is an interesting footnote in the career of a man whose own musical bent was far removed from the Mersey Beat. "[He] had the right sniffer," said Tony Sheridan in a 1994 interview, "but he wasn't able to actually see deep enough into it to see what the Beatles could have done . . . he gave the Beatles away to Brian Epstein."

Despite this lapse of judgment, the German band leader played a major role in the pop instrumental field of the sixties, serving as a bridge between the lush orchestral music of the fifties and the smooth, easy-listening pop of the sixties. Songwriter, band leader, arranger and producer, Kaempfert's considerable contribution to the golden age of instrumentals has largely been overlooked.

He was born in Hamburg in 1923, an only child and spoiled prodigy. At the Hamburg School of Music he mastered the piano, clarinet, saxophone and

The Master of Gemütlich looks like he's been listening to too many of his own records. The multi-talented Bert Kaempfert of Germany is seen here conducting his original score for the 1966 American spy movie A Man Could Get Killed, which produced "Strangers in the Night," later a #1 song for Frank Sinatra. (Archive Photos)

accordion. After graduation, he went to work for the Hans Busch band in Danzig and formed his own band in West Germany after the war. Polydor Records hired him as a producer and in 1959 he had his first hit, "Morgen" (#13 in America), by Yugoslav singer Ivo Robic.

The following year, Berlin songwriter Klaus Neumann brought Kaempfert a lovely ballad he had written, which had been used as the title song in an unsuccessful German film *Our Wonderland by Night*. The film was a disturbing drama about post-war Germany, but the song, while somber, had a romantic lyricism that appealed to Kaempfert, and he agreed to record it with a studio orchestra.

"Wonderland by Night" is one of those full-blown big band ballads that could have been recorded in the forties. Anchored by a solid trumpet solo by Charly Tabor, it had one of the most grandiose instrumental openings since Roger Williams' "Autumn Leaves," complete with blaring trumpet and whooping male and female chorus. Kaempfert added one interesting innovation—an electric bass guitar line that bounced along, adding a distinctive contemporary beat to the music. It would become a Kaempfert signature and be featured on all his subsequent hits.

"Wonderland by Night" became a huge hit in Germany, Japan and eventually the United States, where it went to #1 for three weeks at the end of 1960.

Kaempfert would follow it with a string of upbeat, foot-tapping instrumentals. "Afrikaan Beat" (#42) was supposedly based on an Afrikaan folk tune and was one of a number of South African songs Kaempfert recorded. With its echoing brass and heavy, happy beat it was an oddly optimistic number at a time when the Afrikaans were beating the life out of black South Africans with their system of apartheid. Together with "That Happy Feeling" (#67) and "The Happy Trumpeter" (later retitled "The Magic Trumpet"), it helped create a subgenre of *gemütlich* (German for "good feeling") instrumentals, built on perky brass and woodwinds, soaring strings and that bouncing bass line. The style would later be further refined and packaged by Herb Alpert and the Tijuana Brass.

Kaempfert's best-known composition in this style was "A Swingin' Safari," where the infectious bass beat and a syncopated chorus of twittering woodwinds swung the tune clear up to the jungle canopy. Kaempfert's recording, however, was overshadowed by a cover by American band leader Billy Vaughn which went to #13 in 1962. Vaughn, the king of covers, was the instrumental equivalent of Pat Boone and worked for the same label, Dot. "A Swingin' Safari" was the last of his long string of Top 40 instrumentals, making him the number one orchestral popmeister of the rock era. "A Swingin' Safari" would be reborn a few years later as the theme song of television's *Hollywood Squares*.

Kaempfert's other songwriting credits were equally impressive. He wrote "Wooden Heart," sung by Elvis Presley in *G.I. Blues*, and based on the German folk song, "Muss I Denn." It later was a #1 song for Joe Dowell. Kaempfert provided Wayne Newton with his first and best hit, "Danke Schoen" (#13), with a swinging arrangement that rivaled Bobby Darin's big band hits. His "Red Roses for a Blue Lady" (#11) was that rare song that was a simultaneous hit as an instrumental (for Kaempfert) and a vocal (for both Newton and Vic Dana). "Spanish Eyes," originally titled "Moon Over Naples," gave Al Martino one of his last big hits, and "Strangers in the Night," originally sung in a movie spy spoof, *A Man Could Get Killed*, gave Frank Sinatra his first #1 pop song in over a decade.

The Master of Gemütlich continued to record his tuneful, breezy music into the seventies. He died in June 1980 in Switzerland at age 56.

....

ANOTHER GERMAN WITH a talent for the light touch was jazz pianist Horst Jankowski, who took an orchestral piece for voice and piano called "Eine Schwarzwaldfahrt" and turned it into a lively pop piano tune, "A Walk in the Black Forest" (#12). The walk was a one-way affair, however, and despite numerous albums and singles, Jankowski never again trod through the Top 40. By 1965, homegrown instrumental artists were giving the Europeans a run for their money with their own irresistible brand of ear candy.

FROM ALL OVER THE WORLD

Before we return stateside, there are a few more instrumental oddities from abroad that must be mentioned.

Take the case of Los Indios Tabajaras, a brother duo of Brazilian guitarists. Their official biography reads like something from the overheated imagination of a press publicist. Sons of a Tabajaras Indian chieftain in the jungles of Ceara, Brazil, Natalicio and Antenor Lima happened upon a guitar left behind by a careless group of explorers and taught themselves to play it. Soon they were playing their tribal folk songs in gigs in Rio de Janeiro. An agent promptly discovered them and sent them to Mexico to complete their musical education. In 1957 RCA signed the brothers to a recording contract.

Their album, *Sweet and Savage*, sold poorly and the brothers went back to the jungle. Five years later a producer of the morning show on WNEW radio in New York played a cut from the *Sweet and Savage* LP as filler. Audience response was so positive that RCA released a single. Never mind that "Maria Elena" was no Brazilian folk song but a remake of a 1941 Jimmy Dorsey Orchestra #1 hit. It sounded very sweet on the acoustical guitars and went to #6 on the national charts.

When the rereleased album was a best seller, the cry went out from RCA headquarters to "Find the Indians!" The Lima brothers were discovered living on a ranch outside Rio and were whisked back to the States to resume their recording career. They made a string of successful albums for RCA before once again fading from view. Perhaps they are back in the jungle looking for another abandoned instrument to play.

Looking like they just stepped out of the Amazon jungle, Natalecio and Antenor Lima, better known as Los Indios Tabajaras, pose mysteriously for an album cover. Their sweet acoustical guitars on "Maria Elena" were a refreshing novelty in late 1963 and they continued to record for RCA through the sixties.

Then there was "Hawaii Tattoo" (#33) in the summer of 1965, a rather loopy-sounding island instrumental with a steel guitar, peppy organ, and busy percussion that was the work of the Waikikis who hailed from balmy . . . Belgium?[2]

....

MORE SUITABLY GALLIC was French orchestra conductor Paul Mauriat. His first foray into the U.S. charts was a vocal version of his instrumental "Chariot," which became that most inspirational of girl group songs, "I Will Follow Him," a #1 hit for Little Peggy March in early 1963. Nearly five years later, Mauriat came into his own with "L'Amour Est Bleu" ("Love Is Blue"), a pretty, melancholy ballad that featured a lush string section, beguiling woodwinds and a harpsichord that set the proper pseudo-classical tone. Number one for five weeks in the winter of 1968, it is the only #1 U.S. single, instrumental or otherwise, from France and the first #1 instrumental since "Telstar." The phenomenal success of "Love is Blue" only heightened the sad fact that almost the only instrumentals to reach the airwaves by the late sixties were the rare blockbusters.

....

ALTHOUGH EVEN FURTHER out of our time period, we can't help but take note of what may be the strangest instro hit of them all. The stirring hymn "Amazing Grace" had already been a #15 hit for folk singer Judy Collins in 1971 when the Royal Scots Dragoon Guards tackled it the following year on bagpipes. The original recording was part of an album honoring the joining together of two Scottish regiments and caught the ear of a British disc jockey who started playing it regularly on his late night program. RCA, which seemed to have cornered the market for foreign instrumental flukes, released the droning, hypnotic tune as a single, first in Great Britain, then on the continent, and finally in the United States, where it zoomed to #11. Amazing.

---

[2] Belgium was a veritable hotbed of instrumental groups in the sixties. Two of the biggest were the Cousins and the Jokers, neither of whom managed to translate their popularity across the Atlantic.

Chapter Six

All That Jazz

The teen-ager is at first a rock and roll buyer.
As he matures away from this, he graduates to
rhythm and blues, from which he climbs aboard
the straight jazz bandwagon. Many of them
completely by-pass the straight pop music field.
DICK BOCK, president of World Pacific Records,
independent jazz label (1961)

If a man has the conviction to play his own style,
he's looked upon as a giant. It's morally wrong
to expect people to pay for satisfying your ego.
CANNONBALL ADDERLEY

In his excellent, highly personalized survey, *Rock & Roll: An Unruly History*, Robert Palmer makes a convincing argument that jazz played as major a role in the evolution of rock as did rhythm and blues and country and western. He explains how during World War II jazz split in two directions—the dance "jump" music of masters such as Count Basie, and the arty, modern jazz of the East Coast bebops and West Coast cool school. "Jump jazz," according to Palmer, evolved into rhythm and blues and then into rock 'n' roll.

If Palmer is right, a strange reversal took place in the late fifties. The new cool, intellectual jazz began to feed into pop music, giving new life and vitality to the pop instrumental.

At the start of the rock era, however, jazz artists of any persuasion were a rarity on the *Billboard* charts. Count Basie had a hit version of "April in Paris" (#28) in 1956 but it was strictly traditional big band, as was Louis Armstrong and the All Stars' vocal version of "A Theme from *The Three Penny Opera*" (#20), probably the most recorded instrumental of 1956. Joe Darensbourg and the Dixie Flyers scored in 1958 with "Yellow Dog Blues" (#43), but their traditional New Orleans jazz, while popular in England, had few imitators in the states.

The jazz artist who had the biggest crossover pop success with something far more contemporary was Moe Koffman, Canada's renowned jazz flutist. The

Koffman Quartette's coolly delicious "The Swinging Shepherd Blues" reached #23 in 1958 and brought a rash of cover versions, a sure sign of an instrumental's success. But Koffman paid dearly for his moment of pop fame. Other jazz musicians and critics branded him a sellout —a fate that would befall other jazz artists who dared to dabble in the commercial marketplace. Koffman, who was classically trained at the Toronto Conservatory of Music, didn't let it bother him. He went on to record a highly regarded series of albums of jazz interpretations of Bach and other classical composers as well as more mainstream jazz.

DETECTIVE JAZZ

In September 1958 a new crime-detective series debuted on NBC TV, produced and directed by filmmaker Blake Edwards. As Edwards later wrote, the dilemma facing him was "How do we set the Peter Gunn show apart from other mystery-adventure series? . . . It hit me then—JAZZ. If we could use the music as an integral part of the dramatic action, firing story-line and score, we should have something worthwhile."

Edwards turned to 34-year-old Henry Mancini, who had already proven himself a gifted film composer, most recently with the dynamic, moody score for Orson Welles' film noir *Touch of Evil* released earlier that year. In his main theme for *Peter Gunn*, Mancini created a driving, rhythmic jazzy piece that was the most striking TV theme since *Dragnet*. "The guts of the whole thing was the rhythm section—bass, guitar, drums and vibes and walking bass that opened the show," Mancini noted years later in an interview. "In a normal movie a walking bass would be lost. The sound of `Peter Gunn' was a totally contained sound, and it started a new approach to commercial recording."

It also made modern jazz—with its cool, lean, sophisticated sound—a hot commodity. Mancini's album *Music from Peter Gunn* became a best seller, topping the album charts for three weeks in early 1959. Ray Anthony, dance band leader and creator of the Bunny Hop, covered Mancini's version of the title music and had a Top 10 hit on the singles' charts.

Edwards' claim that Mancini's score was the first jazz score for a television series is not exactly true. *Richard Diamond, Private Detective* debuted a year before *Peter Gunn* and had an authentic jazz score provided by Pete Rugolo, who had composed for Stan Kenton and whose jazz credentials were far superior to Mancini's. *M Squad*, also appearing in 1957, boasted a main theme by Count Basie playing big band jazz in a more modern vein. It was Mancini's bold, aggressive music, however, that best expressed the dangerous world of the detective, a romantic figure from the forties who, like jazz, had gone cool and contemporary in the fifties.

Mancini and Edwards made the music an integral part of the show by putting the top West Coast jazz musicians who played the score in the action as the house band at Mother's, the nightclub that Gunn frequented between cases.

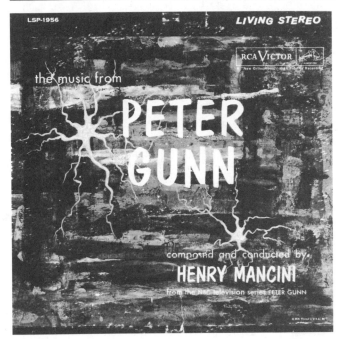

Peter Gunn may have been only a moderate hit as a TV series, but the music by Henry Mancini was a blockbuster. The jazz score, typified by the aggressive main theme, was a smash both as a single and as an album and brought jazz into the pop mainstream.

Most of the numbers on the first *Gunn* LP were more laid back than the main theme—easy-listening cocktail lounge jazz and a far cry from the revolutionary sounds of the likes of Charlie Parker and Miles Davis. Yet, however diluted, jazz had entered the pop mainstream and would stay there for the remainder of the golden age of instrumentals.

A slew of small-screen sleuths followed in Gunn's footsteps with jazz or jazz-flavored scores—*Naked City*, *The Thin Man*, *Ellery Queen* and *Pete Kelly's Blues*, whose main character was a jazz musician and bandleader. The most popular of all these crime shows, however, was *77 Sunset Strip*, Warner Brothers' first and most successful detective series. It not only made a modest hit out of the finger-snapping theme song by Don Ralke (#67), but launched the spectacular, albeit brief, career of teen idol Edward "Kookie" Byrnes, the Fonz of the fifties.

"Jazz is moving into the pop market in every area—records, TV, radio, movies, TV films, singing commercials, etc," reported *Billboard* in a March 1959 issue. Jazz scores enhanced such prestigious motion pictures as *I Want To Live!* and *Anatomy of a Murder*, music for the latter written by no less a jazz luminary than Duke Ellington. Jazz music poured forth from the relatively new FM radio band, offering older discriminating listeners a pleasant alternative to rock 'n' roll, which now all but dominated AM radio.

In the fall of 1959, Mancini and Edwards struck again with another action/crime series, *Mr. Lucky*, based on the 1943 Cary Grant film. But the main theme, while another pop hit (#21), this time with Mancini conducting, was far closer in style to the romantic movie songs he would win a shelf full Grammies and Oscars for in the sixties than the jazz played down at Mother's. Detective jazz, unlike the gangsta rap of three decades later, was not quite authentic. But the real thing lay just around the corner.

COOL KEYBOARDS
Craig Stevens, star of *Peter Gunn*, returned to television three years after the demise of his series in another adult adventure show, *Mr. Broadway*, created by Hollywood writer Garson Kanin. The series only lasted a few months, but it should be remembered as the only television series scored by jazz pianist Dave Brubeck. The *Mr. Broadway* theme, edgy and rhythmically complex, produced no hit single, but then the Brubeck Quartet was already a household name and had made a successful crossover to the pop charts that few other serious jazz groups had attempted or achieved.

Brubeck was born David Warren on December 6, 1920, in Concord, California, northwest of San Francisco. His mother was a noted piano teacher in the Bay area and his father was a rancher and champion rodeo roper who played the harmonica. One of Brubeck's first compositions was "Dad Plays Harmonica."

He studied classical music at Mills College in Oakland with distinguished French composer Darius Milhaud, whose own love of American jazz is evident in such compositions of his as *L'Creation du le Monde*. Milhaud encouraged Brubeck to stay with jazz. Brubeck led an Army radio band during War World II and on his return to California after the war helped form the Jazz Workshop Ensemble, an experimental group of musicians, soon re-named the Dave Brubeck Octet or "The Eight." Brubeck, who had always considered himself "a composer who plays piano," pared down the ensemble to a trio and started tinkering with such traditional musical elements as rhythms, time signatures and keys. In 1951, alto saxman Paul Desmond joined the trio, making it a quartet. A few years later drummer Joe Morello came on board, and in 1958 bassist Eugene Wright joined, establishing the classic Dave Brubeck Quartet that would make jazz and pop history for nearly a decade.

Brubeck's new cool sound was lyrical and contemplative compared to the hard, "hot" bebop of the East Coast jazzmen, but it also had a sinewy strength, driving rhythms and time signatures that could suddenly change without warning. Unlike many jazz musicians of the cool school, Brubeck took his music out of smokey little clubs and coffeehouses and onto college campuses where young people, tired of the Hit Parade but too sophisticated for rock 'n' roll, reveled in his challenging music. The Brubeck Quartet became the first modern jazz group with real youth appeal.

In 1959, Desmond wrote "Take Five," an upbeat but moody jazz waltz with tricky rhythms and playful sax solos. Along with Brubeck's own exotic "Blue Rondo à la Turk," it was the centerpiece of *Time Out* (1960), a breakthrough jazz album that his label, Columbia, was reluctant to release. It wasn't only the orig-

The classic Dave Brubeck Quartet pictured here, made the lean, combo sound of modern jazz commercially marketable. Although not a rocker himself, Brubeck (at the piano) enjoyed the music and was good friends with Buddy Holly before his death in 1959. (Archive Photos/Metronome Collection)

inal, experimental music that Columbia objected to, but the album cover—an abstract painting by Joan Miró. The reservations proved groundless: *Time Out* soared to the top of the *Billboard* charts and became the first jazz album to sell a million copies. "Take Five" was released as a single and peaked at #25 in the fall of 1961, an extraordinary achievement for a serious jazz instrumental. When Brubeck received the National Medal of the Arts more than thirty years later, President Bill Clinton told him that he had learned to play the sax listening to Paul Desmond on "Take Five."

Brubeck had only two more charting singles, the folksy novelty "Unsquare Dance" (#74) and "Bossa Nova, U.S.A." (#69). An unlikely international hit, "Unsquare Dance" became the theme music for popular television shows in both Austria and England, where its rhythmic hand clapping broke in every time there was a punch line to a comedy sketch. The Brubeck Quartet's albums continued to sell well in the pop field for years, and their success opened the door to a number of other jazz trios, quartets and quintets.

·······························

ANOTHER INTROSPECTIVE PIANIST from the Bay area was Vince Guaraldi. After a long apprenticeship in the fifties playing piano in the traditional jazz bands of Cal Tjader, Woody Herman and others, Guaraldi formed his own trio (piano, bass, drums) in the early sixties. One of his most intriguing compositions, "Cast Your Fate to the Wind," had none of Brubeck's stylistic virtuosity, but was eloquent and exuberant in its simplicity. The opening chords, like shimmering ripples on the sea, led to some distinctly playful riffs, including a cowboy nod to Floyd Cramer's slip-notes. Guaraldi's understated lyricism took "Cast Your Fate" to #22 and won him the 1962 Grammy for Best Original Jazz Composition.

Guaraldi's most lasting legacy, however, was the wonderful musical soundtracks he wrote and performed for the Charlie Brown TV specials. Deft mixtures of sophistication and childlike innocence, they perfectly matched Charles Shultz's melancholy comic strip characters. The Charlie Brown scores are perhaps the most listened-to jazz works in the world, enjoyed by millions of adults and children who wouldn't know Duke Ellington from Wynton Marsalis. Guaraldi's career was tragically cut short in 1976 when he died at age 47 of a heart attack during a break between shows at a nightclub.

·······························

WHILE GUARALDI PIONEERED his own original compositions, other jazz combos resorted to the time-honored tradition of taking pop or folk melodies and improvising on them. The Don Shirley Trio cracked the Top 40 with a strikingly original version of the old prison song, "Water Boy" (#40). The instrumental opens impressively with the main melody plucked soulfully on a cello, a most unorthodox instrument for a jazz ensemble, while each phrase is punctuated by a sharp drum beat. Shirley's piano quietly picks up the melody and slowly builds momentum to a gospel-like fervor.

Shirley, who was born in Kingston, Jamaica, had doctorates in musical composition, psychology and the liturgical arts and had been a practicing psychologist before devoting himself to jazz.

....

FAR LESS IS KNOWN OF the David Rockingham Trio, but the group's sole 1963 charter, "Dawn" (#62), was an energetic sunrise jaunt with a pumping organ and a lively jazz guitar riff played by Bobby Robinson, who also produced the single for Josie Records.

....

A FEW MONTHS BEFORE the Brubeck Quartet's pop breakthrough a black jazz combo had reached the pop charts with an African-based cool jazz. Julian Edwin Adderley was born eight years after Brubeck in Tampa, Florida. His father, who played the cornet, was a music teacher and Julian became a music director at a Florida music school in the mid-fifties. But blowing the alto sax was his passion, second only to eating. Both loves took him to New York in 1955, where fellow musicians affectionately called him a "cannibal" because of his gargantuan appetite, which led to the nickname "Cannonball."

New York was the center of the emerging bebop school led by Charlie Parker, who had just died, and Miles Davis, his heir apparent. After working with his own combo and other groups, Adderley joined Davis's Sextet for a while. Then

One of the first jazz artists to cross over into pop, Julian "Cannonball" Adderley had to wait until 1967 for his one Top 40 hit, "Mercy, Mercy, Mercy." A man of gargantuan appetites, Adderley died after a massive stroke at age 47. (Archive Photos)

in 1959 he again went on his own, forming the Cannonball Adderley Quintet, with his brother Nat on cornet. Adderley signed with Riverside Records, a small but ambitious independent jazz label, founded in 1952 by jazz aficionados Bill Grauer and Orrin Keepnews, who named it after their New York telephone exchange. Originally reissuing old RCA Victor jazz albums, the two men began recording new experimental jazz artists in 1956, starting with pianist Thelonius Monk. Adderley became one of their most popular artists and in early 1961 they released his version of "African Waltz," a single that had already been a major hit for English jazz leader Johnny Dankworth in Great Britain. Adderley's version, a colorful celebration of African rhythms and instrumentation in a jazz idiom, went to #64 on the *Billboard* charts, encouraging other independent jazz labels to release 45's of their own artists for the pop market.

Another quintet, led by bebop tenor saxman Eddie Harris from Chicago, recorded a jazz version of the theme from the hit movie *Exodus* on the Veejay label and took it to #36.

Adderley and Harris were adventurous spirits, not commercial sell-outs, and weren't afraid of being ostracized by the jazz establishment for moving in new directions. In his crusade to save modern jazz from the purists and elitists, Adderley eventually moved from Riverside to Capitol records and made albums with strings, big bands and even jazz vocalists like Nancy Wilson. Surprisingly, he lost little of his stature as a leading jazz artist, which encouraged other artists to make the crossover to the pop market.

"Not since the golden era of the big band," wrote Jack Maher in *Billboard* in 1961, ". . . has jazz been as potent a fact to the money-making potential of the recording industry as it is today." Within a year that potential would become far greater, as a new musical trend from sunny South America made jazz more commercial than ever before.

BOSSA NOVA U.S.A.

Despite the seemingly endless configurations that arose from the Almighty Twist in 1962, not even the savviest A & R man in the recording industry would have dreamed that a dance would arise that took its inspiration from modern jazz. And then like a balmy breeze from Brazil, land of the samba, came the bossa nova.

The bossa nova, which literally means "new beat" or "new direction" in English, was not really a dance, but since this delicate weaving of the samba beat with jazz-like melodies first appeared in the tiny, crowded bars of Rio de Janeiro about 1958, Brazilians were dancing to it.

In the spring of 1961, Charlie Byrd, a guitarist who was equally at home playing classical music and jazz, toured Latin America for three months under the aegis of the State Department. When he wasn't performing, Byrd was busy collecting tapes and recordings of the indigenous music of each country he visited.

He was particularly captivated by the new Brazilian music, with its freshness, rhythmic complexity and flowing melodies. It was the kind of music that offered rich possibilities for improvisation, the meat of American jazz artists. Like modern American jazz, which influenced the creators of bossa nova, it was cool, sophisticated, often understated, and played by small musical ensembles, often with a guitar comprising the rhythm section.

Byrd was not the first American jazz musician entranced by bossa nova music. Trumpeter Dizzy Gillespie and members of Woody Herman's orchestra had been to Brazil and heard it around the same time. But Byrd was the first who felt inspired to interpret it in his own musical language back in the States. Here he faced a problem. Riverside, Byrd's label, wasn't interested in putting out a bossa nova album, and neither were any of the other independent jazz labels he approached. So Byrd turned to his friend, Stan Getz, one of the most respected alto saxophonists in jazz, and suggested a collaborative album. At the time, Getz had hit a rough patch in his career and was receptive to something new. Indicted on charges of drug possession, he had been living in Denmark for three years and had just returned to the United States.

A brilliant musician and a deeply troubled man, Stan Getz created authentic-sounding bossa nova music by collaborating with the Brazilian masters. He "discovered" Astrud Gilberto, who had never sung before professionally, and collaborated with her on the enchanting "The Girl from Ipanema." (Archive Photos)

He was immediately attracted to the Brazilian music Byrd played for him and quickly convinced his label, Verve, to put out a bossa nova album. Producer Creed Taylor called the Byrd-Getz LP *Jazz Samba* to attract American record buyers who knew nothing of the bossa nova.

With the release of *Jazz Samba* that all changed. The album was the perfect musical melding of Getz's lyrical sax with the tight rhythmic underpinning put down by Byrd's guitar. Together they made the Brazilian melodies warmly appealing to both jazz buffs and pop music lovers. The album shot up the pop charts and Antônio Carlos Jobim's "Desafinado" ("Slightly out of Tune" in English) was released as a single. It went to #15 on the *Billboard* charts, the highest-selling contemporary jazz single up to that time. Although American listeners couldn't pronounce the composer's name (it came out "Joe Beam"), they were captivated by his music.

Jobim was widely regarded as the most original and gifted of the four or five leaders of the bossa nova movement. He was born in 1927 in Rio and spent most of his childhood in nearby Ipanema, a place he would later immortalize in a song about a girl he saw walking on the beach there. "I was a beach boy," Jobim said in an interview shortly before his death in 1994, "and I believe I learned my songs from the birds of the Brazilian forest."

From the tiny, crowded clubs of Rio called "inferninhos" ("little infernos") to the Brazilian recording company where he worked as an arranger in the early fifties, Jobim developed and refined his elegant music. His biggest break came in 1959 when, in collaboration with guitarist/composer Luis Banfa, he composed the score for the French-Brazilian film *Black Orpheus*, a lyrical retelling of the Orpheus legend set in contemporary Rio during Carnival. The movie became an art house hit in the States and won the Academy Award as best foreign film of 1959.

Jobim now began to write the songs that would make him a celebrated composer and performer in the United States in a few short years—"Chega de Saudade" ("No More Blues"), "How Insensitive" and "Desifinado"—most of them in collaboration with another talented composer, João Gilberto.

"The bossa nova bandwagon gathers more pulling power and more passengers with each succeeding week," announced *Billboard* confidently. "Artists, some in pop, but most associated with jazz, are booming the new Brazilian rhythm in projected concerts, new LP and single releases and increased radio and TV time." Among the jazz artists who released bossa nova albums in the fall of 1962 were Dizzy Gillespie, Herbie Mann, Sonny Rollins, Dexter Gordon, Lionel Hampton, Zoot Sims and the Paul Winter Sextet, which played the bossa nova at the Kennedy White House to a less than enthusiastic audience of Washingtonians. The easy-listening crowd could lend an ear to *Big Band Bossa Nova* by Enoch Light and the Light Brigade. Pop vocalists like Eydie Gorme ("Blame it on the Bossa Nova") and Paul Anka ("Esso Besso") scored hits and

Jazz guitarist Charlie Byrd first heard bossa nova music on a government-sponsored tour of Latin America in 1961. He made beautiful music with Stan Getz on their recording of "Desafinado," but it all turned sour when Byrd later publicly accused Getz of not sharing his Grammy and royalties with him. (Archive Photos/ Metronome Collection)

even Elvis got in the act with the slyly humorous "Bossa Nova Baby," written for him by Jerry Leiber and Mike Stoller.

The pop music establishment was anxious to tie this hot new music into a teen dance that would make it, as *Billboard* put it, "the new Twist." Of course, the Brazilian samba steps were there all along and simply adapted. While the dance never quite caught on with teens, it became popular with adults who were tired of the twist and anxious to try what Eydie Gorme called "the dance of love."

Dance schools gave eager beginners instructions on how to do the bossa nova, although these fanciful liner notes on an album by the Orchestra Saxsambistas Brasilerios might have been taken from one of Jobim's elliptical lyrics:

> The distinctive dance form of Bossa Nova is characterized by a horizontal progression in space, with a floating rib cage action which moves downward through the body to easy flexion of the knees and firm foot placements. . . .

For those who found the step too daunting to attempt, there was always the bossa nova doll that could do it for you.

For all the bright happiness of the music, there was an underlying melancholic strain that ran through it and this darkness soon touched the lives of the musicians who had best captured it. Charlie Byrd was deeply hurt when Getz received a Grammy for Best Jazz Solo Performance of 1962 for "Desafinado." In a statement in *Down Beat* magazine he argued that Getz should have shared the Grammy with him, although, unfortunately, his solo work on the album version had been edited out for the single. He eventually sued MGM, which owned Verve, for royalties and won a $50,000 settlement.

Meanwhile, Getz was busy recording new Verve albums with Jobim, Gilberto and Banfa, who had come to the States with the bossa nova boom. While working on the Gilberto album, Getz was struck by the untrained but distinctive voice of Gilberto's wife, Astrudo, who was the only one of the Brazilian contingent who spoke English. Under Getz's urging, and despite her husband's objections, Astrudo, who had never sung professionally before, recorded two numbers for the album, one of them Jobim's "The Girl from Ipanema."

Astrudo Gilberto's understated but erotically charged reading of "Ipanema," which Henry Schipper has described as a "vocal without makeup," created a new style of jazz singing. A single was released and "The Girl from Ipanema" became a Top 5 hit in mid-1964, right at the peak of Beatlemania. Shortly after making the recording, Astrudo separated from her husband and later had a tempestuous affair with her new mentor, Getz.

The 1964 Grammies were even a greater triumph for Getz than the 1962 Grammies. He took both the Album of the Year and the Best Instrumental Jazz Performance awards for the *Getz/Gilberto* album, the first jazz artist ever to win both categories in one year. "The Girl from Ipanema" won Record of the Year. A few days later, after a night of heavy drinking, the manic depressive Getz attempted suicide by sticking his head in a gas oven in his kitchen.

....

As THE BOSSA NOVA BOOM widened, American songwriters adapted the sound to their own styles. Dave Brubeck's "Bossa Nova, U.S.A." was smooth and jazzy in the Quartet's classic style. Charlie Byrd and his jazz trio, backed by a string orchestra, bounced back with an impressive album. A single from it, Jobim's sublime "Meditation" (#66), gave Byrd his second pop hit.

Composer and band leader Joe Harnell caught the fantastic side of Jobim's music with his fanciful "Fly Me To the Moon—Bossa Nova," a Top 15 hit in Harnell's instrumental version. The pop tune charted four more times, mostly as a vocal, and provided a nice annuity for Harnell who went on to the more mundane work of musical director for such TV shows as *The Bionic Woman* and *The Incredible Hulk*.

....

VERVE'S SUCCESSFUL bossa nova albums encouraged other jazz artists to go in a more commercial direction. Kai Winding was a Danish-born jazz trombonist who started his career playing in a burlesque house. Working his way through the big bands in the forties and his own small ensembles in the fifties, he signed with Verve in 1961. "More," the theme from *Mondo Cane*, a strange Italian documentary about the wilder side of modern life, was unabashedly romantic and most unjazz-like. The soaring organ that carried the inspirational melody and the galloping rhythm section was more than a little reminiscent of "Telstar" and helped boost the record to #8.

Another unorthodox instrumental hit from a jazz group in 1963 was "Washington Square" (#2) by the Village Stompers. (That's Greenwich Village, of course.) An eight-man band of Dixieland devotees, the Stompers were a fixture at Basin Street East, a jazz club in the Village, when their first single was sold to Epic. The melancholy mood set by "Washington Square" is reminiscent of Kenny Ball's "Midnight in Moscow," but the expressive banjo solo that opens and closes the record is evocative of early Americana, making this the only jazz instrumental of the era to reflect the folk revival of the sixties.

....

By 1966, THE BOSSA NOVA was just another discarded dance craze of another era. However, that fall one more bossa nova hit emerged, the laid-back "Summer Samba" (#26) by organist Walter Wanderley, who was Brazilian and a contemporary of Jobim and Gilberto.

A resurgence of interest in the bossa nova in the 1980s brought Jobim back to the States to perform for the first time in years. He played and sang at the fiftieth anniversary of Verve in 1991 and ironically performed Harnell's "Fly Me to the Moon" on Sinatra's *Duets* album in 1994. Jobim died in December of that year at Mt. Sinai Hospital in New York City at age 67. Stan Getz had passed away three years earlier of liver cancer.

Writing of Jobim's music in an obituary in *The New York Times*, William Grimes noted that it "transferred the rhythms and messages of public celebration to an intimate scale . . . and [its] lyrics were sly and elliptical, often sung in a whisper." It has proven to be one of the most seductive whispers in pop music, one that still beckons to the discriminating listener today.

ORGASMIC ORGANS

The bossa nova was just one of the new directions jazz was taking in 1962. A charismatic performer, who had been a leading light of the East Coast movement since the mid-fifties, burst onto the pop scene that year. Although he was definitely a modernist, there was nothing cool about Jimmy Smith. He played one "hot" organ and was, as one jazz critic put it "the best thing to happen to the Hammond organ since electricity."

Smith was born December 8, 1925, in Norristown, Pennsylvania, where his father was a piano teacher. He taught his son to play and at age 9 the boy won the Major Bowes Amateur Show on radio. Smith briefly performed with his father as a song-and-dance team in 1942 before entering the Navy for war service. After the war, he studied at Philadelphia's Hamilton School of Music.

His passion switched from the piano to the organ after hearing pioneer jazz organist Wild Bill Davis perform. For a year Smith played jazz piano in clubs at

Jimmy Smith burns up his Hammond organ in a jam session. His electrifying keyboard style, set against a big band, created a new and exciting form of jazz pop in the early sixties that defied categorization. (Archive Photos)

night and practiced the organ by day. In the early fifties he played organ with Philadelphia rhythm and blues singer Don Gardner, who would much later find his moment of Top 40 fame with the rousing "I Need Your Loving," sung with Dee Dee Ford. Smith found the straight rhythm and blues that Gardner and his group, the Sonotones, played too restrictive. He preferred the free flow of jazz that would allow him more room to improvise. In 1955, he formed his own jazz trio with Eddie McFadden on guitar and Donald Bailey on drums.

The electric organ was as much a novelty in jazz in the fifties as it was in rock. What James Booker and Dave "Baby" Cortez did for the rock organ in the late fifties, Smith did, on a grander scale, for the jazz organ. Smith's style was an original and tantalizing mix of intricate jazz improvising with down-home, funky blues. He played with a percussive power that was, by turns, lean and supple and shrill and frenetic. Upon first hearing Smith's trio at a club in Atlantic City, Babs Gonzales wrote, "I heard 'futuristic stratosphere' sounds that were never before explored on the organ." His first major New York engagement at Greenwich Village's Cafe Bohemia in 1956 was a major event in the world of jazz. Blue Note, the legendary jazz label, wasted no time in signing the Jimmy Smith Trio to a contract and put out a string of albums that solidified his reputation as the country's premier jazz organist.

In early 1962 Smith's single of the old tune, "Midnight Special," made it on the pop charts (#69), followed a year later by "Back at the Chicken Shack" (#63). Like other jazz artists with crossover appeal, Smith was courted by the major labels. His agent, the dynamic Clarence Avant, got him out on loan to Verve, where he worked with band leader/arranger Oliver Nelson on a version of the bold and brassy theme from the film *A Walk on the Wild Side*.

The lean, sparse sound of the trio was gone, replaced by a resplendent big band, which Nelson ingeniously modernized with angular melodies, unusual instrumentation and tight rhythmic brass riffs. "A Walk on the Wild Side" set the pattern for the Smith-Nelson collaboration. The piece opens mysteriously with jangling sleigh bells and a bass riff. Then the full orchestra blares out the theme, much as in a classical concerto before the soloist appears. Then Smith's organ enters in an extended solo, backed only by percussion, wildly improvising on the main theme, twisting and turning it, wringing every ounce of tension and suspense out of sustained notes and chords, building energy at every turn. Finally, the full orchestra returns for a brief battle with the organ. Smith's shrieking pipes duel with blasting brass for an electrifying finale before the orchestra recaps the theme one last time.

"A Walk on the Wild Side" was unlike anything previously heard in pop music. It wasn't big band, it wasn't quite jazz, or rhythm and blues. It was an exciting blending of all three and the single climbed to #21 on the *Billboard* charts.

Smith's success, like that of other jazz artists, started a bidding war for his services. While Verve didn't offer him the most money, they had Oliver and the creative edge. In February 1963 Smith signed a long-term contract with Verve, the first fruit of which was the album *Bashin'—the Unpredictable Jimmy Smith*, which went Top 10 on the LP charts.

I can still remember the first time I heard "Hobo Flats" (#69), Smith's next charting single, on the radio with its dramatic opening—a four-note brass riff followed by a wailing harmonica. Smith's percolating organ was like a funky hobo grabbing you by the throat for a handout. A few months later I bought my first Smith album, *Who's Afraid of Virginia Woolf?* with its spectacular version of "Slaughter on Tenth Avenue." This time Smith pulled out all the stops on his Hammond, hitting a perfect 10 on the Richter scale. He was, as the title on the album claimed, truly "incredible."

By 1965, Smith was ready to return to his roots and resurrected the trio with jazz veterans Kenny Burrell on guitar and Grady Tate on drums. Their first album's title tune, "Organ Grinder Swing," was one of Smith's most succinct and effective singles, although it only went to #92 on the pop charts. On his next outing he added vocals to "Get My Mojo Workin' (Part 1)" (#51) in a voice that Orrin Keepnews described as sounding "like Louis Armstrong with a sore throat."

After twelve charting records, Smith's single sales dropped off and he began a successful series of collaborations with other jazz artists like guitarist Wes Montgomery. In the seventies he opened his own nightclub on the West Coast with his wife Lola. He still plays the organ today, with little of the passion gone.

Despite his undeniable talent and his dominance of an instrument he virtually set the standard for, Jimmy Smith did not escape the old criticism of all jazz artists who dare to popularize their music. But what may have looked to some like a sell-out thirty years ago, today looks more like a golden age, when jazz and pop fused together in the inventive genius of one of the sixties' most dynamic instrumentalists.

....

IN HIS STRIKING CHART DEBUT, Jimmy McGriff may well have been called "Son of Jimmy Smith," for the influence of the older artist on this organist was undeniable. McGriff himself is leery of the comparison, and today insists he is a blues, not jazz, organist. Eight years Smith's junior, he grew up in Philadelphia and was pursuing a career in law enforcement when he heard Smith at a local jam session and decided to become a full time musician. A multi-talented musician who played sax, piano and bass in various local r & b bands, McGriff eventually followed Smith's footsteps into Don Gardener's Sonotones. He first sat down at a Hammond B-3 organ at his sister's wedding and, with Smith's encouragement and the coaching of Richard "Groove" Holmes, he eventually formed his own trio.

In 1961 McGriff laid down a swinging, screeching, almost unrecognizable version of Ray Charles's "I've Got a Woman" on the Jell label. The two-part single got some airplay and was picked up by the bigger Sue label in New York in early 1962. Part I eventually went to #20 on the national charts, making the virtually unknown McGriff a leading rock organist almost overnight. Such later charting singles as "All about My Girl" (#50) and "The Last Minute (Part 1)"

(#99), both from 1963, were in a slower, more bluesy vein. McGriff left Sue in 1966 and has since recorded on a number of labels, most significantly on Milestone Records in the 1980s, where two of his albums made the Top 5 on the jazz LP charts. Whether you call his style blues or jazz, Jimmy McGriff has long since stepped out of the shadow of Jimmy Smith and proved his music can stand on its own.

RAMSEY LEWIS IS "IN"

By 1965, the once daring sound of small jazz ensembles was becoming passé in the onslaught of new musical trends that made instrumentals something of an endangered species. But one more jazz artist's star would rise in the pop world before the party was over.

It is interesting to note that the last major instrumentalist to emerge from the golden age of the genre was a jazz artist. Like Jimmy Smith, Dave Brubeck and Cannonball Adderley, Ramsey Lewis had paid his dues as a serious jazz musician before finding crossover glory on the pop charts, although his popularity at its height in the mid-sixties far outshone that of his colleagues.

Lewis was born in Chicago on May 27, 1935. By age 6 he was playing the piano, which he further pursued at the Chicago College of Music and at DePaul University, studying classical music but loving the free improvisational character of jazz. By the age of 16 he was playing in the rhythm section of a Chicago group, the Cleffs, then went on his own in 1956 with two other ex-Cleffs, bass player Elder Young and drummer Isaac "Red" Holt. The Ramsey Lewis Trio played jazz, but with enough infusion of Chicago blues and rocking rhythm to make the group a hot attraction on the local club circuit. Argo, a subsidiary of Chicago's top blues and r & b label, Chess, signed the group almost immediately.

For nearly a decade the Ramsey Lewis Trio built up a respectable following in the jazz world and its albums sold well in that market. Lewis also recorded with such other jazz artists as drummer Max Roach and Clark Terry. Argo, getting on the crossover bandwagon in the early sixties, put out a number of singles, but the only one that charted was Lewis's version of Chris Kenner's New Orleans' slow rocker "Somethin' You Got" (#63) in 1964, which was also a modest hit that year for singer Alvin Robinson.

The following year Lewis was in a bar when Dobie Gray's hit song "The In Crowd" came on the jukebox. The pianist was captivated by the strong rhythmic drive of the tune and immediately wanted to cut his own version. At the time, the trio was packing them in at the Bohemian Cavern in Washington, D.C., where it had a standing engagement. The group had already made one live album at the club and Lewis insisted that *The In Crowd* LP also be done live. Live albums were not new in 1965, but live singles were still something of a rarity.

The spontaneous sounds of hand clapping, glasses clinking and patrons' shouts of encouragement added a distinctive ambience and excitement to "The

The last instrumental star from the golden age of instrumentals, Ramsey Lewis paid his dues as a jazz pianist for a decade before achieving pop celebrity with "The In Crowd" in 1965. (Photo courtesy of Showtime Archives, Toronto)

In Crowd." The club crowd seemed to inspire the trio's members, driving them to new heights of improvisation and pounding rhythm. The instrumental was released as a single in the summer of 1965, only seven months after Gray's vocal version had peaked at #13. Few pop re-makes had appeared so quickly after the original. Lewis's version surprisingly outsold Gray's, going to #5. The album was also a best seller and the song won the 30-year-old Lewis a Grammy for the Best Jazz Instrumental by a Small Group.

Lewis's playing was always at the service of the heavy beat set down by drummer Holt. The group's lean, rhythmic sound on "The In Crowd" was miles away from the heavily orchestrated original and gave a new meaning to what it meant to be "in." Everyone who heard the Ramsey Lewis Trio's version knew that the "In Crowd" was at the Bohemian Cavern, clapping and laughing and having a good time as the trio played. Lewis himself was quick to point out on the liner notes to a subsequent album that "around 75% of our crowd is professional people—doctors, lawyers, dentists, schoolteachers—and the rest is the college and high school age group."

The group's follow-up, an equally appealing, Latin-tinged version of another big vocal hit, "Hang On Sloopy" by the McCoys, went to #11 at year's end.

The live performance, before a boisterous crowd that seemed several times larger than the one at the Bohemian Cavern, was recorded this time at the Lighthouse, a club in Hermosa Beach, California, on a street that dead-ended at the Pacific. The singalong on the chorus was a bit too deliberate and belied the spontaneity of the live recording technique. Further singles continued to cover proven pop hits by the Beatles ("A Hard Day's Night" and "Day Tripper") and Motown artists ("Uptight" and "Dancing in the Streets").

The trio had stayed together through nearly ten years of modest success in the jazz world, but when it entered the realm of pop superstardom things started to fall apart. "In June of 1965 we were making something like $1,500 to $2,000 a week," said Lewis. "By September we were earning something like $15,000 to $25,000 a week. . . . After that we started finding problems with each other, dissension set in. . . ."

In 1966 Young and Holt left to form the Young-Holt Trio with Don Walker on piano. They signed with Brunswick Records, and had their first hit in January 1967 with the wild and wacky "Wack Wack" (#40). The irrepressible humor of Young and Holt came through joyously in the vocal duo that starts off the record and in Young's springy bass. They pushed the pop style they had developed with Lewis further away from jazz into a more aggressive soul style. Two years later, now renamed Young-Holt Unlimited, with brass added to the ensemble, they continued their former leader's penchant for covering pop songs, but with a new twist. The track of "Soulful Strut" (#3), their biggest hit, was identical to the one used by label mate Barbara Acklin on her "Am I the Same Girl," a minor hit the previous year. It was a very conventional, easygoing soul serenade with just a streak of funk, completing Young and Holt's journey from jazz to pop. The two musicians finally went their separate ways in 1974 after several hitless years, leaving Holt to form Red Holt Unlimited.

Meanwhile, Ramsey Lewis pursued the charts with a new lineup. Bassist Cleveland Eaton and drummer Maurice White were worthy successors to Holt and Young. However, Lewis's next album would abandon the small ensemble sound for the backup of a big band, led by Richard Evans. Evans' arrangements on the album *Wade in the Water* have none of the fire and originality of Oliver Nelson's work with Jimmy Smith, but they ably back Lewis's dynamic piano which produced another Top 20 single with the title tune, based for once, on something other than a pop hit. Lewis continued to chart with singles through the sixties, and nearly all his subsequent albums were best sellers. In 1969, White left to help form the prototypical soul group of the seventies, Earth, Wind and Fire, and was replaced by Morris Jennings.

In 1973 Lewis left Chess's Cadet label to sign with Columbia, where he discovered fusion jazz with *Sun Goddess* (1974), produced by White and featuring Earth, Wind and Fire on backup. Despite a promising *Reunion* album with Young and Holt, Lewis drifted into disco, the latest pop craze, and lost the dynamic attack that made much of his earlier pop material so attractive. He never lost touch with his jazz roots, however, and in 1989 he turned out a creditable, stripped-down jazz album with pianist Billy Taylor, titled *We Meet Again*.

Many jazz and rock critics have castigated Lewis for his less than inventive playing on his cover hits. Paul Evans in *The Rolling Stone Album Guide* hailed him as "the jazz counterpart to country's Floyd Cramer." Yet Lewis's music has held up well for thirty years, thanks to his sense of showmanship and rhythmic drive. If he didn't grow to greater heights as an artist, Ramsey Lewis turned out an impressively high level of music and kept at it far longer than most of his contemporaries. He and his gifted collaborators, especially Young, Holt and White, bridged the gap from modern jazz and pop to funk and fusion, continuing the blending of pop and jazz that began with Moe Koffman back in the fifties.

....

THE LAST WORD IN SIXTIES' FUSION, however, must go to one of the men who championed the cause—Cannonball Adderley. In 1967 he finally found the major crossover hit for which he had been searching for years. "Mercy, Mercy, Mercy" (#11) was laid-back Chicago soul and a fervent cry for tolerance in a year of political and social confrontation. Ironically, it was written by Austrian Joe Zawinul, the Adderley Quintet's drummer. A vocal version by the Buckinghams, with more conventional lyrics, went to #5 the same year. Adderley would continue to cross over until his death from a massive stroke in 1975, working on a folk opera *Big Man*, based on the legend of a man whose gargantuan appetites rivaled those of Cannonball himself—John Henry.

If modern jazz, as some claim, was somewhat diluted by its crossover to pop, at the same time it infused the pop instrumental with a creative energy that greatly enriched the genre.

Chapter Seven

Surfer's Stomp

*I never really understood what surf music had to do
with surfing or surfers. To me, surf music always
sounded like rock-and-roll spaghetti western music.*
QUENTIN TARANTINO

*Friday nights the surfers would go to a stomp and dance
their brains out and get drunk! Saturday morning they'd
get up and go surfing all day. Saturday night meant
another dance. . . . . Life will never be the same again!*
MARK VOLMAN of the Crossfires

I'm here to take people on a sonic ride!
DICK DALE

O f all the styles of instrumental rock, none has had the staying power of
surf music. First heard in the small beach clubs of southern California
around 1960, instrumental surf music has been a part of our national
musical landscape ever since. Vintage surf bands have met annually
since 1977 for a "Surfer's Stomp" convention in southern California that
draws thousands of devotees. Independent labels like Sundazed and Del-Fi regularly reissue CDs of the most obscure sixties' surf bands with loving devotion.
(Have you ever heard of the *Original* Surfaris?) Dick Dale, granddaddy of surf
music, is back on the concert trail following the release of his 1993 album *Tribal
Thunder*, as are other classic groups like the Chantays, who, in 1994, made their
first new album in thirty years. Dale's music, and that of such classic surf bands
as the Tornadoes, the Centurions and the Lively Ones, made up a sizable slice
of the soundtrack of Quentin Tarantino's 1994 crime epic *Pulp Fiction*, while the
Chantays' "Pipeline" can be heard in the Terry Gillian film *Twelve Monkeys*.
New surf groups of the nineties, like the Mermen, Man or Astroman? and
Simon and the Bar Sinisters, are making waves in the contemporary rock world.

All this success is somewhat puzzling. Ask any baby-boomer to name a vintage surf group and they're more likely to name the Beach Boys or Jan and Dean

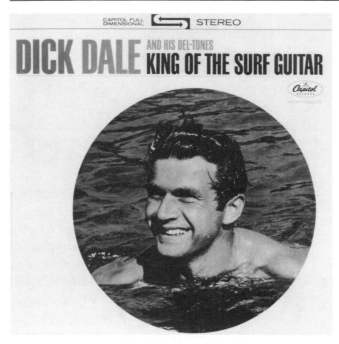

*King of the Surf Guitar,
Dick Dale's phenomenal
regional success never
translated into national
record sales. Capitol gave
him the star buildup,
however, on this first
album for the label. The
liner notes boast that
when he showed up for
the film Beach Party he
was the only surfer "who
didn't need bronze body
makeup."*

than any instrumental group. And no instrumental genre has produced so few bona fide hit records. Surf instrumental is largely the domain of one-hit wonders (the Surfaris, the Chantays) and no-hit wonders. (Dick Dale's highest charting record on *Billboard*'s Hot One Hundred checked in at #60.)

But then surf music, unlike so many "manufactured" rock music movements of the fifites and sixties, was never really about hit records. It was about kids doing a dance called the stomp in rundown beach clubs a stone's throw from the ocean. It was about wild men like Dick Dale shredding his pick into confetti as he burned up the strings on his Stratocaster. It was about the magic charisma of live performance. The only rock music to come out of a sport and the lifestyle that grew up around it, surf music's untamed quality and free spirit has allowed its practitioners to incorporate in their music every style from twangy guitar to country and western, from rhythm and blues to Middle Eastern music. In its grassroots appeal, eclectic repertoire and the often outrageous behavior of the performers, surf instrumental music was the precursor of garage bands, punk and grunge. Once thought to be a southern California phenomenon, it has proven to be as potent a celebration of rugged American individualism as the Western movie.

THE BIG KAHUNA

At the end of the fifties, white southern Californian instrumental groups like the Belairs, the Gamblers and the Revels were playing a kind of wild guitar music that was more urban and anxious than the Western twangy guitar music played by Duane Eddy and his imitators. The connection with surfing did not yet exist, but the surfers who frequented the beach clubs after a hard day's surfing, liked the music's driving beat and adopted it as their own.

The phenomenon might have gone no further than the beach communities of southern California, if not for a young guitarist who created a sound to match the ocean's swell. Dick Dale grew up in Boston, Massachusetts, in a middle class family with a Lebanese father and a Polish mother. His first instrument of choice was the drums and his hero was big band drummer Gene Krupa, whose rhythmic pounding would remain an important influence. Always restless, Dale moved on to the trumpet, the piano and finally the guitar. His proud father, a machinist, would take the underage Dale to bars to compete in country guitar contests.

In 1954, the family moved to southern California where Dale formed his own group, the Del-Tones, and started playing school dances and less formal surfer gatherings. He landed a regular gig at the Rinky-Dink Ice Cream Parlor. When the owner refused to give him a $5 raise so he could hire a drummer, Dale took his band to the Rendezvous Ballroom in Balboa.

The year was 1960 and the Rendezvous was known for its jazz concerts, which drew poorly and nearly drove it into bankruptcy. Dick Dale changed all that. Within weeks, the group was drawing capacity crowds of from 3,500 to 4,000 young people every Thursday through Saturday. The Rendezvous dress code included ties for men and the Del-Tones would hand surfers in shorts and bare feet ties at the door.

But the crowds that came to the Rendezvous Ballroom didn't come merely to listen, but to dance till dawn. The rhythmic, primitive throb of Dale's music as characterized by his signature piece, "Let's Go Trippin'," set the beat for a rather elemental dance step. The stomp, a simple pound-your-feet-on-the-floor dance, became the surfer's dance of choice.

Quickly becoming a local legend at the Rendezvous, Dale decided to record "Let's Go Trippin'" and formed, with the help of his father, his own label, Del-Tone, in September 1961. Although L.A. producer Joe Saraceno beat Dale to the record rack with his copycat but beguiling "Surfer's Stomp" by the Marketts (more on them later), Dale's single sold extremely well regionally and eventually reached #60 on the national *Billboard* charts.

In January 1962, the Del-Tones moved their act to the Pasadena Civic Auditorium. January was normally a down month for the Auditorium because the water was too cold for surfing, but Dale pulled in over 3,000 customers every night he played for the entire month. Pasadena's straight-laced town fathers were shocked at the sight of hundreds of kids, unable to get into the Auditorium, dancing in the lobbies and even on the streets of their fair city.

Dick Dale was on a roll as awesome as any ocean wave. In February, the Del-Tones played a benefit at the L.A. Sports Arena and stole the show from teen idols Fabian and Chris Montez. In November, Dale released his first album, *Surfer's Choice*, on Del-Tone. In three months sales topped 75,000 in southern California. It was the second best-selling album in the region after Vaughn Meader's Kennedy satire, *First Family*.

Dale began experimenting with the "surf music" he and other bands were playing. As he told Jon Pareles in *The New York Times* in 1994, he wanted to recreate in his music "the force of the wave, the screaming of the lip coming over my ears as I stick my finger in the wave . . . the power of Mother Nature, of our earth, of our ocean. . . ."

To help him in this quest, guitar manufacturer Leo Fender gave Dale new equipment to experiment with. Fender's electronic reverb, when attached to Dale's Stratocaster, allowed the guitarist to get an echo effect in live performance that previously could only be done in the studio. The echo and reverb gave the guitar a "wet" sound, as if it were being played underwater. Dale accentuated the reverb by playing the guitar in rapid staccato fashion with his left hand. The effect was as strikingly original as Duane Eddy's twangy bass or Link Wray's fuzztone had been several years earlier. It gave surf music it's own unique sound.

The first composition Dale tried out his new technique on was "Misirlou." The results were astonishing. "Misirlou" is about as good as a surf instrumental gets, although its inspiration came more from the desert than the sea. Dale, attracted to the hypnotic Mid-Eastern melodies of his father's homeland, chose a little-known Greek pop song from the forties and turned it inside out with his dramatic machine-gun rapid reverb, creating a whirling dervish of an instrumental, with able support from a plaintive trumpet, thumping bass and swirling piano figures.

The Del-Tone single of "Misirlou" shot to #2 on the local radio charts, while the vocal "Peppermint Man" went to #1. The big record companies began lining up to bid for Dale's services and in February 1963 *Billboard* announced that Capitol had emerged victorious from "one of the hottest battles for talent in recent disk history." With a guarantee of $25,000, Capital promised Dale an all-out promotion to make him a national recording star. In an unprecedented gesture, they agreed to distribute *Surfer's Choice* and the two singles under the Del-Tone label. Dale's five-year contract called for four more Capitol albums over three years.

Capitol filled the trades with full-page ads praising Dale as the "Pied Piper of Balboa" and compared his phenomenal rise to the young Sinatra and Elvis. Even more importantly, the label presented the athletic, charismatic performer as a positive role model for young people who bordered on the messianic:

> A Dick Dale audience, at first glance, might seem like any crowd of high-
> ly enthusiastic young people. But when you look closely, you notice an

amazing difference. **They are actually well behaved!** The place is filled to capacity . . . but there are no fights, no rowdiness, nobody getting out of line. And here is the secret of Dick Dale's astonishing success. He is the acknowledged "leader" of the kids. They respect him because he speaks to them with an almost evangelical fervor . . . The remarkable thing is that the kids listen to him . . . and **practice what he tells them!** So amazing is this effect that thousands of parents in the area are applauding his efforts. Instead of objecting to their kids attending the dances where Dick Dale appears, they are urging their youngsters to go! If teen-agers could vote, Dick Dale might well be Governor of California.

But the politics of the recording industry was something the "Pied Piper of Balboa" was not equipped to deal with. Although Capitol experimented with recording Dale's live act at the Harmony Park Ballroom in Anaheim, where he now resided, Capitol's first new Dale album, *King of the Surf Guitar*, was done entirely in the studio, where the raw power of Dale's guitar was largely lost. "I smashed the record against the wall," he said years later in an interview. "I never would play it at home because it wasn't the way I sounded on stage."

After the excitement of the live *Surfer's Choice*, *King of the Surf Guitar* was a very mixed bag. The title tune, released as a single, was the kind of girl chorus cum guitar solo number that Lee Hazlewood was producing around the same time for Duane Eddy, but infinitely better. Although best known as an instrumentalist, Dale sang on half the album's tracks. The Beach Boys, whose first single "Surfin'" came out two months after "Let's Go Trippin'," had set the standard for surf vocal music, with their pristine, Four Freshmen-style male harmonizing. Dale was no Brian Wilson. He sang in a raw rhythm and blues baritone. While effective on a number like "Mr. Peppermint Man," it was not a voice that wore well on the ear nor did it fit the clean-cut California image defined by the Beach Boys and Jan and Dean. The album's instrumental tracks were, predictably, much better, especially Dale's amazing take on the Jewish folk song, "Hava Nagila," which became an unlikely standard in every surf band's repertoire.

While Dale continued to turn out fine singles for Capitol like "The Wedge" and "The Scavenger," his only other Hot One Hundred record at #89, his audience was dwindling. He was being overshadowed by younger bands like the Surfaris and the Chantays, who had monster hits with their own original tunes, something that Dale was never able to achieve.

Seeing that its "skyrocketing new star" was about to crash and burn, Capitol tried to change his image. Dale's next album, *Checkered Flag*, heralded the exodus from surf music to hot rods and fast cars. It was a direction even the Beach Boys were moving in to keep selling records. The track titles reflected the move, but Dale continued to play his music in his own inimitable style.

Mr. Eliminator, released in early 1964, had some real gems. The title number was Link Wrayish in its elemental power chords, while "The Victor" was another classic Dale carpet ride into the mystic East, with its gorgeous, sinuous melody line and snappy finger cymbals.

In late 1964 Dale's last Capitol LP, *Summer Surf*, appeared, but the endless summer of surf and sand were about over, not just for Dale, but for all the surf groups except the Beach Boys, who would soon be moving away from the beach and the parking lot and into the studio with its electronic wizardry. High tech had ultimately won out over nature's call.

Dale had mastered new technology, but his forte was still live performance. He felt uncomfortable in the studio and was fed up with Capitol's mishandling of his career. He was also a very sick man. Doctors diagnosed rectal cancer and cut fourteen inches cut out of his rectal tract. Told that he had three months to live, Dale took off for Hawaii where amazingly he recuperated, surfed and waited out the short time remaining in his contract with Capitol. Eventually he returned to California, went into real estate and started raising lions and tigers on his property. Over the next twenty years, he made only a few singles on his own Cougar Record label and a remake of "Let's Go Trippin'" on GNP-Crescendo.

Then in 1987 Paramount Pictures put together the movie *Back to the Beach*, a reunion of Annette Funicello and Frankie Avalon and their beach pictures of the early sixties. Among the vintage surf performers hired for the soundtrack was Dick Dale, who ironically didn't play one of his own compositions but a new version of the Chantays' "Pipeline" with the late blues-rock guitarist Stevie Ray Vaughn. Although it hardly upstaged the original, "Pipeline" showed Dale still in fine form after a quarter century and Columbia released the tune as a single. Dick Dale found himself "rediscovered." Two years later, Rhino Records released a compilation of his best sides from Del-Tone and Capitol. It gave Dale the clout to put together a new album, *Tribal Thunder*, which got good reviews and launched him on a major tour with a new band. Playing at college campuses, Dale received the kind of adulation he hadn't known since the glory days at the Rendezvous Ballroom.

Like Link Wray, Dick Dale is a kind of force of nature with a guitar, who can roar as loudly as one of his lions. Yet his deep excursions into the Middle East, rhythm and blues, and even country and western (his favorite singer is still Hank Williams) show him to be much more than a one-note rocker. If the Beach Boys gave surf music a voice, Dick Dale undeniably gave it a sound, one that continues to reverberate in our collective imagination.

MENACE, MYSTERY AND MAJESTY—THREE CLASSICS

I have a confession to make. As a 14-year-old kid in suburban Connecticut in 1963 who didn't know a gremmie from a gremlin, I thought "Wipe Out" was just a scary song with a maniac laugh and that "Pipeline" was about water or oil moving through a pipe, like the Alaskan Pipeline. (That's what it sounded like, didn't it?) That these instrumentals were both about *surfing* never occurred to me.

More recently, however, I have been relieved to learn that surfing wasn't the first thing on the minds of the kids who composed these instrumentals either. The Surfaris originally called "Wipe Out" "Switchblade," and "Pipeline" began life as "Liberty's Whip," after the villainous title character in the John Ford Western *The Man Who Shot Liberty Valance* (1962). Then the Chantays changed it to "44 Magnum." They only settled on the present title after seeing a surf movie in high school that featured the Hawaiian Pipeline.

It's difficult to believe these two groups weren't inspired by surfing, for few tunes so vividly depict two of the sport's most dramatic moments. It's even more incredible that these classic instrumentals were slapped together at the last minute in studio sessions with the clock ticking away.

"Wipe Out" and "Pipeline" were the only surf instrumentals to crack the Top 10 nationally and remain instantly recognizable to anyone between the ages of 30 and 55, including those who never got any closer to the water than a back-yard swimming pool. For most Americans, these two instrumentals sum up the surfing experience, depicting in musical terms the thrill and danger of riding the curl of a wave and the awesome mystery of entering the wave itself.

....

By 1963, THE SURF CRAZE was at the crest of its popularity. Dozens of surf bands were being signed up by major labels, while Del-Fi, the small California independent that had put many bands into the recording studios, was doing phenomenal business. Everyone from Henry Mancini to Bo Diddley was cranking out surfing albums. Verve even released a surf jazz album, *Soul Surfing*, by Kai Winding that featured "the surf guitar sound backed by Winding's trombone choir sound." (Cowabunga!) Surfing magazines, surf boards and other related paraphernalia were disappearing from the shelves. Surf music spread to Hawaii, Australia and even Japan.

"For the first time," wrote Lee Zhito in *Billboard*, "a sport has emerged with its own music, and its own dance step, thereby combining the appeal of all three."

No instrumental surf group rose more quickly to stardom and struggled harder to live the California dream long after it had ended than the Surfaris of Glendora, California. The group's rise literally started with a dream, one experienced by drummer Ron Wilson. He woke up with a half-formed lyric in his head about a proto-surfer and his travails, based on the real-life brother of a fellow band member, which the rest of the band helped flesh out.

The five young high school students, ranging in age from 13 to 17, had been playing the round of school dances and local clubs, where their act was caught

Like so many of the surf bands of the early sixties, the Surfaris were just a bunch of eager young kids who wanted to cut a record. This picture was taken at the Cinnamon Cinder in Fresno, California, in 1963. Jim Pash (far right) missed the "Wipe Out" recording session because he had to work for his father that night. (Jim Pash)

by agent Dale Smallins. Impressed by Wilson's dream song, "Surfer Joe," Smallins booked the quintet into a small recording studio in nearby Cucamonga for a four-hour session that would cost them $100.

"Surfer Joe" was a fun-loving ode to a stereotypical bleached blond surfer. Like the Elvis figure in Bobby Bare's "All American Boy," the song ends with Joe getting drafted ("They cut off his big, blond locks I'm told, and when he went on maneuvers, Joe caught cold."). The clever lyrics, Wilson's casual but endearing vocal, and the infectious lock-step beat made "Joe" irresistible and Smallins had high hopes for the disk.

Being the amateurs they were, however, the boys had forgotten they needed a song for the record's flip side. Putting their heads together, they quickly improvised an instrumental, speeding up the guitar chords from "Surfer Joe" and throwing in extended drum solos from Wilson, who used the traveling music he played to get the Charter Oak High School Marching Band out onto the football field. Knowing a novel opening never hurt an instrumental, Wilson ducked out into the alley and came back with a deteriorated two by four. He broke it in half before the mike to simulate the sound of a surfer crashing into a wave. Smallins contributed the infamous blood-curdling laugh, which he was famous for at parties, and the title, "Wipe Out."

They recorded the song in just two takes and then were all driven home by guitarist Jim Fuller's father. (None of them was old enough to drive.) Thirteen-year-old Jim Pash, the group's sax player, couldn't make the session because he had to work that evening for his dad in the family business. One wonders what one of the most famous of guitar instrumentals might have sounded like with a wailing sax.

For their $100 investment the Surfaris also got a hundred copies of their record, which they hoped to sell to their friends at school. Richard Delvy, drummer for the Challengers, another surf band whose members were already established recording artists, had other ideas. He was impressed by the disk and made a deal with the Surfaris to distribute it on his Princess label. Airplay on local stations brought a favorable response for "Wipe Out" and Dot Records picked up the tune for national distribution. "Surfer Joe" went to #62 on the charts, but "Wipe Out" took off like a tidal wave. It rose to #2, staying in the Top 40 for ten weeks that summer.

We have been listening to "Wipe Out" for so long that it is hard to hear it with fresh ears. The hypnotic throb of the drum solos, the most famous in rock 'n' roll, with the incisive break-ins from the guitars, give the record a primitive, tribal power that perfectly reflects the tension experienced by a surfer precariously poised on a board before the big wave. Part of its charm is the rough edge to the guitar playing and an unfinished quality to the recording.[1]

Wilson and Fuller admit freely that they got the idea from Preston Epps's "Bongo Rock," while Jim Pash, in a recent interview with the author, points to Duane Eddy's "Yep!" as a source for the guitar line. Whatever other instrumentals inspired them, the Surfaris' made it all their own, creating something fresh and original.

The five teenagers from Glendora should have been enjoying the fame of their smash hit, but fame brought them as much grief as happiness. When their first album *Wipe Out!* was released, they were shocked to hear another group playing all the tracks but their double-sided hit. Without conferring with the Surfaris, Delvy had used his own group, the Challengers, claiming the Surfaris' original material was substandard. Worse still, the Challengers, although uncredited, received the performance royalties from the album, which sold extremely well.

The boys' parents urged them to sue Dot and they became entangled in a long and agonizing lawsuit. To further complicate matters, two other surf groups, in turn, sued the Surfaris. The Impacts from Pismo Beach had recorded

---

[1]Wilson actually dropped a drumstick near the end of the session and finished beating his hand on a cymbal. No one wanted to bother with another take, so it stayed in.

their own original "Wipe Out" previous to the Surfaris' instrumental. The question of whether the Surfaris copied from the Impacts is still hotly debated in surf music circles. A close listening to both "Wipe Outs" by this writer shows the Impacts' composition to be a beguiling and probably more sophisticated guitar instro than the Surfaris', but the similarity between the two tunes is slight. There are no drum solos in the Impacts' version and it has none of the immediacy or drama of the Surfaris' composition.

At the same time another group called the Surfaris from Fullerton, California, claimed they had been performing under that name since 1962, a full six months before the Glendora group formed. Although the Fullerton group lost its case, as did the Impacts, the judge allowed the band to continue to perform under the name the Original Surfaris. The Original Surfaris managed to benefit from their namesakes' fame and even added "Wipe Out" to their act. And, in what must have been an act of sweet revenge, when they recorded the tune they used the Impacts' version of "Wipe Out" and gave them writing credit.

Meanwhile, the Glendora Surfaris were still in the middle of their Dot lawsuit and, while their song was ruling the charts, they were without a label. They finally signed with Decca, a somewhat conservative label that wanted to get onto the surf bandwagon. Decca didn't quite know what to do with its first surf band, so it left the Surfaris to their own devices. The resulting album, *The Surfaris Play*, was quite good and allowed them a degree of artistic freedom they would rarely enjoy again. Their first Decca single, "Point Panic," bore a striking resemblance to "Wipe Out," right down to the opening sound effects and a manic voice crying out the title. It had a rhythmic drive all it's own, however, along with a great B side, "Waikiki Run," and placed a respectable #49 on the charts.

Over the next several years, the Surfaris turned out four more albums and nine singles for Decca, many of them of high quality, but none charted. About half of the singles were vocals, sung in the Beach Boys' style with Ron Wilson doing a smoother, if less interesting, lead than his ingratiating solo on "Surfer Joe." "I Wanna Take a Trip to the Islands" even featured the surf girl group the Honeys, who also did back-up on the Beach Boys' "Be True To Your School."

If their vocal sides were pleasant but derivative, their instrumentals remained fresh and original. "Murphie the Surfie" is a hard-driving number with an attractive country/folk lilt, while the group made a smooth transition to hot rod music with such top-notch entries as "Scatter Shield," which owed more than a little to the Chantays and "Pipeline," and "Dune Buggy."

Ron Wilson, whose drum work continued to be outstanding, was the group's inspiration and its resident bad boy. A kind of surfing Peter Pan, Wilson was married at least three times, had innumerable affairs, and set a world record for continuous drumming (one hundred four and a half hours). Disagreements with other group members led him to quit the Surfaris twice. He was living in near poverty in Dutch Flats, California, when he died of a brain aneurysm in 1989.

Scattering after a poorly produced album by the normally top-notch Gary Usher, several other group members had their own problems. In February 1965 bassist Pat Connolly was convicted of assault with a deadly weapon and spent eighteen months in the California Youth Authority. Ironically, it was Jim Pash, who is not heard on "Wipe Out," who kept the group alive after things fell apart with Decca. He recruited new band members and took over lead guitar.

In the summer of 1966, the Surfaris experienced a renaissance when Dot, which had settled its differences with the group, re-released "Wipe Out" and it became a hit all over again, peaking this time at #16. The second time around, however, was too debilitating for Pash, who got into drugs and then converted to Christianity. In 1967 he went to Vietnam as a chaplain's assistant to avoid the draft. It was a new era and the fun-loving surfing days were a thing of the past.

Pash reorganized the group in the seventies and was later joined by lead guitarist Jim Fuller. Fuller and Pash still perform as the Surfaris today with new group members. Pash, whose many accomplishments include the invention of the gitsitar (a combination guitar and sitar) and an ongoing study of music in the Bible, is a fervent spokesman for surf music. Although his proposals for a Museum of Surf Music and an annual surf music festival have not as yet been realized, Pash is proud of the Surfaris' induction, along with the Chantays, into the Hollywood Rock Walk and the continued popularity of surf music in the nineties. He sees the instrumental surf music his group pioneered as the indigenous folk music of southern California. However, he remains refreshingly modest about the Surfaris' accomplishments. Like so many of the young musicians who helped create this musical form, the Surfaris in the beginning had no high aspirations. "All we wanted to do was play a melody on a guitar so our friends could dance," Pash says.

WHILE THE SURFARIS PERSISTED for years in the quest for another hit, the career of the Chantays was over almost before it began. The rock quintet hailed from Santa Ana, California, where they got together in high school in 1961. After the usual run of school dances, they were signed up by deejay/manager Jack Sands. Sands got them a recording contract with Downey, a local label that already had the surf band the Rumblers under contract. Lead guitarist Bob Spickard and rhythm guitarist Brian Carman wrote two originals, "Pipeline" and "Move It," which they recorded in the same Cucamonga studio where the Surfaris would record "Wipe Out" a few months later. Downey, in its infinite wisdom, plugged the upbeat "Move It" as the A side. Richard Delvy, the Surfaris' nemesis, this time played the good guy and convinced a local radio station to give the B side a chance. "Pipeline" caught on and was picked up by Dot Records for national distribution in March 1963.

The Chantays look like they're ready to be fingerprinted in this publicity shot. Less dramatic that Dale's "Misirlou" or "Wipe Out," their "Pipeline" is, in its quiet way, the most compelling surf instrumental of them all. (Bob Spickard)

If "Wipe Out" captures the thrill and danger of surfing, "Pipeline" (#4) is the supreme expression of the awesome mystery of that experience. Its opening descending wet riff has been as copied and imitated as Dick Dale's flashy reverb from "Misirlou." From the opening sound of breaking surf to its final shimmering chords, "Pipeline" immerses the listener in a watery world full of beauty and wonder. The instruments mesh together perfectly, from Carman's endlessly vibrating rhythm guitar to the clear bell-tones of the Wurlizter electric piano that delivers the simple but beautiful release. The Chantays were not the first or the last surf band to feature a keyboard, but no other group managed to make it such an integral part of its sound. The watery chords that follow the undulating guitar riff are like the gentle tendrils of underwater sea plants pulling the listener deeper and deeper into the mystic sea.

Seductive, mysterious and always intriguing, "Pipeline" is *the* classic surf instrumental, bar none. While other groups skimmed the beaches and the water with their music, the Chantays delved deep under the waves and found a world of muted wonder and beauty. One of the most covered of rock instrumentals, no one, not even Dick Dale himself backed by the incredible Stevie Ray Vaughn, has come close to recreating the Chantays' unique magic.

After "Pipeline," their progress was depressingly familiar. The group caught its manager skimming the profits and fired him. Still in high school, the band members couldn't go on the road to promote their big hit when it really counted. Dot came out with a *Pipeline* album soon after the single, but Downey decided to distribute the follow-up single, "Monsoon," itself, unaccountably waited six months and then botched the job badly. A little derivative, but a decent instrumental in its own right, "Monsoon" never even charted, making the Chantays true one-hit wonders. This is unfortunate, because the originals on the *Pipeline* LP showed real promise. "Banzai" was coolly exciting, proving drummer Bob Welch could keep up with the likes of Ron Wilson, while "The Wayward Nile" was a sinuous river journey with an intriguing oriental flavor.

Disillusioned with Dot's poor handling of their second album, which was half vocals, some members of the original group moved to Reprise in 1965, but a name change to the Ill-Winds didn't help them any. A few Chantays made further releases under the names the Leaping Ferns and Craig and Michael, but those went nowhere.

Looking more ready to take on a round of golf than a ride on a surfboard, original Chantays Brian Carman (foreground), Bob Spickard (behind Carman) and Bob Welch (far right) have started recording again in the nineties with newer members Brian Nussle (far left) and Ricky Lewis (third from left). New tracks like "Killer Dana," however, show they haven't lost their creative edge in the thirty years since "Pipeline." (Bob Spickard)

The good news is that Spickard, Carman and Welch reunited around 1990 and have since then released several CDs. Their most recent release, *Waiting for the Tide* (1996), includes an intriguing acoustical version of "Pipeline" and exciting new tracks like the driving "Killer Dana," which was good enough to be included in Rhino's new definitive surf box, *Cowabunga!* After thirty-five years, the Chantays have lost none of their artistry, although we personally miss that electric piano.

....

JACK NIETZSCHE WASN'T a surfer and never played in a surf band, but he recorded the third in our trio of surf classics. Unlike the Surfaris and the Chantays, he would probably rather not be remembered for his sole Top 40 hit, but for the landmark records he arranged, produced and sometimes composed for Phil Spector and his Philles label in the early sixties. Fresh from the Westlake College of Music and a copyist job for Sonny Bono, Nietzsche was hired as an arranger by Lee Hazlewood. Hazlewood's former partner, Lester Sill, then working with Phil Spector, brought him in to arrange Spector's first classic recording, "He's a Rebel," for the Crystals. Over the next four years, Nietzsche worked on a string of memorable hits for Spector and helped construct his famous "wall of sound."

Between sessions at Philles, where he often played the chimes and bells, Nietzsche signed on as a solo artist with Reprise in 1963. "The Lonely Surfer" (#39), from the album of the same name, was hardly typical of current surf instrumental music. It only featured one guitar backed by symphonic strings, brass, percussion and a trio of French horns. The six-string bass guitar played by Bill Pittman (not Nietzsche himself, as many people believed), opens with a simple rambling melody that gradually grows and swells as it is picked up and embellished by the other instruments until the lonely surfer is transformed into a veritable son of Neptune. "The Lonely Surfer" gives a romantic, majestic view of the surfing experience from the height of an extended wave and remains a high mark in the surf instrumental.

Nietzsche made three more albums for Reprise, including one with the London Symphony Orchestra, and went on to a distinguished career as a film composer for such diverse fare as *Performance, One Flew Over the Cuckoo's Nest* and *Stand by Me*. In a career now spanning more than three decades, Nietzche has worked with everyone from bongo player Preston Epps to pop singer Jackie De Shannon. His excursion into the world of surf music was brief but profound.

....

ANYONE WHO SAYS instrumental surf music was a one-note riff built on a reverberating guitar should give these three classics a listen again. Taken together, they not only conjure up a musical era, but an entire lifestyle. Those are indeed deep waters.

FROM BALBOA BLUE TO THE WILD
BLUE YONDER WITH THE MARKETTS

Like the protean sea, surf music changed and evolved through the early sixties. The progression was an elemental one—from water (surfing) to earth (hot rods) to air (outer space). No group encapsulated this evolution more dramatically than the Marketts. Their ability to transform themselves with the times helped them to achieve the longest chart life of any surf instrumental group—from late 1961 to early 1966.

This enviable track record may seem odd for a group that hardly fit the surf band mode. The Marketts' sound was light years away from the "wet" guitars of most surf groups and was a smooth r & b mix of rhythm guitar, sax, piano, bass and drums. The beat was laid back and easy, more for lying on the beach than riding the waves.

Defining the Marketts' sound is far easier than defining who they were. The brainchild of pop entrepreneur Joe Saraceno, the group was, in his words, "whoever were available to play that day." But the available players included the A list of L.A. session musicians from the "golden quartet" of Rene Hall, Plas Johnson, Earl Palmer and Ernie Freeman, all of whom were black, to top white musicians like Tommy Tedesco (guitar), Leon Russell (keyboard) and Hal Blaine (drums). Who played on which records is a matter of some conjecture, although it is generally believed the black guys played on the Marketts' surfing sides and the white guys in their penultimate outer space phase.

It all started in late 1961, when Saraceno, in search of a new craze to capital-

As can be seen here, the Marketts were primarily a studio group, but composed of the best L.A. musicians. That's Leon Russell at the grand piano and Hal Blaine and Earl Palmer (right) on percussion. (Sundazed Music)

ize on, wandered into a California beach bar and saw the kids doing the surfer's stomp to Dick Dale's "Let's Go Trippin'." Saraceno was impressed and immediately appropriated Dale's bass line to his own melody to create "Surfer's Stomp," which was duly recorded by the "Mar-Kets," released on the tiny Union label, and then picked up by Liberty Records in early 1962. The catchy tune with its slow but soulful bass line, tinkling piano and strutting sax was not the first surf record, but it was the first to break nationally in the Top 40, cresting at #31.

Plas Johnson and company never appeared publicly as the Mar-Kets. They made the records in the studio while a white "cover" group went on the road. The idea of a black surf band would have truly been an anomaly in the sixties.

"Balboa Blue" (#48), the group's second release, was even more memorable. The jangly opening piano riff sets a wistful, mellow mood that leads into a bluesy sax solo that blows like a balmy breeze over a California bay. Few rock instrumentals have captured a place and mood so deftly.

The third Liberty release, "Stompin' Room Only," didn't chart and Saraceno put the Mar-Kets on hold while he used the same musicians to launch the Routers with "Let's Go (Pony)." In 1963 Saraceno revived the Marketts (this time without the hyphen) on Warner Brothers. Their first single was one of the best and least-remembered car instrumentals of surf music's second phase, the rollicking "Woody Wagon." The raucous sax (Plas Johnson?) is the perfect musical equivalent of the dilapidated jalopy of the title and the single has some of the best yakety sax work since King Curtis backed the Coasters. Incredibly, it didn't chart.

Recognizing that the car craze would not have the staying power of the surf boom, Saraceno turned to the skies for his next production with a clever TV tie-in. In September 1963 a new hour-long science fiction anthology series debuted on ABC TV that quickly took the country by storm. *The Outer Limits* was ABC's answer to CBS's long-running *The Twilight Zone.* Saraceno, in a brilliant move, milked the notoriety of both shows. "Outer Limits," written by head Router Mike Gordon, was based on the familiar opening theme of *The Twilight Zone,* but the title came from the newer show. The creators of *The Outer Limits* were not amused and threatened to sue. Saraceno and Warner Brothers quickly changed the title to "Out of Limits," although everyone got the idea. One wonders if *The Outer Limits* people would have been so irate if Gordon had actually used *their* theme music instead of their competitor's.

By any name "Out of Limits" is a classic rock instrumental. The clever development of the eerie four-note theme, the well-crafted orchestration that includes a haunting French horn and the beautiful release with a piping organ and galloping percussion that recalls "Telstar" propelled the instrumental all the way to #3, which it richly deserved.

Capitalizing on his group's biggest hit, Saraceno quickly put out an outer space concept album with the same title. In the liner notes he set out to make a rather tenuous connection between this futuristic space music and car and surf music. He wrote: ". . . the sax-, guitar-, and drums-men wail their way through the world of 1985 with such wild grooves as . . . 'Collision Course' (are they dragging in space, too?) and 'Twilight City' (which is where you go when you've had it in Surf City, of course)."

Unfortunately, the album was filled with mostly uninspired variations on the title hit. Two exceptions are the lovely "Bella Dalena," the B side of "Out of Limits" and a kind of space-age "Balboa Blue" and another ballad, "Bell Star," that features a soulful sax and a synthesizer-sounding organ.

After that it was mostly downhill for the Marketts. "Vanishing Point" (#90) proved a disappointing follow-up single and by the time they had their last Top 20 hit in 1966 with "Batman Theme" (#17), another TV tie-in, the group had lost the last vestiges of the sound that made it so unique. Saraceno retired the Marketts in 1969 and then resurrected them in 1973, but the earthbound likes of "The Song from M.A.S.H." and the theme from "Mary Hartman" failed to generate much interest.

Never a group with a strong identity, the Marketts, in all their configurations, made some memorable music and were a refreshing alternative to all those reverberating guitars. They took surf music out of the water and lifted it up to the stars.

A SURF BAND LEXICON: FROM THE ASTRONAUTS TO THE VENTURES

In the early sixties there were virtually hundreds of instrumental surf bands in California and across the country. Here, in alphabetical order, are twenty of the best of them.

• **The Astronauts.** This group never got any further into the pop stratosphere than #94 for one week in 1963 with "Baja," a seminal surf instrumental written by producer Lee Hazlewood for guitarist Al Casey. Casey's version is heavy on the twang, but the Astronauts' "wet" version is the definitive one. The Astronauts were one of the few surf bands lucky enough to be signed by a major label, RCA. The members hailed from landlocked Boulder, Colorado, and were a bar band until RCA turned them into a surf band. Having created the Astronauts, RCA stuck by them faithfully, putting out eight well-produced albums from 1963 to 1965. If they never really clicked commercially, at least the group couldn't blame its label, something many other bands couldn't say.

• **The Belairs.** These were one of the proto-surf groups that emerged in 1960-61. House band at the Belair Club in California's South Bay (hence the name), the Belairs had a strong influence on new, emerging surf bands. The group had only one regional hit, the Venturish-sounding "Mr. Moto," but three members went on to bigger things. Guitarist Paul Johnson became one of surf music's most astute historians. Co-founder Eddie Bertrand quit to form Eddie and the Showmen, and drummer Richard Delvy left to found the Challengers and had a long, successful career as a record producer and manager. "Mr. Moto," which was named for the fictional Japanese detective and a real California wrestler, became a surf standard, played and recorded by countless surf bands.

• **The Al Casey Combo.** Al Casey was born in Long Beach, California, but grew up in Phoenix, Arizona, where he would meet Lee Hazlewood and play a major role in developing the twangy guitar style of Hazlewood's protégé Duane Eddy. Long languishing in the shadow of Mr. Twang, Casey and his Combo had a few minor instrumental hits before diving into surf music. Hazlewood, temporarily on the outs with Eddy, gave Casey an instrumental that combined the two hot musical trends of 1963—folk and surf music. "Surfin' Hootenanny" didn't do much for either cause, but it did have the Blossoms doing vocal backup (with Eddy they were the Rebelettes, with Casey, the K-C-Ettes) and Casey's big guitar turning out some dead-on imitations of Dick Dale, the Ventures and, of course, Duane Eddy. The single was put out in red vinyl in a clear plastic sleeve by Stacy Records president Jim Gaylord, maker of the Gaylord automobile, who knew something about designing products to catch the consumer's eye. Store owners complained that the transparent sleeve made it difficult for clerks to count copies, but the record nonetheless went to #48. A surf LP followed with some fine cuts, including a killer surfing version of Casey's "Ramrod." Soon after Hazlewood and Eddy patched things up and Casey once again faded into the background. Too bad. He was a great guitar player.

• **The Centurions.** This group was one of the more obscure surf bands, and, in an interesting reversal, put out an album but no singles. Their "Body Surfin'" is a mean instro with a driving, Dick Dale-like guitar riff.

• **The Challengers.** The Challengers never had a monster hit like the Chantays or the Surfaris, but remain one of the most popular and high profile of the southern California bands. Founded by the enterprising Richard Delvy, they put out one of the first completely instrumental surf albums, *Surfbeat*, in January 1963. Their best-known single, "K-39," was inspired by a popular surfing spot 39 kilometers south of the Mexican border. The Challengers played at the Grammy Awards in 1965, but by then surf music, at least nationally, was reaching low tide. The Challengers, with numerous personnel changes, continued to perform and record to the end of the decade. Their final single may be the last word in hot rod tunes—"Chitty Chitty Bang Bang."

• **The Cornells.** This group may have had one of the nerdiest names of any surf band, but its lineup had real star quality. Four out of the five band members were the sons of Hollywood celebs—Bob Linkletter (TV host Art Linkletter), Jim O'Keefe (actor Dennis O'Keefe), Peter Lewis (actress Loretta Young), and Charlie Correll (one half of radio's *Amos 'n' Andy*, Charles Correll). The parental connections didn't hurt, getting them such posh gigs as the Hollywood Bowl in 1964, but the group had talent, too. One of their specialties was updating old songs like "Shortnin' Bread" ("Mama's Little Baby") and "Deep in the Heart of Texas" ("Lone Star Stomp"), both of which were regional hits. Another single, "Agna Caliente," later became a vocal hit for the Beach Boys as "Sloop John B." The only Cornell to go on to bigger things was lead guitarist Peter Lewis, who discovered folk rock in the mid-sixties, formed his own group Peter and the Wolves and later was a member of San Francisco's Moby Grape.

• **The Crossfires.** This was one of the rowdiest and raunchiest of the surf bands. The six members all went to Westchester High School and came together in early 1963, when the surf boom was at its height. An obscene version of "What'd I Say" played at a Westchester Women's Club social got them banned from the area by the local Chamber of Commerce. Their raunchy antics were better appreciated at the Revelair Club at Redondo Beach where the crowd's favorite number was "Chunky." A band member's cry of "Chunky!" during the instro was a cue for the guys in the crowd to whip out spoons and press them between their dates' legs while doing the Surfer's Stomp. Hot stuff! "Fiberglass Jungle," the B side of the first of the group's only two released singles, and one of the great surf titles, is a moody, sax-heavy number with a Dick Dale-inspired Eastern melody. By mid-1965 the Crossfires were ready to call it quits when two record executives looking for a folk rock band to promote suggested they change their act. The group bought a twelve-string guitar, shifted their repertoire and were promptly signed to the White Whale label. And thus one of the scruffiest surf bands was transformed into one of the most successful folk rock bands of the sixties, the Turtles.

• **The Frogmen.** Does anyone know who the Frogmen were? Ace producer Joe Saraceno does. Another one of his studio bands, the boys just missed the Top 40 in early 1961 with "Underwater" (#44). The catchy guitar riff was further enlivened by a searing sax and a Spanish percussion instrument, called a *guiro*, that sounded like a croaking frog. The silvery guitar work, along with the wet title, may qualify this as the first charting surf instrumental, released five months before the Marketts' "Surfer's Stomp."

• **The Impacts.** This group had the misfortune to go up against the Surfaris with a competing version of "Wipe Out" and lost. But its members deserve to be remembered for more than that. Natives of Pismo Beach, on California's central coast, they were the house band at the Rose Garden Ballroom, owned by sax player Jack Rose's father. Prolific surf band producer Tony Hilder recorded the group's classic *Wipe Out!* album in November 1962 and never paid the players a penny in royalties, according to lead guitarist Merrell Fankhauser, who wrote the title tune. The Impacts were one of the few surf bands to feature a lap steel guitar, which gave their music an authentic Hawaiian flavor. Fankhauser, who left the group in 1963, moved to Maui a decade later with his psychedelic, blues-rock band MU, named after a lost mystical continent that has obsessed this multi-talented musician for years. After thirty-odd years pursuing the elusive hit record with four different bands, Fankhauser has recently reunited with other members of the original Impacts and returned to his surf rock roots while pursuing other projects.

• **The Lively Ones.** These might have become the new Del-Tones, but for band loyalty. Dick Dale was ready to hire them as his new band, on the condition they drop lead guitarist Jim Masoner. The other members refused. Despite the bad break, they remained one of the most popular of the California surf bands and twice beat the Ventures in the Battle of the Bands contests. Interestingly, their sole hit single, "Surf Rider," an intriguing twisty guitar instro, was a cover of an original by Nokie Edwards, lead guitarist of the Ventures.

• **The Original Surfaris.** This band may only be remembered for coming up with a great name that another group appropriated, but it made some good music nonetheless. The group had established itself as a popular band in Orange County and even played the Rendezvous Ballroom, Dick Dale's famous haunt, when the controversy with the Glendora Surfaris stopped their career in midstream. "Although we had a good case and the judge agreed, he had to award the name to the other group as we didn't have a hit record," philoso-phized keyboard player Al Valdez recently in an interview with Robert J. Dalley. Their debut album, *Bombora!*, produced by Tony Hilder, was put in storage and the group broke up in 1965. *Bombora!* was finally released on Sundazed Records thirty years later.

• **The Pyramids.** One of the last big surf bands to emerge, the Pyramids were undoubtedly one of the best marketed. When the Long Beach, California, group's first single, "The Pyramid Stomp," fizzled nationally, bassist Steve Leonard carefully analyzed the Chantays' "Pipeline" and came up with a very clever variation on its famous opening reverb riff. "Penetration" (originally called "Eyeballs") went all the way to #18, helped by the promotional savvy of the group's manager, John Hodge. The British Invasion had begun only weeks earlier and Hodge convinced the Pyramids to shave their heads and become

Their bald heads aside, the Pyramids made some fine surf music, most notably their Top 20 hit, "Penetration." Willie Glover on guitar, the unshaven one, was black, making the Pyramids possibly the only bi-racial surf band of the sixties. (Sundazed Music/John Blair)

"America's answer to the Beatles." During their concerts, the group would wear Beatle mop wigs and hurl them off halfway through the show to reveal their bald heads, while a bevy of girls, hired by Hodge, stormed the stage screaming. Other Hodge gimmicks included having the group arrive at a gig atop an elephant or in a helicopter. The gimmicks worked and the Pyramids quickly found themselves appearing on *American Bandstand* and *Hullabaloo*, and in the third Frankie and Annette beach movie, *Bikini Beach*. Unfortunately, Hodge was not as good at investing their money as he was helping them earn it. Several bad investments blew their nest egg and the group's members soon grew back their hair and disbanded.

• **The Revels.** This was perhaps the first band to play the kind of wild guitar and sax music that would become associated with surf music. The group's members were part of a larger dance band at San Luis Obispo High in 1957 but formed a smaller group to play rock 'n' roll. They called themselves Gil Serna and the Rockets, but their career didn't take off until tenor saxman Norman Knowles assumed control and changed their name to the Revels, which reflected their love for wine, women and song. Knowles also loved rhythm and blues, and was a friend of sax great Earl Bostic. Guitarist Dan Darnold's reputation for drinking a beer in four seconds flat inspired him to write "Six Pak," which the Revels recorded in 1959 and which was the first of a string of raucous alcohol-related instros. The group's r & b sound was so genuine that one black L.A. station started playing "Six Pak," thinking the group was black. "Church Key," slang for a can opener (this was before the invention of the poptop can), was a delirious follow-up with its popping beer can (the real thing) and strange girly giggling. Both "Church Key" and its eruptive flip side, "Vesuvius," became surf classics, performed by countless groups. "Church Key" was banned on many radio stations because of its celebration of booze and its sacrilegious title. The group continued unrepentant, even kicking out Darnold when he got married because "he wasn't fun anymore." Despite their reputation as a primo party band, the Revels were respected as one of California's best backup bands with a versatility few other groups could match. More singles, including the delicious "Intoxica," and an album, *On a Rampage*, didn't further their chart status, but did confirm their cult status to this day. After all, what can you say that's bad about a rock band that was once the mascot of the Hells' Angels?

• **The Rhythm Rockers.** Coming out of Santa Ana, California, the Rhythm Rockers were in the enviable position of replacing Dick Dale when he left the Rendezvous Ballroom in 1962. While they never drew the crowds that Dale did, the management was impressed enough to pay for their first recording session, which produced "Foot Cruising" on Wipe Out Records. They returned the favor by naming their second single on the bigger Challenge label "Rendezvous Stomp." Their subsequent LP, *Soul Surfin'*, was a fine collection, but, like so many surf records, was poorly distributed. Unlike some bands, the Rhythm Rockers were homeboys and never left the Santa Ana area to tour and promote themselves nationally. They broke up in late 1963, but three of the seven members continued to do well in the music business. Drummer Tracy Longstreth and pianist Mike Patterson worked with the Righteous Brothers and other top acts in the sixties and seventies, while saxman Dave Garland later became Paul Williams' musical director.

• **The Rumblers.** Like the Revels, the Rumblers, who took their name from Link Wray's biggest hit, started out as a rhythm and blues group and only drifted into surfing music much later in their careers. "Boss," a hip adjective for excellence, was a fine rocker with a down-and-dirty bass guitar riff. It was recorded on the small Downey label and rose to #87 on the national charts in 1963, after peaking at #2 in the L.A. area. Eclipsed by the Chantays, who also recorded for Downey, the Rumblers changed their name to the Nylons and then the Bel Cantos, during which time they recorded with a then little-known arranger and back-up singer named Barry White. They rumbled into oblivion in late 1965 when lead guitarist Johnny Kirkland was drafted.

• **The Sentinals.** This band brought an attractive Latin lilt to surf music. Another California group with a love of rhythm and blues, its "Latin'ia," released on three different labels in 1962-63, was a soothing concoction of shimmering guitars and beating tom-toms. The flip side, "Tor-chula," sounded like a surfin' "Tequila" but was as much in debt to the Fireballs as to the Champs. Both tunes became standard fare for other surf bands.

• **Eddie and the Showmen.** This group was founded by ex-Belair Eddie Bertrand. He got the Showmen a contract with Liberty Records, which put out five of the band's singles in 1963-64. Its seminal single, "Mr. Rebel," is a catchy, folk-like tune with Bertrand's lead guitar sounding like a banjo. The title, however, doesn't refer to the Confederacy but to L.A. disk jockey Reb Foster, a good friend.

• **Dave Myers and the Surftones.** Initially calling themselves the Beach Boys, they changed their name because people felt it wasn't "musical." Too bad. Myers took surf guitar lessons from the master, Dick Dale himself, and proved one of Dale's most talented students The Surftones had a less aggressive sound than the Del-Tones, due in part to their curious brass choice of an alto sax. It brought a sweet lyricism to such hard surf fare as "Moment of Truth."

• **The Tornadoes.** The Tornadoes (not to be confused with the English instro group of "Telstar" fame), were offered a recording contact with Capitol, but turned it down for the higher royalties offered by the New York-based Aertuan label. Another local surf group from Riverside, California, signed with Capitol the same day. They were the Beach Boys. The Tornadoes' first single, "Bustin' Surfboards," featured lots of splashing water (taped from a local radio station's weather report track), a heavy drum beat and neat Hawaiian guitar riffs. They later aligned themselves in the Revels/Crossfires raunchy party band camp with such offbeat offerings as "The Gremmie, Parts 1 & 2" and "The Inebriated Surfer," which brought the booze right into the water. But the song that gained them the most notoriety was "Shootin' Beavers." When parents found out that the record's interjected cries of "shoot that beaver" and "bag that pelt" weren't

referring to furry little animals, they barraged local radio stations with com-
plaints, and the promising single was pulled from the play lists. Renaming
themselves "The Hollywood Tornadoes" to avoid confusion with the other
Tornadoes didn't help their career, either. The group finally abandoned the surf
for strictly Top 40 fare and in 1968 changed its name to Gross Prophet. How
gross can you get?

• **The Ventures.** Although the Ventures adapted easily to nearly every style of
rock music, their affinity for surf music was a genuine one. Unlike the questionable surf records of such established artists as Duane Eddy and Bo Diddley,
theirs were among the best of the genre. "Walk—Don't Run '64" was an imaginative surf version of their first hit, while "Diamond Head" (#70), a huge hit in
Japan, had great guitar runs and electronic blips reminiscent of Jorgen
Ingmann's version of "Apache." Their "Surf Rider" was one of the more
thoughtful and melancholy surf instrumentals.

Chapter Eight

Memphis
Soul Stew

> *Maybe it was the physical location. Maybe it had*
> *something to do with the water, or the temperature.*
> *Who knows? . . . Maybe it takes that one guy, that one*
> *executive, who says, "Go ahead, make me a record."*
> BOOKER T. JONES on the Memphis record industry

> *Today's special is Memphis Soul Stew. We sell so much*
> *of this people wonder what we put in it. We gonna tell*
> *you right now. Give me about half a teacup of bass.*
> *Now I need a pound of fatback drums. Now give me*
> *four tablespoons of boiling Memphis guitar. . . . Now*
> *just a little pinch of organ. Now give me a half a pint*
> *of horn. Place on the burner and bring to a boil.*
> KING CURTIS

O f the three pioneering rock capitals of the South, New Orleans was predominantly the domain of black musicians and Nashville predominantly of white musicians. Memphis, however, was a different matter. Here, music for a long time was created by and for blacks, but enjoyed by white listeners, too, who came to emulate it. Thus in the mid-fifties, Sam Phillips of Sun Records went from producing mostly black blues men to white artists who sounded black—most significantly Elvis Presley. But the rockabilly sound from Sun was just one ingredient in the thick stew of Memphis music that included liberal helpings of blues, jazz, rhythm and blues and rock 'n' roll. Out of this simmering pot emerged a new delicacy, a genre that would explode in the sixties and become the dominant form of rhythm and blues for the best part of a decade—soul music.

Like the surf music of California that was born about the same time, Memphis soul music was at first mainly instrumental dance music, played by some of the finest musicians in the South. One of the most prominent of these groups would be interracial—a rarity at that time in the still largely racist South.

The music these craftsmen made was down home, bluesy and downbeat, but at the same time warm, passionate and at times highly sophisticated. Gimmicks and novelty, replete in much of rock instrumental music, is hardly to be found in that of the Memphis masters. The music says it all.

SLAP THAT BASS

Bill Black is surely one of the forgotten figures of the golden age of rock instrumentals. Pioneer of the Memphis soul sound, Black's Combo scored six Top 20 hits from 1959 to 1962 and two more in the Top 30. The group earned *Billboard*'s "Most-Played Instrumental Group" award three times and almost single-handedly saved Memphis's Hi Records from closing in 1959 with its first hit single. John "Ace" Cannon, Black's star sax man, went on to a successful solo career in 1962.

For all this, Black is barely mentioned in most rock chronicles and few if any of his hits are heard on oldie stations or found in instrumental anthologies. If he is remembered at all, it is as the man who played bass for Elvis in his early, classic recordings for Sun and RCA.

William Patton Black, Jr., was born September 17, 1926, in Memphis. His father drove a streetcar and in his spare time played the fiddle. When Bill was age 8 his Dad made him a guitar out of a cigar box. The young man took up the bass in high school and later went to work loading freight for the railroad. He was drafted near the end of World War II and met his future wife while stationed at Fort Lee in Virginia. By the early fifties Black was back in Memphis playing country and western music with vocalist Doug Poindexter and his Starlite Wranglers, a group which he helped form. The bass player was typically the clown in country bands and Black dressed the part of a barefoot Ozark hillbilly, slapping his big doghouse bass with joyful abandon.

His break came when Sam Phillips, who produced the Wranglers' records, hired him and fellow Wrangler guitarist Scotty Moore to play back-up to his latest discovery, Elvis Presley. At the time the skeptical Black didn't see it as a move upward. He questioned the young truck driver's talent and experience, which, compared to that of the two musicians, was very limited.

But in time, a mutual respect developed and Moore's skillful guitar picking along with Black's driving bass provided the perfect background for Presley's breakthrough Sun singles. "Bill could slap the fire out of a bass. No notes, just wood . . . ," drummer D. J. Fontana noted in a 1991 interview. Fontana later joined the trio, but the drums are hardly missed in the early Sun recordings, with Black's strong, percussive plucking and slapping providing a rocking rhythm for such classic sides as "Good Rockin' Tonight" and "I Don't Care If the Sun Don't Shine."

Moore's and Black's importance on these recordings was reflected on the labels that often read "Elvis Presley with Scotty and Bill" or "ELVIS PRESLEY,

Hi Records president Joe Cuoghi (right) has good reason to look pleased with Bill Black. Black's Combo saved the company from bankruptcy with its first hit "Smokie —Part 2." Black produced so many hits for Hi over the next few years that it became known in the industry as the "Hit Instrumental" label. (Photo courtesy of Showtime Archives, Toronto/Colin Escott)

SCOTTY AND BILL." When Presley's new manager, Colonel Tom Parker, made a deal with RCA to buy out his Sun contract, the boys went right along. But things changed. Their role was reduced from respected musicians to hired help with no royalty cut. According to Black's brother Johnny, they were making only $200 a week, less than many mediocre session musicians. Disillusioned and bitter, the two men quit in 1958, leaving Fontana, who worked with Elvis on a free lance basis, to carry on.

Moore used the money he had saved to buy into Fernwood Records and in 1959 produced a major hit—Thomas Wayne's moving ballad "Tragedy." But Black floundered on his own. He spent his days servicing air conditioners in Memphis to pay the bills for his growing family and his nights trying to put together a new group with top session guitarist Reggie Young. Rockabilly singer Ray Harris, who knew Black at Sun, was a partner in a small, struggling record company, Hi. Harris offered Bill Black's Combo a recording contract, but with Hi on the verge of bankruptcy, the future didn't exactly look promising.

The combo consisted of Black, who had turned in his old upright bass for an electric model, Young on guitar, Martin Willis on sax, Joe Louis Hall on piano and Jerry Arnold, country singer Eddy Arnold's nephew, on drums. When a Hank Thompson tune they were trying to record wasn't getting anywhere,

Young pulled out a riff he had been working on and they started improvising. The result, "Smokie," was an infectious rocker with a delicious tinkly piano riff and a powerhouse rhythm section led by Willis's pumping sax.

Harris and Hi President Joe Cuoghi put out the instrumental as a doubled-sided single and "Smokie—Part 2" caught fire. It climbed the national charts to #17, giving Hi its first much needed hit record.

Ironically, the two men who musically contributed the most to "Smokie" were quickly gone from the combo. Hall, who was black, felt poorly treated by Harris because of his color and quit. Willis, also black, left in disgust because he had taken a mere session fee to pay his electric bill instead of a percentage of the hit record. Carl McVoy, Jerry Lee Lewis's cousin, took over on keyboards and alto saxophonist Ace Cannon from Grenada, Mississippi, replaced Willis. Now all white, the combo was thought to be black, due to its greasy rhythm and blues sound and probably Black's name. Hi was anxious to preserve this perception. It issued no publicity shots of the band and pictured the musicians on only one of their many album covers. This could hardly have hid their identity from their fans, however, since ninety-five percent of their live dates were for black audiences.

The combo's next release was a rock cover of the pop vocal hit, "White Silver Sands." Cannon's melodious sax carried the tune effortlessly, backed by a piping Hammond organ that McVoy dragged over to the studio on a truck from his construction company. But the most distinctive sound was the bottomed-out rhythm section formed by a tight blending of Black's bass, Arnold's drums and Young's guitar that gave all the combo's recordings a thumping shuffle beat, perfect for dancing. The easy rocking "White Silver Sands" went all the way to #9 in March 1960 and eventually sold a million copies—the group's biggest hit.

The Black Combo and Hi were on a roll. The company pushed the group's recordings, both singles and records, to such an extent that they became known as the Hit Instrumental (HI) label in the industry with "the untouchable sound of Bill Black's Combo." The group racked up three more hits in 1960 with covers, including Elvis's "Don't Be Cruel" (#10), its second-biggest seller. The following year saw two more hit covers, "Hearts of Stone" (#20) and Hoagy Carmichael's "Ole Buttermilk Sky" (#20). All these sides followed the same winning formula—a strong, gritty sax solo, pulsating rhythm section, and McVoy's cheesy organ, the one wrong note that mars most of the singles after "White Silver Sands."

The group's last big hit, and one of its best, was 1962's "Twist-Her" (#26), one of the few twist instrumentals to make the Top 40. An original composition, it gave Cannon the freedom to really rock it out and McVoy blessedly put the Hammond aside for a piano that was, according to Jim Dawson, in his book *The Twist*, "powered . . . so high and distorted in the mix that it must have kept the recording console's frequency needle in the red zone."

Hi Records was careful not to put Bill Black's Combo on their album covers to reinforce the belief that the group was black for their legions of African-American fans.

WHILE "TWIST-HER" WAS whirling up the charts, Ace Cannon had a hit all his own, a self-composed deep bluesy riff called "Tuff," which went to #17. Like Black, Cannon had a successful career as a rockabilly artist before joining the combo. He had been a member of wild man Billy Lee Riley's Little Green Men since the early fifties, while holding down a day job with a water pump manufacturer. Cannon's replacing Marty Willis in the combo was ironic, for Willis had earlier replaced Cannon in Riley's group.

"Tuff" was a reworking of the old country song "Columbus Stockade Blues" and when it took off in the charts in January 1962 Cannon promptly left the Combo, formed his own group for Hi and went on the road. His gut bucket, bluesy sax guaranteed him a long run of jukebox hits and a few more chart items, including a fine version of the Coasters' "Searchin.'" He stayed with Hi through the seventies and succumbed to easy listening when his brand of r & b fell out of fashion. However, he returned in fine form on the *Class of '55* album, backing his old Sun colleagues Jerry Lee Lewis, Johnny Cash and Carl Perkins.

By the time Cannon left the Combo, Black, suffering from periodic headaches and memory loss, was ready to step back from touring. His absence was barely noticed by the public. Most audiences thought front player Cannon or McVoy was Bill Black anyway.

Hi bankrolled Black's own subsidiary label Lyn-Lou, named after two of his children, but his one potential hit in 1962, the vocal "Lover, Please" was quickly covered by Clyde McPhatter, who had the hit record.

The Combo's formula was beginning to run dry, thanks to overexposure from Hi, but the group was still capable of creative growth. In late 1962 it moved into a more modern soul sound with multiple horns in the excellent "Do It—Rat Now" (#51) and enlivened its 1964 version of Chuck Berry's "Little Queenie" (#73) with a truly stinging guitar chorus.

In the summer of 1965 Bill Black's poor health was discovered to be the result of a large brain tumor. After two painful operations, he was told that a third operation would probably leave him a vegetable. He turned over the combo to bassist Bob Tucker and sold his studio. Bill Black died quietly on October 21, 1965, but the combo bearing his name lived on for years, scoring a few more minor hits before drifting off into country and western music.

Black may have remained largely behind the scenes in his combo, but his signature bottom-heavy rhythm section picked up where Bill Doggett and the other great r & b men of the fifties left off. Now a new generation of gifted Memphis musicians would take Black's groove and widen it considerably.

KING SAX

In the twisting summer of 1962, Sam Cooke paid rare homage to an instrumental in the celebratory but thoughtful "Havin' a Party." Among several current hits he requested from his local deejay were "Soul Twist" by King Curtis and the Noble Knights. "No other songs will do," sang Sam.

"Soul Twist" may have been King Curtis's first Top 40 hit, but he had been the premier East Coast tenor saxman since the mid-fifties, bringing the indelible stamp of his lyrical horn to scores of hit records. If Dick Dale was the King of the Surf Guitar, King Curtis was without question king of the soulful sax, which in his hands could be as expressive as the human voice.

He was born Curtis Ousley in Fort Worth, Texas, on February 7, 1934, and was raised by adoptive parents in nearby Mansfield. His adoptive father played guitar with church groups, but it was the music of rhythm and blues pioneer Louis Jordan, blues guitarist T-Bone Walker and others artists he heard on the radio that inspired him to become a musician.

Like Memphis, central Texas was rich in down-home, rural music traditions. The Texas musical stew was flavored with tasty country blues, pungent "sanctified" gospel music and high-energy big city r & b dominated by sax players like Illinois Jacquet and Earl Bostic. It was the alto sax that was Curtis's first instrument of choice at age 12, but he later switched to the tenor sax, which offered him a larger emotional range. During high school, he alternated between playing in the school band and jamming in Fort Worth's clubs and juke joints at night. At age 18, while visiting an uncle in New York City, he made an extraordinary debut at the Apollo Theater's Wednesday night amateur contest. Curtis was immediately hired to play on a package tour through the Northeast.

Both in his own instrumentals and on the recordings of other artists from the Coasters to Aretha Franklin, King Curtis was the king of the East Coast sax players for more than a decade. (Archive Photos/Frank Driggs Collection)

He later returned to Fort Worth and joined Lionel Hampton's jazz band. When the band broke up in New York a few months later, Curtis decided to stay. The young saxophonist quickly established himself as a top session man who could adapt his highly personal style to almost any kind of music when required. At the beginning, he averaged sixteen recording dates a week, which fell off only slightly when he raised his price for a three-hour session from under $50 to $100.

Few musical bridges in rock 'n' roll have been more celebrated than Curtis's memorable backing on the Coasters' "Yakety Yak" and other recordings. His rollicking, stuttering sax breaks were as integral a comedic element to their brilliant "musical playlets" as Bobby Nunn's bass or Leiber's and Stoller's music and lyrics. But he was also memorable on other Atlantic/Atco hits, lending mournful support to Chuck Willis on his swan song, "What Am I Living For?" and giving some added zing to Bobby Darin's early string of rockers.

While his contributions to other people's recordings was considerable, Curtis's own solo efforts sold few records. Then along came the twist in late 1960. Between session work, Curtis headed the house band at Smalls' Paradise in Harlem, a sort of uptown version of the Peppermint Lounge. RCA Records and the Arthur Murray Dance Studios collaborated on a twist album performed by Curtis and his band, the Noble Knights. The single taken from the album, "The Arthur Murray Twist," was, predictably, a dud. But the experience made

Curtis something of a dance party specialist and his first release on the Enjoy label in 1962 was a low-down dance number he called "Soul Jay Walk."

Producer Bobby Robinson suggested two changes that raised the saxman's hackles. Robinson assured Curtis the instrumental would be a hit if his honking sax took a back seat to a catchy opening hook for Billy Butler's bass guitar. Second, Robinson wanted to change the title to "Soul Twist" to give it a higher profile in the marketplace. Curtis wisely conceded on both counts and "Soul Twist" zoomed to #1 on the r & b charts and peaked at #17 on the pop charts. A gritty, deep-beat instro and a refreshing alternative to fluffier twist fare of the day, "Soul Twist" was also one of the first hit records to carry the word "soul" in its title.

While Curtis's reputation continued to grow in the music industry, it would be another two years and a new record label, Capitol, before he had another hit—the sublime "Soul Serenade" (#51), written in collaboration with Luther Dixon. Glissando Memphis guitars and a Floyd Cramer-like piano start the tune off with a surprising country flavor. Then Curtis enters, playing his heart out on a B-flat soprano saxophone, called a saxello, made all the more haunting by echo feedback. The high, pure tones of his saxello wind their way through the ravishing melody like a snake charmer's pipe. Soul music never sounded so sweet.

Despite the high production values on "Soul Serenade," Curtis was generally dissatisfied with Capitol's creative restrictiveness and soon after jumped ship to Atlantic, where he had played on so many sessions as a free agent years before. With the rise of Aretha Franklin, Wilson Pickett, Don Covay and other artists, Atlantic was in the forefront of soul music and King Curtis became a key player in the movement. He continued to back top Atlantic and Atco acts like Franklin, Covay and Solomon Burke, while scoring more hits of his own—a soulful version of Ben E. King's "Spanish Harlem" (#89) and a funky dance number, "Jump Back" (#63), on which he was backed by a female chorus.

But the piece de resistance came in 1967 with "Memphis Soul Stew" (#33). This novelty instrumental, a rarity for Curtis, opens with Curtis reciting in his rich baritone the recipe for "today's special." The same idea was used a decade earlier by Cole Porter in the number "Now You Has Jazz" in the film *High Society*, where Bing Crosby explains each musical element in Louis Armstrong's band. Curtis's culinary approach is more inventive and includes such ingredients as "half a teacup of bass, a pound of fatback drums, four tablespoons of Memphis guitar, a little pinch of organ and half a pint of horn." Curtis goes from server to chef in the number's last minute and a half, honking his heart out.

"Memphis Soul Stew" is a good example of how Curtis could dominate a record while still allowing each member of his band, the Kingpins, plenty of room to express their own creativity. "There was always space, always room to do your own thing," recalled ace drummer Bernie "Pretty" Purdie in an interview with Max Weinberg. "Curtis gave me the opportunity to play a twelve-bar or sixteen-bar solo, which was long enough for me to get into something sweet, and short enough not to get boring."

Curtis himself was never boring, even when covering other people's hits, which he did frequently in the late sixties. Like his peers, Booker T. and the MG's, he had a gift for taking familiar tunes and making them his own. His bewitching version of "Ode to Billy Jo" (#28), his last Top 40 single, for example, is just as haunting and mysterious as Bobby Gentry's original, even without the cryptic lyrics. As the song unravels, Curtis begins to brilliantly riff on the melody, while never losing the center of the song's pervading darkness.

The meaning of the music was always central to Curtis's art, which makes his tragic end all the more senseless. On a scorching August day in 1971, he was carrying an air conditioner into his apartment at 50 West 86th Street in Manhattan. Two men using drugs blocked his way. He asked them to move and they erupted in violence. One of the two pulled out a knife and stabbed the musician in the heart. He was pronounced dead on arrival at Roosevelt Hospital. Jesse Jackson spoke at his funeral and the Kingpins played "Soul Serenade" for an hour. Aretha Franklin, who had just hired Curtis days before as her musical director, sang the spiritual "Never Grow Old."

King Curtis, dead at 37, would never grow old, but neither will his music. Neither jazz nor pop, it took the best of both and made an expressive, personal statement that reflected the deep soul of its creator.

TIME IS TIGHT

About the time Hi Records was finding its feet with the instrumental hits of Bill Black's Combo, another modest Memphis record company was struggling to make a name for itself.

A 40-year-old housewife and former schoolteacher and her 28-year-old brother who worked in the bonds department of the First National Bank in Memphis seemed an unlikely pair to open a recording studio dedicated to black rhythm 'n' blues. However, Jim Stewart, who played a mean hoedown fiddle and harbored Walter Mitty dreams of becoming a record producer, was determined. Estelle Axton believed in her brother's dream enough to mortgage her house, buy a one-track Ampex recorder and set up the tiny Satellite Record Company in a vacant grocery store in nearby Brunswick, Tennessee, in 1959.

Among Satellite's first recording artists was an instrumental group called the Royal Spades, formed in 1958 by 16-year-old Steve Cropper, a gifted guitarist who grew up in Missouri, a stone's throw from the Ozark Mountains. Originally a quartet of guitar, bass, drums and keyboard, the group expanded by 1960 into a septet with three brass players, including Wayne Jackson on trumpet and Charles "Packy" Axton, Estelle's son, on tenor sax. Although nearly all white, the group specialized in rhythm and blues, and honed their craft in local clubs and at endless sock hops.

As their sound improved, the Spades worked out a catchy two-note riff that had the insistent beat of a colossal hangover after a night on the town. Over a period of months they developed the riff into a full-blown instrumental that Estelle Axton thought was "a catchy little deal." She convinced her reluctant brother and Satellite's A & R man Chips Moman to press it on wax.

With its brief but insistent brass riff, one of the shortest hooks in all rock 'n' roll, the flavorful organ playing of Jerry Lee "Smookie" Smith and the effective moaning of the title by baritone sax player Don Nix in the musical breaks, "Last Night" was the instrumental blockbuster of 1961. It was only shut out of the #1 position on the pop charts by the seven-week reign of Bobby Lewis's "Tossin' and Turnin'."

"Last Night" put Satellite on the musical map and gave Memphis music a tight, rhythmic, horn-dominated sound that would set the standard for sixties' soul music. Success brought trouble, however, when a California company with the same name sued Satellite. The company quickly changed its name to Stax, formed from the first two letters of St-ewart and Ax-ton. Estelle didn't like the name Royal Spades and rechristened the group the Mar-Keys, after the garish marquee on the company's new headquarters, a former movie theater on McLemore Avenue in Memphis.

Stax was on its way to becoming the main purveyor of sixties' soul music, but the Mar-Keys would never duplicate their initial success. "The Morning After," a logical follow-up, had a longer riff that was nearly as memorable as its predecessor, yet rose only to #62. Further releases didn't even chart that high, but the group never lost its touch and provided strong backing for a number of Stax and Volt, its subsidiary, acts. As late as 1966 the band was putting out fine dance instrumentals of its own, like "Philly Dog" (#89), a bouncy brass reworking of Rufus Thomas's "The Dog."

Wayne Jackson would go on to form the Memphis Horns with saxophonist Andrew Love, who came to Stax from Hi at the urging of drummer Al Jackson, Jr. The duo spent the better part of the next decade providing endlessly inventive and memorable brass riffs that would become the signature of Stax soul. After being discovered by the mainstream rock audience while backing Otis Redding at the Monterey International Pop Festival in 1967, the Memphis Horns' services would be in demand for artists from Petula Clark to Elvis Presley who wanted to rejuvenate their careers with a shot of Memphis soul.

Another alumnus of the Mar-Keys who would go on to bigger and better things was Steve Cropper. He left the group in 1962 and joined forces with another precocious teenager and Stax newcomer, Booker T. Jones. Jones grew up in Memphis, where his father was a high school science and math teacher. A musical prodigy, he mastered in quick succession the clarinet, oboe and trombone before settling down on keyboard. At age 16, he auditioned at Stax and was hired to play baritone sax on Stax's first modest hit, Rufus and Carla Thomas's "Can I Love You."

An older musician both Jones and Cropper wanted to play with was drummer Al Jackson, Jr., whose reputation as a rock steady time keeper with Willie Mitchell's house band at Hi was already legendary. Another veteran who sat in with these musicians at Stax was bassist Lewis Steinberg, another member of Mitchell's band.

On one memorable day in June 1962 the four musicians had finished a demo session with the old Sun rockabilly artist Billy Lee Riley when they started to jam. The engineer was struck by the bluesy number they were playing. They called the piece "Green Onions" because of its nasty disposition, but another more rhythmic dance number that Cropper and Jones had been fooling around with for a while was more to the liking of Jim Stewart. He suggested they switch the titles, which is how "Green Onions" got to be "Green Onions" instead of "Behave Yourself."

"Green Onions" made nearly as big a splash on the pop charts as "Last Night," going all the way to #3. The only common denominator between the two instrumentals was the cool organ, which Jones started playing because the tune "sounded a lot better on the organ than it did on the piano." Lacking a brass section, the group balanced Jones' organ with Cropper's sharp, stinging guitar, which cut through the heavy rhythm section like a razor-sharp paring knife. You could feel the tightness of Steinberg's strings and Jackson's skins working together as one. This was soul music that was clear, precise, economical and carefully crafted. The group decided to call themselves the MG's after Chips Moman's little sports car which was parked every day outside the Stax studio. The car company, however, disapproved of its automobile being associated with rock 'n' roll, so the group made MG stand for "Memphis Group."

Booker T. and the MG's protean talents made them a top Stax recording act into the early seventies, maintaining a remarkable high standard of musical excellence on a dozen albums and twenty singles, three-fourths of which charted.

Jones was appropriately the leader; his keyboard playing took stage center on nearly all their tracks. His intuitive mastery of both organ and piano was truly astonishing. Jones' knack for sustained notes to build intensity at times recalled Jimmy Smith, but his subtle, rhythmic style was completely original.

Cropper's stinging style of Memphis guitar was modeled after Lowman Pauling, guitarist with the Five Royales, but Cropper took the slash-and-burn technique to another dimension. His sharp "sound bursts" created a tension that was at times almost subliminal. His timing, as with all the MG's, was as exquisite as his playing, which could go from sweet to stinging at the drop of a downbeat, as in the underrated, hypnotic "Soul Dressing" (#95).

Steinberg and his replacement, Donald "Duck" Dunn, spun out rhythmic bass figures that interplayed skillfully with Cropper's lead guitar.

Individually and collectively, Booker T. and the MG's contributed to nearly every soul classic on Stax Records in the sixties. Still going strong in the nineties, although without drummer Al Jackson, Jr. (right), they remain the "fathers of the Memphis Sound."

Jackson was a human metronome, "the Godfather of Time," who kept the beat on nearly every Stax release in the sixties. His beat was unwavering, eschewing self-indulgent fills and flourishes. When he did let rip with a fill, it was timed to have the maximum effect.

Together the four formed a formidable unit, playing with such economy and control that every guitar slash, drum fill and sustained organ chord seemed inevitable. They knew exactly what they were doing every moment of every record, which is what makes the bulk of their work hold up as well today as on the day it was recorded.

But Booker T. and the MG's were much more than *the* soul instrumental group of the sixties. Their masterful hand can be seen on nearly every classic side to come out of Stax in the sixties, mostly as back-up musicians, often as arrangers, sometimes as songwriters (Cropper alone wrote or co-wrote a score of classics with the likes of Wilson Pickett and Otis Redding), and occasionally as producers.

If the group didn't have another Top 40 hit for four and a half years after "Green Onions," it wasn't for want of good material. Follow-up singles like "Jelly Bread," "Chinese Checkers," which featured Booker T. on a very Oriental-sounding Wurlitzer electric piano and overdubbed trombone, "Soul Dressing" and "Mo' Onions," another serving of the band's first hit, were all excellent exercises in deep groove soul and none scored higher on the pop charts than #78. "Can't Be Still," a snappy, handclapping dance number, and the hard-driving "Red Beans and Rice" amazingly didn't chart at all.

With "Boot-Leg" (#58), a Top 10 r & b hit in 1965, the group added a new member to the ensemble. Donald "Duck" Dunn, Cropper's old school chum and fellow Mar-Key, replaced the talented Lewis Steinberg, whose heavy drinking had become a problem. The group was now fully integrated—two white members and two black. "For us, music had no color," Cropper has said.

About the same time, Booker T. made the surprising decision to temporarily walk away from performing with his hit group and go to college to study musical theory, something Stewart couldn't understand. It was the beginning of a riff between Jones and Stax that would widen over time. While the MG's carried on with Isaac Hayes taking over keyboard duties, Jones was at Indiana University transcribing Bach fugues for the school band.

When Jones returned in 1966, it was with a new musical maturity. The results can clearly be seen on the sublime "My Sweet Potato (#85), where he plays the acoustic piano with the jazzy authority of Ramsey Lewis but with a quiet, gospel-like fervor that Lewis never achieved. "My Sweet Potato" showed that soul music could rock and be reflective at the same time. With "Hip Hug-Her" (#37) in 1967, the group returned to the Top 40 in a more contemporary vein, while the delicious "Soul-Limbo" (#17), with Isaac Hayes on cowbell, was a graceful melding of soul and calypso, inspired by a cruise Cropper took to the Bahamas.

Until now, nearly all the group's singles had been originals the members had developed together from riffs to complete compositions, while most of the cuts on its albums were covers of other people's material. With "Groovin'" (#21), the band turned more and more to covers for its singles. The group actually heard the Rascals' laid-back paean to a Sunday afternoon on a test recording and had to hold back its own version until the original was released. As on nearly all its covers, the band brought a fresh originality to its playing, making the material its own with unexpected rhythm changes, jazzy improvisations and inventive chord progressions. "Hang 'Em High" (#9) is an evocative, soulful revisit of the theme to a Clint Eastwood Western, with Cropper's reverberating guitar providing an electrifying climax. It was as expressive as Hugo Montenegro's splashier "The Good, the Bad and the Ugly"—an excellent example of how the

MG's could do more with less. Their "Mrs. Robinson" (#37) is a joyful jam on the Simon and Garfunkel hit, while their version of the Beatles' "Something" (#76) has Cropper's guitar and Jones' piano going from pretty to potent, transforming the gorgeous ballad into an intensely rhythmic riff.

In 1969 Jones extended his range by writing the score for the Jules Dassin film *Uptight!*, a well-intended but flawed updating of John Ford's *The Informer* from Ireland in the thirties to Harlem in the sixties. One of the few mainstream movies of the sixties to be scored and performed by a rock instrumental group, it is undoubtedly the best. "Time is Tight" (#6), the single from the score, became the group's second-biggest selling record and, as the title suggests, summed up the heart of the MG's artistry. Cropper's guitar sets the steady, unrelenting rhythmic beat, quickly joined by drums and bass. Then Jones' soothing organ quietly enters with the compelling melody, built on powerfully sustained chords. Jackson raps out a sharp fill that signals the bridge. Then it's back to the beat, growing in intensity with every opened organ stop. Cropper's jaunty guitar breaks keep the ball rolling. The organ swells with emotion, the drum fills rattle like machine gun fire and the soul train glides on down the track out of sight.

Other gems from the score, which has been re-released on Rhino Records, include "Johnny, I Love You," in which Booker T. reveals himself to be a gifted soul singer; "Children Don't Get Weary" (vocals by Judy Clay), as strong as any black anthem the sixties produced; and "Deadwood Dick," an eerie, off-center waltz, with Booker's Hammond sounding like a haunted calliope, counterpointing with an electric piano.

The same year saw the beginning of the end for the original MG's. Jones, tired with the restrictive bounds of the new Stax, bought by Gulf and Western in 1968, left for California with his new wife, Priscilla Coolidge. There he signed with A & M and produced two popular albums, the second of which, *Home Grown* (1972), was a soulful set of duets for him and Priscilla that included two Bob Dylan songs. Jones played on two more MG's albums, one of which, *Melting Pot* (1971), was deemed not "commercial" enough by Stax. By then Cropper, too, had had enough and left, leaving behind a small fortune in uncollected royalties and benefits. Jackson and Dunn stayed on at Stax, where an attempt to restart the MG's with new members failed. "It wasn't the same without Booker and Steve," Dunn recalled.

It wasn't the same for their once small but creative company, either, where sudden corporate growth ended in bankruptcy in 1975. By now Al Jackson was the only one left, working in the front office and preparing to testify before a Senate committee about "irregularities" in the company's finances. The night before his appearance, according to the police report, he surprised a burglar at his Memphis home and was found shot dead. Rumors that his death had something to do with dirty dealings in the record business persist.

The loss of Jackson, the beating heart of the MG's, made the thought of a reunion painful to imagine, although two years later the surviving members attempted it, with Willie Hall of the Bar-Kays filling in on drums. The album, *Universal Language*, for Asylum, was a flop, mostly because the label didn't know how to promote the premier soul group of the sixties.

Dunn and Cropper signed on for a three-year tour with the Blues Brothers (Dan Ackroyd and John Belushi), whose comic antics didn't hide the tribute their film and concert appearances made to American soul music and two of its principle architects. Jones' string of producing triumphs culminated in one of Willie Nelson's finest albums, *Stardust* (1978), a collection of pop standards in a Country and Western vein.

The MG's finally got it together again in 1988 for Atlantic Records' fortieth anniversary party at Madison Square Garden and played together sporadically until their triumphant 1993 tour of North America and Europe with Neil Young, reclaiming their title as "the best back-up band in the universe."

In 1994 they released a new CD, *That's the Way It Should Be*, with Steve Jordan on drums, that recaptured their early sound on such fine original tracks as "Slip Slidin,'" "Mo' Greens" (can't get enough of those onions) and the title tune, a reggae-like anthem to peace and light. Over three decades after their auspicious debut, they are still *the* Memphis group.

While Duane Eddy may have had more hits and the Ventures and the Tijuana Brass may have sold more albums, no rock instrumental group can match the consistently high artistry of Booker T. and the MG's, who richly deserve the title "the fathers of the Memphis Sound."

MADE IN DETROIT

While the Mar-Keys and Booker T. and the MG's were creating a new brand of rhythm-driven instrumental music at Stax, the company's main competitor, Detroit's Motown Records, was surprisingly devoid of instrumental groups.

Motown owner Berry Gordy, Jr., did have a jazz label, Workshop Jazz, that recorded some fine jazz from Detroit, but his interest in jazz was minimal and he never marketed it the way he did his more commercial r & b labels—Motown, Gordy and Tamla. Gordy did, however, have the good sense to hire older, experienced jazz musicians for his core house band, who came to be collectively called the "Funk Brothers."

The Funk Brothers were as much the architects of the "Motown sound" as the MG's and the Memphis Horns were of the "Stax sound." Benny Benjamin's thundering tom-toms and fierce snare drums, James Jamerson's ingenious, often complicated bass hooks, the skillful keyboard work of Earl Van Dyke and the interplaying rhythmic guitars of Robert White, Eddie Willis and Joe Messian defined the Motown sound on dozens of classic sides by the Temptations, the Four Tops, the Supremes and other groups.

Unfortunately, Gordy could be as tight-fisted with his musicians as he was with his vocal acts. The Funk Brothers received no royalties or credit for their work, were paid well but not extravagantly as session musicians, and were forced to supplement their income by playing nights and weekends at other studios and in local Detroit clubs. Perhaps most regrettably they were never given the opportunity to record on their own and have only in recent years gotten the recognition they deserved.[1]

....

MOTOWN DID, HOWEVER, produce one outstanding instrumental group, Junior Walker and the All Stars. They were brought to Motown as an answer to the Stax/Volt artists, whose gritty Memphis soul music was, by the mid-sixties, becoming a serious threat to the more sophisticated sound of Motown soul.

Junior Walker, born Autry DeWalt in Blythesville, Arkansas, in 1938, was nicknamed "Walker" in high school, as the legend goes, because he was always walking places. DeWalt's family moved to South Bend, Indiana, where he started playing saxophone in the high school band. After performing with several Midwest groups, Walker formed his own band, the Jumping Jacks (aka the Stick Nix Band after the group's drummer, Billy "Stick" Nix) in the early fifties. Years of honing their craft in dances halls and small clubs turned them into professionals who could play any song request on demand. Hence, they came to be called the "All Stars."

Operating out of Battle Creek, Michigan, by the late fifties, the group was signed by Harvey Fuqua, former leader of the Moonglows, to his Harvey label in the early sixties. Harvey was actually a subsidiary of Motown and it wasn't long before the All Stars were signed to Motown's new "down-home" affiliate Soul, where they became a vocal group by one of those fateful accidents that make the history of rock so intriguing.

After an initial release that flopped, the All Stars were set to record a Walker song inspired by a dance he had seen in several local clubs. The dancers moved their arms like they were cradling a shotgun, which is what Walker named his tune. The designated vocalist failed to show up at the recording date and the other band members encouraged Walker to take a stab at the vocals himself. His rough-as-sandpaper voice was earthy and appealing, even if what he was singing was at times incomprehensible. (What was that line "we're gonna pick tomatoes" about?) Coupled with the heavy rhythmic groove of Willie Woods' guitar, Vic Thomas's red-hot organ riffs and Walker's explosive sax breaks, "Shotgun" skyrocketed to #4 on the pop charts in early 1965 and gave Motown its first soul hit in the Memphis mode.

A string of Top 40 dance hits followed, sometimes backed with an instru-

---

[1]Earl Van Dyke did some solo singles and albums at Motown, but they were generally poorly produced and did not serve the artist well.

When they weren't cranking out dance hits like "Shotgun," Junior Walker and the All Stars made some moody, masterful instrumentals, among the few to come out of Motown's music machine in the sixties.

mental that was in stark contrast to the wild goings-on on the A side. "Hot Cha," the flip of "Shotgun," is a relaxed, soulful serenade that should have easily charted on its own. The more intriguing "Cleo's Back," which backed "Shake and Fingerpop," did chart, going all the way to #43. Best of all was "Cleo's Mood" (#50), a rare A-side instrumental for the group, which was originally recorded in 1963 on the Harvey label. It gets off to a truly creepy start with Thomas's haunted house organ that gives way to a down-and-dirty rolling guitar riff coupled with Walker's echoing honking sax that sounds like it was recorded in an empty warehouse. "Cleo's Mood" remains one of the most mood-drenched instrumentals of the soul era.

As the sixties progressed, the All Stars turned more and more to gritty covers of other Motown hits ("How Sweet It Is," "Money," "Come See about Me"). In 1969 Walker displayed a more lyrical side of his sax on "What Does It Take (To Win Your Love)" one of the great Motown love songs, and the instrumental, "Walk in the Night," his last Top 10 r & b single in 1972. The latter's length and lack of strong thematic material led Don Waller to refer to it as "Jr. Walker Plays Variations on a Theme in Search of a Television Cop Show." But his music got much worse, drowned in overripe arrangements and lush string accompaniment. Leaving Motown didn't help, and he returned to the label in 1983.

A true original, who, like King Curtis, could blow hot or cool, Junior Walker died in November 1995 of throat cancer. One only wishes this double-barreled talent had taken more time off from the dance floor to produce more instrumental gems like those two mysterious "Cleos."

THE SOUL EXPRESS

Near the end of "Shotgun," Junior Walker, a vocal improviser if ever there was one, howled a few bars of "Twine Time," a raucous rhythm and blues instrumental by Alvin Cash and the Crawlers, which had been a hit only a few months earlier.

Like Walker, Cash grew up in the Midwest, in St. Louis. While the All-Stars were an instrumental group that went vocal, the Crawlers were, despite their name, dancers who literally never appeared on their own records.

Alvin Cash (born Welch) formed a song and dance group with his three younger brothers—Robert, Arthur and George—in 1960. The Crawlers played St. Louis clubs for a few years and then moved to Chicago in 1963, where they landed a contract on the Mar-V-Lus label, a subsidiary to the equally marvelous One-Der-Ful label. Their first release, "Twine Time," was actually performed by the Nightlighters, a band from Louisville, Kentucky, that Cash had been performing with. Cash himself, who played no instrument, provided the memorable opening "It's Twine Time!" and various cries of encouragement to his dance partner that punctuate the record. Many radio stations found his remarks a little too suggestive (was "twine" actually a dance or another euphemism for sex, like rock 'n' roll?) and it was banned from the air waves in numerous markets. But the heavy-laden bass hook with its syncopated groove and punchy horn section made it one of the most infectious dance tunes of the year and "Twine Time" went to #14 on the pop charts, selling nearly a million copies.

A forerunner of seventies' funk, Cash went on to make a string of increasingly outrageous dance instro/vocals, from the "The Barracuda" (#59) to "The Philly Freeze," "The Boston Monkey" and "Funky Washing Machine." The Nightlighters changed their name to the surprisingly bland Registers, while the Crawlers, probably tired of doing nothing on these records, left to form the Little Step Brothers, a dance act. Cash combined his dubious singing career with acting bit parts in movies. (He was one of the Five Satins in *The Buddy Holly Story*.) One of his last releases was "Doin' the Ali Shuffle," a tribute that must have made Muhammad Ali smile.

IF ALVIN CASH WAS a dancing fool, the Bar-Kays, the third and last big instrumental group to come out of the Stax stable, were true party animals. The group was formed by MG drummer Al Jackson, who helped get them a gig as back-up band for singer Norman West. Closer in sound to the Mar-Keys than the MG's, the group featured two brass players—Phalen Jones on sax and Ben

After four of their members died with Otis Redding in an airplane crash in 1967, the Bar-Kays reorganized as the funky seventies' band, pictured here.

Cauley on trumpet. They worked out a raucous vamp that, like "Last Night," evolved into a full-length instrumental. The group played the number during a recording break for Stax president Jim Stewart. Stewart was impressed, but before recording the number grabbed some kids off the street and brought them into the studio for insurance. He bought them cokes and encouraged them to carry on as if they were at a party. Background party noises, which had worked for such disparate artists as Gary U.S. Bonds and the Swingin' Medallions, contributed greatly to the Bar-Kays first and biggest hit. Titled "Soul Finger" after the James Bond film *Goldfinger* of a few years earlier, the instrumental starts off with a sassy brass break of "Mary Had a Little Lamb" and then rolls into the main vamp, which sounds suspiciously like the first half of the melody of Little Richard's "Lucille." The warbling brass, fatback drums and the neighborhood kids yelling out the title at regular intervals keep things rolling until a striking two-note barking brass riff brings the number to its exciting climax. With all this going for it, "Soul Finger" (#17) couldn't miss and stayed in the Top 40 for nine weeks in the summer of 1967.

The group scored two more Hot One Hundred charters by the fall, "Knucklehead" and "Give Everybody Some." Otis Redding, the reigning king of soul at Stax, was so impressed with the Bar-Kays' work that he hired them as his new backup band. They were on their way to joining the MG's as one of the top bands of soul, when they departed with Redding on his winter tour. Their twin-engine Beechcraft was on its way to a date at Madison, Wisconsin, on the rainy morning of December 10, 1967. Three miles from the Madison airport it crashed into a frozen lake. Trumpeter Ben Cauley, who awoke moments before the crash, was the only survivor. Redding, the pilot and four of the six Bar-Kays died in the accident. Bassist James Alexander had not been on the plane. The exact cause of the crash has never been determined. Three months later, Otis Redding had his first and only #1 hit, "(Sittin' on) The Dock of the Bay," written with Steve Cropper and recorded only three days before his death.

Alexander re-formed the band in 1968 with Cauley and four new musicians, all top Memphis session men, the eldest of whom was only 20. The original Bar-Kays were inspired; the new band were skilled professionals. They went on to play back-up for such top Stax acts as the Staple Singers and Johnny Taylor. Their own releases gravitated toward heavy funk in a dance groove, culminating in 1976 in their biggest pop hit, "Shake Your Rump to the Funk" (#23) on Mercury. Bar-Kay drummer Willie Hall was good enough to be asked to fill the considerable shoes of the late Al Jackson in the reunited MG's in the mid-seventies. Thus the soul tradition carried on.

....

BY THE MID-SIXTIES, new changes were coming to Hi Records. Bill Black was dead and a new hitmaker had emerged with a distinctive sound of his own. Willie Mitchell had been a black trumpet player and band leader since the early fifties. With his pencil-thin mustache and matinee idol looks, the women fans flocked to him. According to Hi's Ray Harris, he first met Mitchell while the musician was reupholstering Harris's Cadillac on his day job. If that was the case, it was Mitchell's top-notch Memphis band, featuring future MG's Al Jackson and Lewis Steinberg, that brought him into the company as a recording artist and then as an arranger and house band leader.

In 1964 Mitchell had his first instrumental hit, "20-75" (#31), which was the number on the record label. A catchy instro, it largely eliminated the heavy bottom sound of the Black Combo and replaced it with clean, crisp horn riffs, syncopated hand clapping and a slippery organ line. Mitchell's band was a slightly smoother version of Stax's Memphis Horns, just as riffy but with a little less grit. By the time of his biggest hit, a reworking of King Curtis's "Soul Serenade" (#23), with sweet Memphis guitars taking most of the melody from the sax, Mitchell had redefined soul in a more commercial and sophisticated vein that would appeal to white listeners as much as black ones.

His organizational skills extended well beyond his band and in 1970 Mitchell became executive vice-president of Hi and turned increasingly to new vocal performers like Ann Peebles and later Al Green to fill out the lush wash of strings and horns that had become Hi's new "untouchable sound."

....

TWO SOUTHERN GUITARISTS—one white and one black—also rode the soul express before it derailed at the grand funk station in the seventies, and must be mentioned.

Lonnie Mack, despite only two hit records, both back in 1963, is today considered one of the most influential of rock guitarists with a style and technique as unique in its way as Duane Eddy's twang. Mack's playing was not so different from Dick Dale's, maximizing the vibrato and feedback from the tremolo bar. But while Dale drew his inspiration from the surf, Mack looked to the

THE
WHAM
OF THAT
MEMPHIS
MAN!

*One of the most distinc-
tive guitar stylists of the
sixties, Lonnie Mack has
made several comebacks
since his initial success in
1963 with Chuck Berry's
"Memphis." (Photo
courtesy of Showtime
Archives, Toronto)*

swamp. His country blues technique was always grounded and the balance of
wild abandon and steady control made for a guitar style that was exciting but
far more artistically self-disciplined than that of many of his imitators in the seventies and eighties.

Raised in Aurora, Indiana, Mack's first guitar was a Lone Ranger model that
cost $9.95. He formed his own country band in 1954 and by the early sixties was
making the club circuit in the Midwest with his brother Alvin. As a session
musician, Mack worked for the Fraternity label in Cincinnati that had put
Jimmy Dorsey back on the map in 1957.

In a scene reminiscent of the turning point in Junior Walker's career at
Motown, Mack was set to play Chuck Berry's seminal rocker "Memphis" in a
Cincinnati club when the regular vocalist didn't show. So Lonnie and the boys
played it as an instrumental. The crowd loved it. Later, when finishing a recording session at Fraternity, Mack was told to play something of his own in the
twenty minutes of studio time remaining. He chose his wild swamp rock version of "Memphis." The record was released and zoomed into the Top 5 in the
summer of 1963. Within a few months, Mack struck again with "Wham!" (#24),
an original instrumental on which he loosened his vibrato in escalating power
chords that would shake the rafters of any Southern roadhouse.

Two more singles only reached the lower echelons of the charts and soon
Mack was back on the roadhouse circuit until he was re-discovered in 1968 by
a new generation of guitarists, some of whom found Mack's stratospheric blues
style more of a kick than psychedelic drugs. Such adulation, however, was not

enough to sustain a second career, and Mack retired from the music business in 1971, only to re-emerge once again in 1985, when he returned to touring. The re-release of his classic album *The Wham of That Memphis Man!* by Alligator in 1987 assures that his unique brand of guitar picking will continue to be appreciated.

....

BLUES GUITARIST Slim Harpo was primarily known as a singer until he produced one of the biggest instrumentals of 1966, the infectiously rhythmic "Baby, Scratch My Back."

Harpo, so named for his wily harmonica playing, was born James Moore on February 11, 1924, in Lobdell, Louisiana, where he helped raise three siblings after the sudden death of his parents. Always conscious of needing a "day job" to pay for his musical career, Harpo went to work as a longshoreman in New Orleans at age 18 and much later operated his own trucking business in Baton Rouge while recording for Excello Records.

On a club date in the early forties, he met guitarist Otis Hails, also known as Lightning Slim, who would become his musical partner for the next two decades. At the suggestion of recording studio owner J. D. Miller, Harpo developed a unique nasal singing style to separate himself from the other Southern blues artists. He wrote and recorded the seminal blues "I'm A King Bee," later recorded by the Rolling Stones, but didn't have a national hit until "Rainin' in My Heart" in 1961.

"Baby, Scratch My Back" (#16), which hit five years later, was not only his biggest single (going to #1 on the rhythm and blues charts), but was one of the last classic rock instrumentals in a year dominated by the easy-listening sounds of the Tijuana Brass. "Baby, Scratch My Back" was a different kind of easy listening, a rolling Memphis blues guitar that actually did scratch, with Harpo's wailing harmonica alternating with his sly, suggestive asides to his partner. It made the itch simply irresistible.

On the eve of his first trip to Europe, Harpo was working on one of his trucks when its engine fell on his chest. He seemed to have recovered from the accident, but died the next day, January 31, 1970, of a heart attack.

By then Memphis was rapidly fading as the capital of instrumental soul. The MG's had had their last Top 40 hit, the Bill Black Combo was a nostalgia act, Stax was only a few years away from bankruptcy and Willie Mitchell at Hi Records, once the home of the instrumental, was just a year away from launching the career of the last of the big soul singers, Al Green.

Soul would soon be making way for funk and then disco, which would return the instrumental briefly to prominence with such chart-toppers as one-hit-wonder Van McCoy's "The Hustle." Disco, with its mechanical dance beat and big ensemble, however, had none of the personality, the tang and the raw, rhythmic power of the great soul music that came out of Memphis in the sixties. The flavor of the stew was gone.

Chapter Nine

Country Licks

We try to emphasize the solo sound,
one guitar man or one bass. We like to hear what
one guy has to say when he gets wound up.
CHET ATKINS

It's a bunch of good musicians getting
together and doing what comes naturally.
Of course, you've got to have a referee.
OWEN BRADLEY on "the Nashville Sound"

I just look at music like it's music
and it's not to me whether it's got a name
on it or not; it's whether I like it or not.
BUCK OWENS

A large part of country music grew up as instrumental music. On Saturday night in the rural South the whole family would gather around and jam, everyone playing a different instrument, even if it was only a washboard. But for all the emphasis on teamwork, it was solo performers who would emerge from Nashville in the late fifties and early sixties as the premier country instrumentalists, crossing over to the pop charts with a clutch of classic recordings.

MR. GUITAR

The first musician to make the solo player a force to be reckoned with in country music was also the man most responsible for rejuvenating the genre so it could survive the onslaught of rock 'n' roll.

Chet Atkins was hardly a hit when he first appeared at the Grand Ole Opry in 1950. Although his guitar picking was flawless, the fans didn't immediately cotton to a guy who played guitar and didn't sing. Seventy-odd LPs and dozens of hit singles later, Atkins is country's "Mr. Guitar," or as he prefers to be called these days a "Certified Guitar Player."

He may never have had a Top 40 pop hit, but Chet Atkins is among the most respected figures in country and pop—both as a guitarist of flawless technique and the producer who brought country music into the pop mainstream with the "Nashville sound." (Photo courtesy of Showtime Archives, Toronto)

Chester Burton Atkins was born on June 20, 1924, in Luttrell, Tennessee, about twenty miles from Knoxville. His father was a voice coach and piano teacher; his half brother Jimmy, who first encouraged him to play guitar, was one-third of the Les Paul Trio. The story goes that nine-year-old Chet traded an old pistol for his first guitar. But he first found work as a fiddler on local country radio stations in his teens. After a five-year apprenticeship as a radio performer, he was signed by RCA in 1947 and played as sideman for numerous country acts including the comedy duo of Homer and Jethro, some of whose whimsy rubbed off on the newcomer.

Although his first RCA single was a vocal number ("Money, Marbles and Chalk"), it was his distinctive finger-picking guitar style that caught the attention of record buyers and gave him his first country hit in 1949, "Gallopin' Guitar."

Atkins' skillful, clean technique was as meticulous as the classical guitar work of a Segovia and his repertoire was far-ranging—embracing pop, classical, blues and even rock.

With his keen intelligence and sound musical instincts, he was the perfect choice for consultant and A & R man at RCA's Nashville operation in 1953. By 1957, he was running the studio, virtually recreating country music in a more contemporary and urban style that brought it into the pop mainstream.

Atkins' method was one that would earn him the ire of country purists. He did away with the standard steel guitars and fiddles and replaced them with rhythm guitars and drums. He sweetened the sound with the smooth background vocals of the Anita Kerr Singers and the male gospel group the Jordanaires and a wash of soft strings. On the technical side, he overdubbed the harmony, something pop singers had been doing for years. In the process he turned country artists like Jim Reeves, Skeeter Davis and the Browns into pop stars.

Ironically, Atkins himself never placed a tune in the pop Top 40. It wasn't for lack of trying. Singles like "Boo Boo Stick Beat" (#49 in 1959) and "Teensville" (#73 in 1960) were decent rockers. Anyone who think Atkins is a square should listen to his rocking, slashing guitar work on these sides. But the country gentleman was probably too old and didn't have the ambition to become another Duane Eddy. He was far too busy anyway, running RCA Nashville.

Atkins' schedule was so hectic that he converted his garage into a recording studio so he could record his own music at night. "I'd fall asleep every night with a guitar in my hands," he recalled years later in an interview with Jim Ohlschmidt.

The sidemen Atkins drew to Nashville were as versatile and skillful as himself. He had a knack for finding players who were creative and could bring a spark of originality to the most mundane recording sessions. In a *Billboard* interview in 1960, Atkins chided the New York labels and studios for their mediocrity:

> Sidemen blow the notes and do what they're told. . . . Down here, we have arrangements but we never write them down. We create them in the studio. Every musician offers suggestions, so we have seven or eight creative minds at work for every record. The a & r man acts as an editor, pulling these ideas together and unifying them.

ATKINS' COUNTERPART AT Decca in the fifties and sixties was Owen Bradley, who shared his ideas about widening the commercial appeal of country music. There the resemblance between the two men ended. Atkins was slim and urbane; Bradley was big and looked like a bumpkin. He hated to wear a tie and liked to refer to himself as "just a hilly-billy." But this hilly-billy knew how to rock. When not producing Brenda Lee and other crossover artists, he led the Owen Bradley Quintet and played a mean, boogie-woogie piano. He can be heard to good effect on "Big Guitar," his biggest pop instrumental that went to #46 in 1958.

Bradley's greatest achievement, however, may have been providing a studio for Nashville's finest that is still in demand today. In 1956 he bought a dilapidated barn twenty miles outside of town and renovated it to provide his oldest son with a place to cut demonstration tapes for his new publishing company. The out-of-the-way location and the state-of-the-art equipment soon brought country's top artists by to record at "Bradley's Barn," along with such pop instrumentalists as organist Lenny Dee and clarinetist Pete Fountain. In 1968, the rock group the Beau Brummels were so pleased with the results of their country rock foray at the legendary studio that they named the LP *Bradley's Barn* in his honor.

From Decca, Bradley moved to MCA, where he helped guide the crossover careers of Bill Anderson, Loretta Lynn and Conway Twitty. When asked by a *Newsweek* writer to define the Nashville Sound some years later, Bradley said, "It's a song that's our kind of song and a bunch of musicians who can put it over." Some of these same musicians would soon be "putting themselves over" and moving into the solo spotlight.

FROM SIDEMEN TO SUPERSTARS

Pianist Floyd Cramer was only 21 when Chet Atkins invited him to come to Nashville and join RCA, but he was already a seasoned professional. Cramer had taken up the piano at age 5 in his hometown of Huttig, Arkansas, known at that time for its sawmill. After high school, he signed on to Shreveport, Louisiana, radio station KWKH's country cavalcade of stars, "Louisiana Hayride." Over the next four years Cramer toured with several Hayride stars including Hank Williams and a very young Elvis Presley. He played sessions for other artists at local Abbot Records, where he first came to Atkins' attention.

At RCA, Cramer became the most in-demand pianist, playing on everything from Elvis's "Heartbreak Hotel" to Jim Reeves' "He'll Have to Go." He made his solo debut on the label with "Flip, Flop and Bop" in 1958, a rocking boogie woogie instrumental that only went to #87 on the charts.

One day in early 1960 Atkins called Cramer in to listen to a demo record he had just gotten. The song was "Please Help Me I'm Falling," written and performed by pianist Don Robertson. It was a lovely country ballad, but it was Robertson's unusual style of playing that caught Atkins' ear. He would start to hit one note and quickly slip his fingers over to another, bending the notes to create a strikingly melancholy sound. Atkins asked Cramer if he could play Robertson's "slipnote" style and the pianist replied that he had used that technique himself, but never in the recording studio. He agreed with his boss that the "lonesome cowboy sound" of the slipnote was distinctive and could sell country records. Cramer chose his own composition, a somber but beautiful ballad, "Last Date," to try it out on.

With its quiet, mournful piano, warm strings and soft background vocals by the Anita Kerr Singers, "Last Date" was the epitome of the new sophisticated Nashville sound—misty, understated, urbane, immensely commercial—country music for the city folk. It not only topped the country charts but peaked at #2 on the pop charts, blocked from the top position by Elvis's "Are You Lonesome Tonight," on which Cramer also played. "Last Date" was the first and biggest country crossover instrumental and helped make the slipnote style

Floyd Cramer was Elvis's favorite pianist for years, but it wasn't until he recorded his ballad "Last Date" in the slipnote style that he became a star in his own right. He once described the slipnote technique as "a sort of near-miss on the keyboard. . . . The result is a melancholy sound." (Photo courtesy of Showtime Archives, Toronto)

de rigueur not only on country songs but pop records as well. No instrumentalist at the time had as powerful an influence on pop music as Floyd Cramer.

Skeeter Davis, another of the new breed from Nashville, collaborated with songwriter Bouldeaux Bryant on lyrics to the tune and had her own hit with "My Last Date with You." Conway Twitty put different lyrics to the song in 1972 and took "(Lost Her Love) On Our Last Date" to #1 on the country charts.

With his next single, the rollicking "On the Rebound," Cramer proved that life goes on after the last date and, for those who had missed "Flip, Flop and Bop," that he was no sedate cocktail pianist. Another Top 5 pop hit, he quickly followed it with a high-strutting, only slightly more subdued version of the country classic "San Antonio Rose" (#8).

Although his last Top 50 hit was his version of Allen Toussaint's "Java" (#49) in 1963, Cramer cemented his title as "Mister Keyboards" with a busy touring schedule and a highly successful series of LPs called "Class of . . ." that covered each year's top hits starting in 1965. Best known for the slipnote style he made famous, Cramer has mastered nearly every style of music from boogie woogie to classical, although we doubt we'd ever want to listen to his 1967 release, *Floyd Cramer Plays Monkees*.

....

BASED ON HIS ONE BIG HIT, Bill Pursell's pedigree as a country pianist may be suspect, despite his many years in Nashville. A graduate of the Peabody Conservatory of Music in Baltimore, he served in the Air Force Band in Washington, D.C., during World War II. After picking up an M.A. in music at the Eastman School of Music in Rochester, New York, Pursell moved to Tennessee, where he played with the Nashville Symphony. Country music called, however, when a recording contract with Columbia led him to record an album of country tunes arranged by Mr. "Raunchy" himself, Bill Justis. "Our Winter Love" was perhaps the least country-sounding track on the album, but this quiet, simple tune built on continually escalating piano chords backed with the ever-present strings, was chosen as the single and went Top 10 during the winter of 1963. One of the most romantic pop instrumentals of the early sixties, it remains the perfect background music for a tryst by a warm fireplace on a

"Yakety Sax" is a seminal sixties' instrumental, but it took Boots Randolph three tries and at least five years to make it a hit. The top country saxman for more than three decades, Randolph closed his famed Nashville dinner club in 1994 after seventeen years in business. (Photo courtesy of Showtime Archives, Toronto)

snowy evening. Pursell never charted again, but has had a long and successful career as a teacher and session musician.

....

BOOTS RANDOLPH, another Atkins's acquisition, waited five years to see his signature tune become a hit, but it proved worth the wait. Homer Louis Randolph III was born in Paducah, Kentucky, on June 3, 1927. True Southerners, the family formed a band during the Depression featuring Dad on fiddle, Mom on guitar and sis on bass. Little Homer played ukulele. Boots graduated to the trombone in junior high and then picked up the tenor saxophone in high school, where he played in the marching band. After a hitch in the Army band during World War II, he married and did odd day jobs while working nights as a sideman.

The Randolphs now lived in Illinois and for four years Boots and his sax were a regular attraction at a club in Decatur. Homer and Jethro caught his act and told their old friend Chet Atkins about the promising young jazz artist. Atkins liked hiring jazz musicians because they were flexible and creative and could usually play anything. When he heard Randolph's tape of what may have been an early version of an original instrumental, "Yakety Sax," he hired him to come to Nashville. The tune, written with guitarist Spider Rich, was named after the current Coasters' hit "Yakety Yak," and was a kind of homage to King Curtis's rollicking sax bridge in that same song, although Randolph claims the main melody was based on "When the Saint Come Marching In."

Randolph adapted quickly to the new Nashville style and quickly rose to the top ranks of sessionmen. Atkins produced his "Yakety Sax," adding some ingenuous touches to broaden its humorous appeal. He had towels stuffed over the strings of accompanist Floyd Cramer's piano and lay a section of copper tubing over the high strings to create a crazy clanking sound that dominated the rhythm section. RCA released the single and an accompanying album in 1960 in its new Living Stereo. Both sold poorly, perhaps because they were marketed in the wrong way: an ad in *Billboard* claimed the *Yakety Sax* LP "places Boots Randolph in the top ranks of today's jazz artists."

In 1961, Randolph left RCA and signed with Monument, where another top Nashville sessionman, bassist Bob Moore, had just struck gold with his proto-Tijuana Brass instrumental, "Mexico" (#7). Monument released "Yakety Sax," this time gearing it toward the country market, where it scored a modest success. Two years later it reissued the single and album, when the tune got national exposure on ABC TV's *The Jimmy Dean Show*, on which Randolph was a regular musician. Sears and Roebuck had just come out with a new stereophonic system and store demonstrators used the *Yakety Sax* album to show off the system for prospective customers. They ended up selling more albums than stereos.

The third time proved the charm and "Yakety Sax" reached #35 on the pop charts and made Boots Randolph a household name. On the basis of his hit, he put out a string of successful albums for Monument, had several more charting singles, played sax with the King on the memorable 1968 TV special *Elvis is Back* and eventually opened his own dinner club, which remained a Nashville institution for seventeen years.

Although he drifted into the easy listening groove in the mid-sixties with such albums as *Boots with Strings*, Randolph has remained a top-flight saxman, able to bring his distinctive melodious touch from country tunes to movie fare pap like "The Shadow of Your Smile."

······································

THE STEEL GUITAR OF Pete Drake didn't "yak," but it did talk, most eloquently on his sole pop hit, "Forever" (#25), in 1964. Drake, a native of Atlanta, Georgia, would have appeared to be one of the "old guard" musicians that had no place in Chet Atkins' new mellow Nashville.

Drake bought his first steel guitar in an Atlanta pawnshop for $33 and taught himself to play. Besides forming his own band, Sons of the South, he played with such top country acts as Ernest Tubb's Troubadours and Wilma Lee and Stoney Cooper. He followed Lee and Cooper to Nashville in 1959, where his individualistic style of playing steel guitar didn't get him any work. An adapt-

Pete Drake not only gave the steel guitar a new lease on life with his novel "talking" technique, but brought its unique sound into rock music, contributing to such landmark albums as Bob Dylan's Nashville Skyline and George Harrison's All Things Must Pass. (Photo courtesy of Showtime Archives, Toronto)

able musician, Drake switched to the more conventional country steel guitar style in order to find employment. Fortunately for him, the old way was on the way out and he was able to revert to his own unique style, thus becoming more popular in the recording studio than ever. At one point, it is said, Drake played on more than three-quarters of the seventy-five singles on the *Billboard* country charts.

Keenly aware that his instrument needed to keep pace with all those shimmering strings and cooing choruses, Drake came up with a novel gimmick. Getting the idea from an old Kay Kyser film, he discovered how to pass the notes he played on the guitar through a driver and into a plastic tube that he pushed into the side of his mouth. By forming words in his mouth he was able to make the steel guitar appear to talk. "The guitar is your vocal chords," he explained in one interview, "and your mouth is the amplifier." He used the gimmick on an early Roger Miller record and one by Jim Reeves.

Then in 1964, Drake took the ballad "Forever," which had been a hit for the Little Dippers a few years earlier, and recorded it with his steel guitar echoing key words from the lyric, sung by the omnipresent Anita Kerr Singers. "Forever" (#25) sold over a million copies and "Pete Drake and His Talking Steel Guitar" became a country sensation.

But Drake was smart enough to see that the novelty would soon wear off. He eventually went back to his traditional style of playing and took his steel guitar into the halls of rock 'n' roll. He played on Bob Dylan's breakthrough country album *Nashville Skyline*. That's Drake playing those lingering sweet strains on the hit single, "Lay Lady Lay." In the early seventies he played on albums by two ex-Beatles, George Harrison's *All Things Must Pass* and Ringo Starr's Nashville LP *Beaucoups of Blues*, which he also produced. His tasteful production of B. J. Thomas's *Amazing Grace* album won him a Grammy in 1982.

The greatest ambassador of an often under-appreciated instrument, Pete Drake died in Nashville on July 29, 1988.

SNAPPY GUITARS, BLARING BRASS

Not all the top country instrumentalists in the fifties and sixties were soloists. Two innovative groups in particular further blurred the line between country and pop.

BUCK OWENS AND the Buckaroos played their own contemporary style of country swing that kept them at the top of the country charts for nearly a decade. While most of their hits were vocals, they turned out some wonderful instrumentals, usually sneaking one or two in at the end of an album recording session, both with and without their famous leader.

Buck Owens was always something of a square peg in the round hole of country music. The son of a share-cropper, his childhood reads like a chapter

Buck Owens and the Buckaroos were country's answer to the Ventures. Their electric guitars and rock-beating drums brought a fresh new sound to country music in the sixties. Head Buckaroo Don Rich (to the right of Owens, who is at the far left) played the Telecaster and fiddle. (Photo courtesy of Showtime Archives, Toronto)

out of *The Grapes of Wrath*. When a move from Texas to Arizona failed to improve the family's economic situation, Buck quit school in ninth grade and went to work as a farm laborer. He got his first instrument, a mandolin, when he was 13 and by age 17 had taught himself guitar. He was soon working with a radio band at a station in Mesa, Arizona. Still 17, he met and married 14-year-old Bonnie Campbell, who sang with a group called Mae's Skillet Lickers.

The Owens moved to Bakersfield, California, in 1951, where Buck formed his own band, the Schoolhouse Playboys. A multi-instrumentalist by now, he played saxophone and trumpet with the group, but became far better known as a guitar sessionman. He started his own solo recording career as a rockabilly singer, under the name Corky Jones, to avoid the disapproval of his country fans. Capitol Records signed him up in early 1957.

The next year he met and hired a gifted 16-year-old fiddle player, Don Rich, from Olympia, Washington. When Owens formed the Buckaroos in 1962, Rich took over lead guitar. The rest of the classic Buckaroos included Doyle Holly on bass, Tom Brumley on pedal steel guitar and Willie Canter on drums—each a master of his instrument. The Buckaroos had one foot firmly planted in country and one in rock. Brumley's steel guitar wept with the best traditional country bands, if in his own unique style, while Rich, who still filled in on fiddle when needed, could scratch away like an old timer at a barn dance. But the sharp attack of the Buckaroos' electric guitars and the crisp, audible drum beat, all but unheard of before in country music, were something new.

The "Bakersfield Sound," as it came to be called, was tight, clean and clearly rocked. It made Bakersfield the Nashville of the West and was often referred to by Owens fans as "Buckersfield."

"People used to moan at me about the guitar and the drums in the 60's but it was what I felt," said Owens in a 1990 *Goldmine* interview. "It's probably a little bit more raw . . . has more of an edge to it, unpretentious and unpolished, unhurried."

The Buckaroos' best instrumentals, like their signature tune, the #1 country hit "Buckaroo" (#60 pop), were simple, upbeat numbers with intricate interplay between Rich's Telecaster and Holly's bass. The group favored high-kicking dance steps, like polkas, that gave Rich a chance to show off his skill with tricky rhythms.

Winner of the Instrumental Group or Band of the Year for four years running in the County Music Association polls, Owens and the Buckaroos played every venue from country fairs to Carnegie Hall, a celebrated performance that was captured on a live album.

Rich died in an motorcycle accident in the early seventies in California. Soon after, Holly left the group and it was never the same. Owens left Capitol for Warner Brothers and the TV show *Hee Haw* and the classic Buckaroos were no more. As much the quintessential country instrumental group of the sixties as the Ventures were in rock, the Buckaroos brought a new zest and excitement to country music, without betraying the music's finer traditions.

....

SOME CRITICS WOULD not say the same about Danny Davis and the Nashville Brass. Brass instruments had been more of an alien sound in country music than a rocking drumbeat. Chet Atkins had used them sparingly in his new Nashville Sound, until Davis, his production assistant at RCA, suggested the idea of a country brass group in the mid-sixties. The Nashville Brass's first album appeared in 1968 and was castigated by some country critics, an opinion that persists to this day. Hugh Gregory, writing in *Who's Who in Country Music*, damns Davis for creating "a country-ish type of muzak. . . . The best that can be said of his career was that it demonstrated how susceptible the Nashville establishment was to opportunism. . . ."

But the average listener was quickly won over to a sound that tailored the peppy, patented rhythms of the Tijuana Brass, Davis' model, to the country market. "I never liked no horns," admitted one country fan on the liner notes of a Brass album, "but I like what you do."

Like Herb Alpert, Davis made his crossover sound more palatable with tight,

Despite the awful costumes, Danny Davis and the Nashville Brass weren't as bad as many country music critics made them out to be. Davis, the one in the tux, came to country via big bands, pop and rock. Their horn-driven music broke one of the last taboos in country music.

clean arrangements, mostly by Bill McElhiney, and above-average production values overseen by Bob Ferguson. The attention to good product paid off. The group's first fourteen albums all sold over 100,000 copies and for fives years (1969-74) the Nashville Brass was voted Instrumental Band of the Year by the Country Music Association.

Born George Nowlan in an Irish family in Randolph, Massachusetts, in 1925, Davis came to country music relatively late in his career. His mother was an operatic vocal coach who helped steer him toward classical music. A trumpet soloist with the Massachusetts All State Symphony Orchestra at age 14, he left the New England Conservatory of Music the following year to go on the road with drummer Gene Krupa's band. Throughout the forties he played in several big bands and even scored a solo hit with "Trumpet Cha Cha Cha" in the fifties. As a producer at MGM later in the decade, he learned the craft of turning out pop hits while working with the young Connie Francis. An Atkins' protégé, Davis was moved from RCA's New York office to become executive A & R director in Nashville, where he conceived the idea for the Brass.

Although rarely scoring on the pop charts, the Nashville Brass had a string of country hits, starting with Hank Williams' classic "I Saw the Light." McElhiney's brisk arrangements for the trumpets and trombone, often backed by a banjo rhythm section, breathed new life into such standards as "Wabash Cannon Ball" and "Columbus Stockade Blues." Admittedly, the group's squeaky clean sound can quickly wear thin, but the band could bring unexpected pleasures to familiar material, as in its striking rendition of Williams' "I'm So Lonesome I Could Cry" that captures all the sweet bleakness of this country classic in a chorus of mournful horns.

THE INNOVATIVE PRODUCERS and artists that used instrumentation and the instrumental to explore new directions in country music helped lead the way, for better or worse, to the country explosion of the eighties and nineties.

Chapter Ten

Pop Goes the Instrumental

*Jerry [Moss] and I never had this master plan of
starting a record company. It just sort of happened.*
HERB ALPERT on the genesis of A & M Records

*Here we were, almost all Jewish guys,
pretending to be Mexican musicians.*
HAL BLAINE on playing drums for the Tijuana Brass

*[I want to create] a better music . . . keeping
within the commercial boundaries
and retaining a teenage, yet adult appeal.*
Producer JOHNNY SCHROEDER of Sounds Orchestral

B y 1964, the year of the Beatles, the rich stream of rock instrumentals that had been running strong since 1958 was dwindling down to a trickle. The previous year had seen twenty-two instrumentals in the Top 40; in 1964 there were ten, only four of which qualified as rock. And one of these was a re-entry from 1959 (the Wailers' "Tall Cool One").

The following year the instrumental would revive briefly, brought back to life by the emergence of the biggest-selling pop instrumental group in recording history. That odyssey began three years earlier when an ex-Army bugler recorded a few tunes in a West Hollywood garage. The sleek, slick sound of Herb Alpert and his Tijuana Brass would at once give the instrumental its last big hurrah and seal its fate.

MONEY IN THE HORN

Herb Alpert was born March 31, 1935, in the Fairfax section of Los Angeles, a lower middle class ghetto for European immigrants, like his father, Lou Alpert, a tailor from Kiev. Every member of the family played an instrument and Herb started on the trumpet at age 8, but preferred football and baseball to practicing. When he did practice and a neighbor complained about the noise, his mother suggested the neighbor consider moving.

In high school, Alpert studied classical trumpet with the first trumpeter of the San Francisco Symphony Orchestra, but steadily gravitated toward jazz and pop. After less than two years of college, he joined the Army and served as a bugler at the Presidio in San Francisco. When he finished his two-year hitch, he returned to Los Angeles and landed a job at Keen Records as an apprentice artist and later a producer along with his friend and classmate from L.A. City College, Lou Adler.

Alpert and Adler were there at the birth of the California "beach sound," producing Jan and Dean's first recording session. The two proved they had a knack for slick commercial pop by writing Sam Cooke's last and highest-charting song at Keen since "You Send Me"—"Wonderful World" (1960). The same year the twosome showed their savvy as producers by rushing out a hit cover of the Hollywood Argyles' chart-topping novelty, "Alley Oop," with the hastily assembled Dante and the Evergreens.

But Alpert had ambitions to perform himself as an actor and musician. His acting career got no further than playing an extra in *The Ten Commandments*. (He also played trumpet on the soundtrack.) As a musician he only found modest work as a studio session man and a band leader for weddings and bar mitzvahs. Then he met relocated East Coast promotion man Jerry Moss and his luck started to change. Moss suggested they start their own record label to promote Alpert's talents. They formed Carnival Records on a shoestring and recorded in Alpert's garage studio on Westbourne Drive.

"I was intrigued with the sound of Les Paul and Mary Ford, the way Les would double his guitar and stack Mary's voice," Alpert told writer Joe Smith in his book *Off the Record*. "I had two tape machines, and I'd go from machine to machine, back and forth, seven, eight times. It started sounding interesting. I felt I was on to something."

The partners recorded two singles, one featuring "Dore Alpert" singing the original tune "Tell It to the Birds." It made the Top 20 on a local L.A. radio station and, with the record's modest profits, Alpert and Moss attempted their third single.

Sol Lake, a neighbor of Alpert's who refinished furniture, wrote a melancholy tune called "Twinkle Star" that Alpert liked. Giving it a Latin flavor, Alpert renamed the song "The Lonely Bull," overdubbed himself on trumpet, and for $200 recorded the instrumental in a commercial studio. To add some authenticity, he drove down to Tijuana, Mexico, with a sound engineer and suspended a microphone over the local bull ring during a bullfight. He then edited the crowd noises and "Olés!" into the beginning and end of the record, an arresting gimmick that caught the ear of many a deejay. At Moss's suggestion, Alpert called himself the Tijuana Brass just so nobody would miss the point. Rather than lease out the recording, Alpert and Moss took the risk of putting it out themselves. Carnival became A & M, for Alpert and Moss. "We went for broke," recalled Moss in 1964.

The gamble and hard work paid off. "The Lonely Bull" with its evocative, mournful trumpets, all played by the overdubbed Alpert, shot to #6 by November 1962—one of the biggest instrumentals in a year of many hit instrumentals. The subsequent album, with Alpert hoisting a cup of tequila on the cover and liner notes by one Hernando Cortes, sold over 125,000 copies.

However, A & M Records' promising start soon came to a standstill. "Marching to Madrid," another ersatz mariachi tune by Sol Lake with the opening gimmick of clip-clopping horse hooves, failed to chart, as did the album named after it. Two more albums did passable business, but a single released from the second, "Mexican Shuffle," shuffled no farther than #85 on the Hot One Hundred. People were saying Alpert had reached a dead end with his "south of the border" sound and would go down as just another one-hit wonder.

But "Mexican Shuffle," for those who were listening, was a departure from his earlier records. The heavy, melancholy trumpets had been replaced with a lighter, perky brass sound. It was no more authentically mariachi than "The Lonely Bull," but instead of trying to imitate the real thing, Alpert had come up with something fresh and original.

It all might have been for naught, if not for a stroke of luck. The Clark Teabury Gum Company was looking for a jingle for its new TV ad campaign and found "Mexican Shuffle" catchy and commercial. Alpert and Moss, struggling to stay alive, gratefully sold the rights to the instrumental and "Mexican Shuffle," rechristened "The Teabury Shuffle," was heard throughout the land on these rather clever TV commercials. Typically, a person would be walking down the street, pop a stick of gum into his or her mouth and immediately break into a ridiculous dance to Alpert's music.

Buoyed up by the exposure, Alpert put out his fourth album in early 1965, *Whipped Cream and Other Delights*, which featured on its cover an alluring senorita totally swathed in whipped cream. The confections inside were all in the new, lighter Tijuana Brass style and two were released as singles—the title tune, a good-time, syncopated dance, and a new version of the popular movie theme, "A Taste of Honey," which had already charted twice instrumentally, once by Martin Denny. "Whipped Cream" peaked at #68, but "A Taste of Honey" soared to #7 and remains one of Alpert's most impressive efforts. A masterful if eminently commercial arranger, Alpert gave the ballad a beat, set by ace drummer Hal Blaine on the bass drum, and an edge that made it provocative and captivating. The crisp attack of the brass, Blaine's thumping percussion and the moody, minor key, gives what could have been a bland, middle-of-the-road instrumental some real bite.

After a triumphant return to the top of the charts, Alpert decided it was time

The Tijuana Brass only existed on a record label for three years. After the success of "A Taste of Honey" in 1965 Herb Alpert went out and hired full-time musicians to play with him. Alpert is the one in the picture, appropriately, holding the horn.

that he formed a real "Tijuana Brass" to take on the road. A *Billboard* review of the group in one of its first live appearances in Santa Monica found "Alpert was nervous and awkward. . . . At this early point the Tijuana Brass shapes up as a potential TV and concert act, but will have to get out of its unpolished state."

The polishing came quickly. By the end of 1965, the group had three million-selling albums on the charts and was one of the country's top performing groups. The Grammies awarded "A Taste of Honey" both Best Instrumental Arrangement and Best Instrumental Performance. The new year brought no less than six Top 40 singles, including another bouncy, programmatic piece, "Tijuana Taxi" (complete with honking horn), a robust, full-bodied version of "Zobra the Greek," and another lean and muscular Alpert arrangement of a familiar tune, "The Work Song."

The sound of the Tijuana Brass was more pervasive in 1966 than any British rock group, as anyone who has perused a used record bin at a garage sale lately can tell you. Not only was the group's music everywhere on the radio but on television as well. "Spanish Flea" (#27) and "Lollipops and Roses" were both theme songs on daytime TV's popular *The Dating Game*, while its version of the big band tune "Tangerine" was put to work selling Sego diet drinks.

A & M Records' stock went up 800% by 1965 to earn $32 million. The record company that had started three years earlier in Alpert's garage was soon to become the biggest independent record company in history. A & M began adding promising new groups to its stable.

....

THE BAJA MARIMBA BAND never achieved a fraction of the popularity of the Brass, having only one Top 50 single, "Comin' in the Back Door," but its albums consistently sold well and the band's live shows were full of boisterous vaudeville humor.

More percussion-based than the Brass, but with the same Ameriachi-pop sound, the nine-man ensemble was led by marimbaist Julius Wechter, who had previously worked with Martin Denny and was a good friend of Alpert's. Sporting fake Pancho Villa-like handlebar mustaches, sombreros and cigars, the Baja Marimba Band veered on the border of bad taste in its Latin stereotypes. What saved the group was a self-depreciating humor that is fully reflected by these liner notes on an early album by comedian Bill Dana, aka Jose Jiminez, another skilful practitioner of the art of Hispanic exploitation: ". . . the Baja Group has again produced an album of major proportions (approximately 12 x 12). . . . Add this to the already mounting apathy of musicologists everywhere, and there you have it . . . the Baja Marimba Band: another millstone around the neck of A & M Records."

The Baja Marimba Band was one of the easy-listening acts that Alpert and Jerry Moss signed to their growing A & M label. Similar in style musically to the Tijuana Brass, the group played it more for laughs, which took the edge off what today would be considered rather tasteless Mexican stereotypes.

....

MORE AUTHENTICALLY LATIN, but just as pop-oriented, was Sergio Mendes Brasil '66. While never strictly an instrumental group, the sextet fit in nicely with A & M's slick brand of sophisticated pop. Born in Niteroi, Brazil, in 1941, Mendes was a popular jazz pianist in Rio when still in his teens with his group Bossa Rio. He arrived in the United States in 1965 with a new group of musicians and singers called Brasil '65 and recorded for Atlantic Records with little success. Alpert, sensing a kindred spirit, signed Mendes to his label the following year and his first A & M album produced the Top 50 hit "Mas Que Nada" (#47). Mendes' bossa nova beat melded nicely with the sexy vocals of Karen Phillips and Lani Hall, who later married Alpert. Less artistic in its intentions than the American and Brazilian musicians who rode the first bossa nova wave, the group put across appealing pop covers of contemporary American pop material, hitting its stride in 1968 with the ballad "The Look of Love" (#4) from the Bacharach-David score to the James Bond spoof, *Casino Royale.*

Brasil '68 and '69 (same group, new years) continued to chart with slick covers of tunes by the Beatles, Simon and Garfunkle, Glen Campbell and even Otis Redding. Never one to lag behind the times, Mendes switched to Arista Records in 1977 with Brasil '77, which he inexplicably changed to Brasil '88 the following year. These new editions of the group, however, did not improve record sales and Mendes only returned to the charts after coming back to A & M in the early eighties with, for a change, male vocals on "Never Gonna Let You Go" and "Alibis."

Casino Royale proved a bonanza for A & M, and gave the Tijuana Brass one of its most appealing sides. The "Casino Royale" theme (#27) had a delightful cat-and-mouse melody by Burt Bacharach, who himself had signed on as a vocalist with A & M. Alpert's arrangement captures the sneaky humor of the composition, while never losing his characteristic sunny, upbeat style. The following year Alpert scored again with another Bacharach-David song, the rather lugubrious "This Guy's in Love with You," which his laid-back vocal matched perfectly. He originally sang it on a CBS Tijuana Brass special to his then-wife Sharon on Malibu Beach. Thousands of viewers called CBS wanting to know where they could get the record, which led to its release two days later. It became Alpert's first #1 hit, and the first for the popular songwriting team as well.

Having saturated the marketplace with his "Ameriachi" sound, Alpert retired the Brass in 1969 and stopped performing for nearly five years. Always a shy, very private person despite his Hollywood good looks, he devoted his considerable energies to producing for A & M, which by the late sixties had become more adventurous, adding such artists to its roster as Procol Harum, Joe Cocker and Captain Beefheart. In the seventies Alpert discovered his prototypical easy-listening act—Richard and Karen Carpenter.

While he re-formed the Brass briefly in 1973, it wasn't until 1979 that Alpert recorded the biggest instrumental hit of his career. Entering the studio to record an ill-advised disco version of "The Lonely Bull," he quickly abandoned the idea and instead recorded a disco-style dance tune co-written by his nephew Randy Badazz. The hard, infectious beat of "Rise" was made warm and cozy, if also a little melancholy, by Alpert's lyrical horn. The instrumental was helped to #1 by its use as a recurring theme for a rape scene (!) on the ABC soap opera "General Hospital." His keen commercial instincts had not deserted Alpert after nineteen years in the business.

In 1990 Alpert and Moss sold their company to Polygram for half a billion dollars. Since then, like some enlightened nineteenth-century industrialist, Alpert has plowed much of his millions back into society through his foundation for new recording artists and by backing such high-tone Broadway plays as "Angels in America" and "Jelly's Last Jam."

When Alpert performs today, it is in a slightly more jazzy vein that in his brassy heyday. However, in a 1996 concert date in New York, Jon Pareles of *The New York Times* called his new material "cheerful, mid-tempo tunes, symmetrical and free of surprises." Surprises he may not have up his sleeve, but after all these years Alpert has given his audience a high quota of pleasurable ear candy. And no one's complaining.

ANOTHER CONSUMMATE purveyor of ear candy in the closing years of the instrumental's golden era, but a trumpeter of far more playing power, was New Orleans' Al Hirt. Hirt began his illustrious career studying trumpet at the Cincinnati Conservatory and first performed with the New Orleans Symphony Orchestra. After touring for several years with some of the top big bands, he served a four-year hitch in the Army, leaving with the rank of sergeant. Hirt returned to New Orleans, opened his own club, raised eight children with his wife Mary and was content to bask in his local celebrity, until RCA Victor came knocking at the door with a recording contract. With much persuasion from RCA and his manager, the 300-pound trumpeter reluctantly left home and quickly became one of the nation's most-recorded instrumentalists. His powerhouse trumpet was showcased in a string of best-selling albums that included *The Greatest Horn in the World*, *Horn A Plenty* and *Honey in the Horn*.

But it wasn't until 1964 that Hirt struck gold on the pop singles' charts with the simple but catchy "Java" (#4). The tune, written and performed in 1958 by another New Orleans' legend, Allen Toussaint, had nothing to do with the Far East or coffee, but was named after a racehorse. Originally written for piano, "Java" had already been a minor hit for Floyd Cramer, but it was Hirt's blaring horn that put "Java" in the Top 5.

Hirt followed it with two equally catchy little confectioneries—"Cotton Candy" (#15), which sounds like jingle music par excellence and "Sugar Lips"

Al Hirt's insatiable appetite for life is captured in this picture. A reluctant recording artist at first, Hirt produced a string of best-selling albums for RCA before striking gold on the singles' charts with "Java" in 1964. (Photo courtesy of Showtime Archives, Toronto)

(#30), which gave him a chance to really show off his chops. He continued to chart through 1968 and still packs them in at his New Orleans club with his robust virtuoso style.

....

"WHIPPED CREAM," "Cotton Candy," "A Taste of Honey" . . . by the mid-sixties the pop instrumental was indeed suffering from an acute sugar attack. The sweetened sounds pioneered by A & M were a contemporary return in many ways to the good old days of the mid-fifties, when middle-brow orchestras and romantic soloists whisked the listener away from the worries of the workaday world to faraway vacation lands and exotic locals. Only it wasn't fifties' conformity that drove millions to seek refugee in the carefree strains of the Tijuana Brass, but a much grimmer world of drugs, hippies, political assassinations and Vietnam.

While much of rock music was exploring and experimenting with older forms (blues, folk, country) and leading rock into its second golden age, the instrumental was retrogressing, providing ear candy for those who wanted escape from the problems of the contemporary world. Not much nutritional value, but flavorful in three-minute doses.

AND NOW FOR A WORD FROM OUR SPONSOR . . .
The Tijuana Brass had shown how a clever little instro could become a successful commercial jingle or television theme. It was only a matter of time before popmeisters were reversing the process and turning to TV jingles for their next

Top 40 hit. The first to succeed at this novel kind of "cross marketing," not surprisingly, was ace instrumental hitmaker Joe Saraceno. In 1965, Saraceno was entranced by the latest Alka Seltzer commercial jingle, which played while cameras zoomed in on a variety of stomachs of people on the move. The catch line of the commercial was "no matter what shape your stomach in" you need Alka-Seltzer. The jingle was written by Sascha Burland, who had been one-half of the Nutty Squirrels, a hip version of the Chipmunks, whose jazzy novelty, "Uh-Oh, Part 2" had been a big hit in 1959.

Saraceno had his latest instrumental group, the T-Bones, record the jingle as the title tune of their fourth album and released it as a single. The T-Bones, a shifting trio of studio musicians on guitars and drums, seemed destined, despite all Saraceno's efforts, to just miss the mark on each passing musical craze. They came to surf music a little late in 1964, quickly shifted to hot rod music, and then combined both genres in typical Saraceno fashion in an album called *Boss Drag at the Beach*. They even tried their hand at dance crazes, when instrumentals were no longer a viable vehicle for them either. What did they have to lose in recording an Alka-Seltzer jingle?

Apparently nothing—and everything to gain. "No Matter What Shape (Your Stomach Is In)" was a catchy tune with an ambling beat and a clever guitar hook. That, and the familiarity of the amusing Alka-Seltzer commercials, turned this modest instrumental into a monster hit. It not only went to #3 but became the #1 instrumental of 1965, outselling releases by the Tijuana Brass and the Ramsey Lewis Trio.

Saraceno scoured the tube for follow-ups jingles, but only "Sippin' and Chippin'" from Nabisco, not half as clever as "No Matter What Shape," scored, peaking at #62. By 1967 the T-Bones—Donny Robert Hamilton, Joe Frank Carollo and Tommy Clark Reynolds—were reduced to making covers of *real* songs, like Sonny and Cher's "The Beat Goes On" (flip side, "Bonesville").

Wisely, the trio gave up on instrumentals, dropped the dumb name and re-emerged in 1971 as the vocal group Hamilton, Joe Frank and Reynolds to score three Top 40 hits, including the #1 "Fallin' in Love" in 1975.

Saraceno was not the last producer to see the potential bonanza in commercial jingles. Bob Crewe, songwriter and producer extraordinaire of the Four Seasons and other top groups, heard a hit in Sid Romin's aggressive but tuneful Diet Pepsi jingle, "Music to Watch Girls By," which followed the time-honored Madison Avenue tradition of using sex to sell the product. Taking an idea from another Pepsi jingle ("You're in the Pepsi generation"), Crewe called his loose gathering of studio musicians, the Bob Crewe Generation, had them record the jingle and landed a Top 15 hit in early 1967.

Another immensely popular television commercial in 1967 was for the British

A number of TV commercial jingles were transformed into pop hits in the waning days of the instrumental's golden era. A good example is the Benson and Hedges' cigarette jingle, "The Dis-Advantages of You," recorded by the Brass Ring. The producers wisely shifted the title's meaning from smoking to romance on the album cover.

cigarette, Benson and Hedges. Considered in one poll as one of the 100 best commercials of all time, "Oh the Dis-advantages" showed these unusually long cigarettes in a series of visual gags getting caught in elevator doors and burning holes in newspapers and beards. In these innocent days before the Surgeon General banned cigarette ads from television, lung cancer was not one of these disadvantages.

The sly, syncopated jingle music, backed by a "lalaing" female chorus, was snapped up by producer/arranger Phil Bodner, who recorded it with his New York studio band, the Brass Ring. "The Dis-Advantages of You" (#36) shifted the tune's theme from cigarettes to romance. The cover of the album containing the hit single featured a short, bald, middle-aged man in the embrace of a tall blonde. Smart move, Phil.

The Brass Ring's biggest hit the previous year was "The Phoenix Love Theme" (#32), a sax-laden ballad from the action-adventure film *The Flight of the Phoenix*.

....

MOVIE THEMES CONTINUED to provide grist for the lumbering instrumental mill in the mid to late sixties, providing veteran Henry Mancini with the biggest pop hit of his career, "The Love Theme from *Romeo and Juliet*" (#1 in 1969) and another old hand, Roger Williams, with his biggest hit since "Autumn Leaves," the stirring theme from "Born Free" (#7 in 1966).

But Hollywood was getting stiff competition from TV land as record producers and artists turned to the theme music of hit TV series, years before they discovered the jingles during the commercial breaks. "Bonanza" (#19), "The Ballad of Paladin" (#33), "Route 66" (#30) and "Ben Casey" (#28) were all Top 40 instrumental hits, the last played by the classically trained pianist Valjean, whose flair for dramatic orchestral openings rivaled that of Roger Williams. Despite his chic European moniker, Valjean hailed from Shattuck, Oklahoma.

Another TV theme of sorts was "Shangri-La," a theme for Reggie van Gleason on Jackie Gleason's popular variety show. The song had been a big vocal hit for the male harmony group the Four Coins in 1957. The composer, harpist Robert Maxwell, turned out a lush instrumental cocktail lounge version in 1964 that went to #13. A consummate showman, Maxwell's favorite ploy in concert was to set off blinking colored lights on his harp when he pressed his foot pedal.

At the other end of the television spectrum was the riffy cartoonish "Batman" theme, which, besides providing the Marketts with their last hit, also charted at #35 for its composer, trumpeter Neal Hefti, who built a career on writing TV theme music.

Another astute composer of TV themes was Lalo Schifrin, whose groundbreaking theme for "Mission—Impossible" (#42) with its bold, angular rhythms, jazzy flute, percussive piano and throbbing tom-toms was as groundbreaking in 1968 as Mancini's "Peter Gunn" theme had been a decade earlier. But unlike "Gunn" it led to no renaissance of instrumentals on the pop charts.

THE RETREAT TO commercial jingles and TV themes seemed a natural development for instrumental artists who had no other suitable genres left to look to for inspiration. Twangy guitar music, dance music, old style r & b, surf music . . . they were all gone, largely swept away by the self-contained bands of the British Invasion that both played *and* sang.

Among the flood of British groups to cross the Atlantic in 1965 was a studio oddity, Sounds Orchestral, whose producer, John Schroeder, saw it as his mission in life to bring back good taste to instrumental music for teen audiences long dulled by the raucous sounds of rock 'n' roll. With BBC producer Johnny Pearson on piano, backed by drums and three bass players, Schroeder remade Vince Guaraldi's "Cast Your Fate to the Wind." A somewhat prettified version of Guaraldi's lean, jazzy composition, it swept to #10 on the *Billboard* charts, surpassing sales of the superior original.

Another studio group that tried to "raise the level" of musical taste, but with an infectious rocking beat, were the San Remo Strings, who scored the same year with "Hungry for Love" (#27). While Joel Whitburn in his usually reliable *The Billboard Book of Top 40 Hits* describes them as "a group of master violinists," rumors abound that master bassist James Jamerson and keyboardist Earl Van Dyke of Motown's Funk Brothers played on the recording session.

....

By 1966, THE REIGN OF the pop instrumental was coming to an end. The only hit rock instros that year were both re-releases of classics—the Surfaris' "Wipe Out," whose throbbing drum solos now sounded positively nostalgic, and the Viscounts' "Harlem Nocturne," which hailed all the way back to 1959.

The year 1967 was the first since the start of the rock era in which not a single instrumental made *Billboard*'s Top One Hundred Singles' List for the year. Outside of the soul music being made by such Stax artists as Booker T. and the MG's and the Bar-Kays, the rock instrumental was all but dead.

Disco breathed a little life into the instrumental and created a brief demand for instro bands, but the artists were by and large one-hit wonders, who shot to the top with one mega-hit and then vanished from sight, despite such pompous names as the Love Unlimited Orchestra, MFSB, and Van McCoy and the Soul City Symphony. There were no new Duane Eddys or Ventures or MG's who had the talent and craft to build a career on instrumental music. A promising group like the Average White Band from Scotland followed its #1 instrumental "Pick up the Pieces" in late 1974 with several vocal hits. It wasn't cool for any respectable rock band to make music that didn't sing.

By the eighties, the appearance of an instrumental in the Top 40 was a rarity. According to Fred Bronson in his *Billboard's Hottest Hot 100 Hits*, only five of the one-hundred top-selling instrumentals of the rock era appeared in the eighties. So far the nineties have produced only one, Kenny G's "Forever in Love" (1993).

What killed off the instrumental? There was, as mentioned earlier, the British Invasion. Rock instrumentals may have survived where their pop brethren were banished to easy-listening bins and elevators, but, after the Beatles, they were no longer a breeding ground for new groups. Like novelty songs, another casualty of the mod sixties, instrumentals were increasingly looked upon as a relic of an earlier, simpler era of rock 'n' roll. With the appearance of a new generation of songwriter-singers in the early seventies, instrumentals, as a genre in pop music, were no longer commercially viable. New and innovative artists were no longer drawn to them.

Yet in their heyday instrumentals attracted many important performers not normally associated with the genre. Which leads us to the last chapter in our story. . . .

Chapter Eleven

They All Played Instrumentals

> *I'm gonna play my fingers off!*
> FATS DOMINO from "Hey Fat Man" (1950)

> . . . *when I started out, to make sure the piano didn't get
> lost, I gave it the brightest, clangiest, bangiest damn
> sound I could. I put it way out front and cranked that
> mother up, then let my boys try to keep up with me.*
> PAUL REVERE

ince the end of the big band era, vocal music has dominated the pop charts, and yet many a vocalist and vocal group have been drawn to the charms of wordless music. Many rock artists during the fifties and sixties threw in an instrumental or two on their albums or used an intro as a B side to a vocal track for a little spice and variety. A surprising number of these artists produced memorable instrumentals, some of them hits.

Fats Domino, pioneer of rock, started out his celebrated career at age 10 as a boogie-woogie and blues piano player working for hand-outs. By the late forties, he had his first professional gig playing with Billy Diamond's band at New Orleans' Hideaway Club, sometimes mixing in vocals with instrumental music. A few years after his first hit record, "The Fat Man" (1950), he recorded two of his best instrumental performances—"Fat's Frenzy" and "Swanee River Hop." The latter was an updated version of the Stephen Foster song, adapted by Ray Charles. Charles' vocal recording of the number is slow and bluesy, while Domino's is a wild, non-stop romp on the keyboard set to a boogie woogie beat. An excellent instrumental that may well have charted, it was never released as a single because of an excess of material and only appeared in 1956 on the album *Rock and Rollin' with Fats Domino* and on an Imperial EP.

Fats Domino began his career playing boogie woogie piano at age 10 in New Orleans clubs. His signature piano triplets are heard on many of his vocal hits, but on his lesser-known instrumentals he played in a more frenzied, frantic style, as in the memorable "Swanee River Hop."

WHILE THE OTHER great keyboard wild men of rock's first generation—Jerry Lee Lewis and Little Richard—seemed to have little interest in making music without their imitable vocals behind it, the two great guitar rockers of the fifties, Chuck Berry and Bo Diddley, gave us quite a few gems of the genre. Both men were multi-talented musicians: Berry also played piano, tenor sax, steel pedal guitar and drums, while Diddley began his musical career on the violin.

Berry never had an instrumental hit, although you get a taste of what might have been on the extended guitar solo that ends "No Particular Place to Go" (1964). Most of his other recorded instrumentals were in a more jazzy, blues, or Latin vein, and sometimes all three. Four instrumentals were included on his second album for Chess, *One Dozen Berrys* (1958), and his "Guitar Boogie" was included on an EP the same year. It was adapted a decade later by the Yardbirds as "Jeff (Beck)'s Boogie." Perhaps Berry's best-known instrumentals are his two extended jams with Bo Diddley, aptly called "Chuck's Beat" and "Bo's Beat," on the classic *Two Great Guitars* LP from 1964.

Bo Diddley's beat, derived in part from tribal African drumming, was more varied and rich than most critics give him credit for. Like Les Paul, Bo, born Ernest MacDaniels, was, in the words of Robert Palmer, "a tireless sonic experimenter." Some of his more ear-bending experiments with distortion and feedback are the instrumentals "The Clock Strikes Twelve," the B side of his biggest pop hit, "Say Man" (1959), with Bo playing a very bluesy fiddle, and "Mumbling Guitar," a reckless run through the classic Bo Diddley beat with Bo's guitar sounding like some huge reverberating rubber band, wangy instead of twangy.

A subtler side of this gifted musician is revealed in the sensual and sinuous "Aztec," the flip side of "Not Guilty" (1961). He almost sounds like the Ventures, but with his characteristic humor coming through in every slide note, blip, and plucked string.

AMONG THE PIONEERING white rock and rollers, none were as instrumental-driven as Bill Haley and the Comets. Although Haley garnered most of the glory, the Comets were a crack band whose tight playing stands up better today than Haley's only serviceable vocals. The group's stand-out musician was saxman Rudy Pompilli, whose honking style and wild stage antics put him in a league with the great black Texas tenors of the early fifites. His finest moment was the justly titled "Rudy's Rock" (#34), which may qualify as the first white rock instrumental hit, coming out just three months after Bill Doggett's "Honky Tonk" in 1956. Perhaps the highlight of the otherwise uninspired rock film, *Rock around the Clock*, was Pompilli blasting "Rudy's Rock" while astride bassist Al Rex.

That Haley appreciated the musicianship of his band is clear from the 1956 vocal hit "The Saints Rock 'N' Roll." Haley changes the lyric of the traditional spiritual to "When the Comets Rock 'N' Roll" and pays tribute to both Pompilli and lead guitarist Frannie Beecher by name during their solo breaks, although curiously doesn't do the same for either drummer Ralph Jones or bassist Rex, referring only to "when the rhythm starts to go."

The Comets managed to have their own instrumental hit, "Week End" (#35), without Haley, while moonlighting in 1958 as the Kingsmen (not to be confused with the Portland, Oregon, band of "Louie Louie" fame). "Week End" became something of an instrumental standard, recorded by Link Wray and many other artists.

As Haley and the Comets' trajectory headed earthward in the late fifties, they turned more and more to the booming instrumental market. Ironically, as their vocal music was becoming woefully archaic, their instrumentals were right in the pop mainstream. Their last two charting singles, "Joey's Song" (#46) and "Skokiaan, South African Song" (#70), were both instrumentals. The group's final Decca album in 1960 was titled *Strictly Instrumental* and, according to critic Milt Gabler had "a Billy Vaughn sound today."

Bill Haley's Comets were a crack band. Saxman Rudy Pompilli (upper left) followed in the wild footsteps of r & b pioneers like Big Jay McNeely. "Rudy's Rock," one of several of the Comets' instrumental hits, may have been the first successful rock instrumental by white musicians.

When the Comets moved to Warner Brothers that same year, a full-page *Billboard* ad described their new single "Tamiami" as "a colorful reading of a catchy and cute instrumental theme." But "catchy and cute" couldn't save this pioneering rock band from its downward spiral. While the other Comets went their separate ways, the ever faithful Pompilli stayed with Haley until the sax-man's death in 1976 at age 47.

....

RAY CHARLES TURNED to the instrumental not out of desperation, but to display another facet of his musical genius. In the fall of 1961 he exchanged his small back-up combo for a full-fledged big band with five saxophones, four trumpets, four trombones and a full rhythm section. "I loved my small band to the draw-ers," he wrote in his autobiography, "but my heart was set on something big-ger." To inaugurate the new band, he recorded *Genius Plus Soul Equals Jazz* and extracted from it for a single, "One Mint Julep" (#8), a big-band flavored instru-mental of a song by Rudy Toombs. With Brother Ray playing a mean organ, "Julep" bore a striking resemblance to Cozy Cole's "Topsy." Charles never toured without his big band again.

Ray Charles had his first instrumental on the pop charts in 1958 with "Rockhouse, Pt. 2," but his biggest instro was "One Mint Julep" in 1961, which featured his new big band and Brother Ray at the organ.

ANOTHER SOUL MASTER with a monster touring band was James Brown. Instrumentals were a big part of the Brown band, giving the other players a chance to strut their stuff while their leader took a break from his vocal pyrotechnics. With Brown leading, they scored several charting instrumentals, including an instro version of his vocal hit "Try Me" (#63). Brown's biggest-selling and best instrumental was the seminal "Night Train" (#35) in 1962, which had been a minor hit for the Viscounts two years earlier. The Brown band lays down a brassy, chugging beat while the Godfather of Soul calls out the stops ("Washington, D.C., Atlanta, Georgia") like some funky conductor.

The air-tight sound of the Brown band was no accident. A strict taskmaster, he would fine musicians for the slightest infractions. "You didn't make mistakes when you played with James Brown," recalls band member drummer "Pretty" Purdie. "You'd make a mistake while he was singing, and he'd turn around and say, `Ten dollars.'"

Brown and the band also turned out some delicious danceable instros under the alias Nat Kendrick (who was one of his drummers) and the Swans. Their "(Let's Do) The Mashed Potatoes (Parts 1 and 2)" was later appropriated by the Dartells as "Hot Pastrami."

ANOTHER VERSATILE performer was pop singer Bobby Darin who, in the midst of his busiest chart year, 1960, in which he placed seven singles in the Hot One Hundred, managed to find time to crank out "Beachcomber," an intriguing keyboard instrumental with an inventive riff, which crested at #100. Darin "at the piano," as the single's label reads, was a fine musician and is nicely backed by jazzman Milton "Shorty" Rogers leading a chorus of sublime strings. Rogers—aka Boots Brown and his Blockbusters—had his own instrumental hit a few years earlier with "Cerveza." When Darin moved from rock to folk a few years later, he abandoned the piano for guitar. "Beachcomber" remains a fascinating footnote to a fascinating career.

PAUL REVERE WAS ANOTHER talented pianist who, unbeknownst to most of his fans, began his group the Raiders as an instrumental band. Seventeen-year-old Revere was a barber in Bosie, Idaho, when he teamed up with pal Mark Lindsay to form the Downbeats, later the Raiders, in 1959. Like many Northwest groups at the time (the Ventures, the Frantics, the Wailers), Revere opted to play instrumentals, centered around his rocking Jerry Lee Lewis style of keyboard playing.

The group's third release on the Gardena label, "Like, Long Hair" (1961), took off and spent a week in the Top 40 at #38. The title of the rocking instro did not refer to hippie hair styles, but classical "long hair" music. The opening bars had Revere putting down some serious concerto-like chords, based on Rachmaninoff's C Sharp Minor Prelude, that quickly morphed into a rocking

The Raiders an instrumental band? That's how they started back in 1959 and even made the Top 40 with a piano rocker based on a Rachmanioff prelude. According to leader Paul Revere, they would buy an old upright for the night and then all but destroy it in their stage act.

boogie woogie beat, in a style similar to the work of B. Bumble and the Stingers. This isn't surprising since Kim Fowley, who wrote the tune with Revere, also produced the Stingers. Further attempts to "rock up" other musicals genres ("Like, Charleston," "Like, Bluegrass") went like, nowhere.

In 1962 Revere and Lindsay moved to Portland, Oregon, and enlisted a new band of Raiders. A year later they signed with Columbia, which gave them *real* long hair, powdered wigs, and cute Revolutionary uniforms. By early 1965 they had their first vocal hit "Steppin' Out" and never looked back.

WHILE MANY SURF instrumental groups of the early sixties, particularly the Surfaris, also recorded vocals, the top vocal surf group, the Beach Boys, rarely dabbled in instrumental music. A few crop up on their first Capitol album, *Surfin' Safari*, and on *Surfin' USA* (1963) they do creditable covers of Dick Dale's "Let's Go Trippin'" and "Misirlou."

IF VOCAL HARMONIES were Brian Wilson's passion from the beginning, rock instrumentals of the late fifties and early sixties played an important role in the formative years of the Beatles.[1] A number of John Lennon's and Paul McCartney's earliest compositions were instrumentals, one of which, the fragmentary "Cayenne," is included on *The Beatles Anthology I.* In their lean and hungry years at the Star Club and other venues in Hamburg, Germany, the boys included numerous instrumentals in their repertoire, such as Duane Eddy's "Ramrod" and "Moovin' 'N' Groovin'."

It was after a long night at the nearby Top Ten Club that they were whisked with vocalist Tony Sheridan in a taxi to a school where Bert Kaempfert oversaw their first commercial recording session on Polydor. The session produced "Cry

---

[1] Before becoming a Beatle, George Harrison auditioned for Paul McCartney on a bus by playing "Raunchy" on his guitar.

In their salad days, the Beatles had a thing for instrumentals. Duane Eddy's tunes were a permanent part of their Hamburg repertoire and their first professional studio recording was the original instro "Cry for a Shadow." (Photo courtesy of Showtime Archives, Toronto)

for a Shadow," George Harrison's tongue-in-cheek tribute to England's reigning guitar instro group, the Shadows. Actually, "Cry for a Shadow," with its wry, weepy lead riff and solid back-up rhythm and bass is a very adept piece of work and shows the Beatles could have given Britain's all time greatest rock instrumental group some stiff competition if they'd had a mind to.

A discography collected by Charles Reinhart lists 131 instrumentals played or composed by the Beatles or the group's individual members. But the group only recorded two of them commercially—"Cry for a Shadow" and "Flying," from the *Magical Mystery Tour* album. "Flying," with its lofty organ theme and ethereal vocalizing may be seen as much a tribute to the Tornadoes' "Telstar" as "Cry for a Shadow" was to the Shadows.

....

WHILE A NUMBER OF other members of the British Invasion—Jimmy Page, Jeff Lynn and Richie Blakeman, among them—had served their apprenticeships in instrumental bands, only a few "first wave" groups found chart success with instrumentals. One of Manfred Mann's first U.K. releases was the instrumental "Why Should We Not?" But the only British Invasion instro to chart high in the United States, if one discounts George Martin's orchestral version of "Ringo's Theme (This Boy)" (#53), was "Mystic Eyes" (#33) by the Belfast band, Them, led by Van Morrison. After hitting the American Top 30 with the excellent vocal "Here Comes the Night," in 1965, the group struck again that year with this quirky instrumental that featured a wailing harmonica, a Bo Diddley-like beat, some great guitar runs and Morrison's growling vocal break about a stroll past an old graveyard. Heady stuff! And an appropriate end to this survey of instrumental artists manqué.

....

THE GOLDEN AGE OF the pop instrumental ended more than three decades ago. But the music keeps reverberating all around us. Vintage instrumentals are experiencing a mini-renaissance, as witness the success of Rhino Records' five-volume *Classic Rock Instrumentals* and countless other collections and anthologies that have appeared in recent years.

Movie soundtracks are awash with vintage instros. In *Forrest Gump*, Tom Hanks runs for his life from a carful of Southern rednecks to the twangy strains of Duane Eddy's "Rebel-'Rouser." In *Mr. Holland's Opus*, Richard Dreyfuss inspires a timid student to stick with the clarinet as he teaches her to play Acker Bilk's "Stranger on the Shore." The soundtrack of Quentin Tarantino's *Pulp Fiction* is a veritable smorgasbord of vintage surf instrumentals, with some classic Link Wray thrown in. Television commercials enlist classic instros like "Patricia," "Wipe Out" and "Take Five" to sell everything from frozen waffles to luxury cars. Late night TV house bands on David Letterman and Conan O'Brien regularly belt out nuggets like "The Lonely Bull" and "Walk—Don't Run" between guest interviews. Even the Olympics are not immune. In the 1996

Summer Games in Atlanta a female gymnast jumped and gyrated in her floor exercises to the semi-classical strains of "Nut Rocker" by B. Bumble and the Stingers.

Is it simply baby-boomer nostalgia that has brought these records back into our lives? I think not. If my own children are any indication, new generations of listeners are finding this music just as exciting as I did at their age. The classic rock instrumental has become as much a part of the pantheon of rock 'n' roll as Chuck Berry, Elvis and the Beatles. Its energy, ingenuity, melodic richness and yes, even gimmickry, are there for each new generation of listeners to enjoy and cherish.

Just as rock instrumentalists kept the beat alive in the late fifties and early sixties when other artists were jumping ship for softer pop, today new groups are revitalizing rock with instrumental music from surf to space age bachelor pad (but that's another book). Whether these new groups and artists remain in the underground or start an instrumental renaissance, this distinctive music, made with such skill, professionalism and love will remain a permanent part of our popular culture.

One day while riding in the car with my nine-year-old daughter, I slipped a Les Paul cassette into the tape player. As the sonic strains of Paul's version of "Lover" circa 1948 came out of the speakers, she turned to me, eyes wide as saucers, and exclaimed, "Daddy, what kind of music is *that*?" Good music. Great music. Music for the space age . . . and beyond.

Bibliography

BOOKS

Baines, Anthony. *The Oxford Companion to Musical Instruments*. Oxford, England: Oxford University Press, 1992.

Bronson, Fred. *Billboard's Hottest Hot 100 Hits*. New York: Billboard Books, 1995.

———. *The Billboard Book of Number One Hits*. New York: Billboard Books, 1985.

Brown, Ashley, ed. *The Marshall Cavendish Illustrated History of Popular Music* (6 vols.). New York: Marshall Cavendish, 1989.

Carr, Ian, Digby Fairweather, and Brian Priestley. *Jazz—The Essential Companion*. New York: Prentice-Hall, 1987.

Case, Brian, and Stan Britt. *The Illustrated Encyclopedia of Jazz*. New York: Harmony Books, 1978.

Chalker, Bryan. *Country Music*. Secaucus, N.J.: Chartwell Books, 1976.

Charles, Ray, and David Ritz. *Brother Ray: Ray Charles' Own Story*. New York: Dial Press, 1978.

Cianci, Bob. *Great Rock Drummers of the Sixties*. Milwaukee, Wis.: Third Earth Productions, 1989.

Clifford, Mike, consultant. *The Harmony Illustrated Encyclopedia of Rock*. New York: Harmony Books, 1988.

Collins, Ace. *The Stories behind Country Music's All-Time Greatest 100 Songs*. New York: Boulevard Books, 1996.

Dawson, Jim. *The Twist: The Story of the Song and Dance That Changed the World*. Boston: Faber and Faber, 1995.

DeCurtis, Anthony, and James Henke, eds. *The Rolling Stone Album Guide*. New York: Random House, 1992.

Dellar, Fred. *The Harmony Illustrated Encyclopedia of Country Music*. London: Salamander Books, 1986.

Dickerson, James. *Goin' Back to Memphis: A Century of Blues, Rock 'N' Roll, and Glorious Soul*. New York: Schirmer Books, 1996.

Doerschuk, Bob, ed. *Rock Keyboard*. New York: GPI Publications, 1985.

Friedlander, Paul. *Rock and Roll: A Social History*. New York: HarperCollins, 1996.

Gillett, Charlie. *The Sound of the City*. New York: Pantheon, 1970.

Gioia, Ted. *West Coast Jazz: Modern Jazz in California 1945-1960*. New York: Oxford University Press, 1992.

Gregory, Hugh. *Who's Who in Country Music*. London: Weidenfeld and Nicolson, 1993.

Guralnick, Peter. *Sweet Soul Music: Rhythm and Blues and the Southern Dream of Freedom*. New York: Harper and Row, 1986.

Hall, Fred M. *It's about Time: The Dave Brubeck Story*. Fayetteville, Ark.: University of Arkansas Press, 1996.

Hardy, Phil, and Dave Laing. *Encyclopedia of Rock*. New York: Schirmer Books, 1988.

Hemphill, Paul. *The Nashville Sound: Bright Lights and Country Music*. New York: Simon & Schuster, 1970.

Heslam, David, ed. *The Rock 'n' Roll Years*. New York: Crescent Books, 1990.

Jancik, Wayne. *The Billboard Book of One-Hit Wonders* (2nd ed.). New York: Billboard Books, 1997.

Kernfeld, Barry, ed. *The New Grove Dictionary of Jazz* (2 vols.). New York: Macmillan, 1988.

Lanza, Joseph. *Elevator Music: A Surreal History of Muzak, Easy-Listening, and Other Moodsong*. New York: St. Martin's Press, 1994.

Lees, Gene. *Jazz Lives: 100 Portraits in Jazz*. Buffalo, N.Y.: Firefly Books, 1992.

Maggin, Donald L. *Stan Getz: A Life in Jazz*. New York: William Morrow, 1996.

Marsh, Dave, and James Bernard. *The New Book of Rock Lists*. New York: Simon & Schuster, 1994.

McNeil, Alex. *Total Television*. New York: Viking-Penguin, 1984.

Medved, Harry, and Michael Medved. *The Hollywood Hall of Shame: The Most Expensive Flops in Movie History*. New York: Perigee Books, 1984.

Millard, Bob. *Country Music: 70 Years of America's Favorite Music*. New York: HarperCollins, 1993.

Miller, Jim, ed. *The Rolling Stone Illustrated History of Rock and Roll*. New York: Random House, 1980.

Nite, Norm N. *Rock On: The Illustrated Encyclopedia of Rock 'n' Roll—The Solid Gold Years*. New York: Thomas Crowell, 1974.

———. *Rock On: Vol. II, The Modern Years: 1964-Present*. New York: Thomas Crowell, 1978.

Palmer, Robert. *Rock & Roll: An Unruly History*. New York: Harmony Books, 1995.

Perry, David. *Jazz Greats*. London: Phaidon Press, 1996.

Ritz, David. *Ray Charles: Voice of Soul*. New York: Chelsea House, 1994.

Roxon, Lillian. *Lillian Roxon's Rock Encyclopedia*. New York: Grosset and Dunlap, 1971.

Scherman, Tony, ed. *The Rock Musician*. New York: St. Martin's Press, 1994.

Schipper, Henry. *Broken Record: The Inside Story of the Grammy Awards*. New York: Birch Lane Press, 1992.

Shaw, Arnold. *Honkers and Shouters: The Golden Years of Rhythm and Blues*. New York: Macmillan, 1978.

———. *The Rockin' 50s: The Decade That Transformed the Pop Music Scene*. New York: Hawthorn Books, 1974.

Smith, Joe. *Off the Record: An Oral History of Popular Music*. New York: Warner, 1988.

Stambler, Irwin. *Encyclopedia of Pop, Rock and Soul*. New York: St. Martin's Press, 1989.

———, and Grelun London. *The Encyclopedia of Folk, Country and Western Music*. New York: St. Martin's Press, 1984.

Tobler, John. *Guitar Heroes*. New York: St. Martin's Press, 1978.

Waller, Don. *The Motown Story*. New York: Charles Scribner's Sons, 1985.

Weinberg, Max, with Robert Santelli. *The Big Beat: Conversations with Rock's Great Drummers*. New York: Billboard Books, 1991.

Whitburn, Joel. *The Billboard Book of Top 40 Hits*. New York: Billboard Books, 1992.

———. *Pop Singles Annual 1955-1986*. Menomonee Falls, Wis.: Record Research, 1987.

PERIODICALS AND NEWSPAPERS

Ackerman, Paul, and June Bundy. "Film Themes Spark Multi-Coverage in Singles Field." *Billboard*, September 26, 1960, pp. 1, 28.

Arnson, David, and Monica Rex. "Dick Dale" [interview]. *Pipeline*, Autumn 1993, pp. 17-28.

Asbell, Bernie. "Nashville on Rise as Hit-Making Hub." *Billboard*, February 1, 1960, pp. 1, 6.

"Bar-Kays Rise Like Phoenix." *Rolling Stone*, May 25, 1968.

Biro, Nick. "Sea or No, Chicago Goes Surf." *Billboard*, July 13, 1963.

Booth, Dave "Daddy Cool." "Chris Barber the Original Sultan of Swing." *Goldmine*, July 10, 1992, pp. 36, 38, 40, 45, 140.

Bundy, June. " '60 Could Be That Band Revival Year." *Billboard*, April 25, 1960, pp. 1, 159.

——. "Late '50s Bid for Posterity Fame as Real 'Jazz Age.'" *Billboard*, March 9, 1959, pp. 1, 42.

Burke, Dave. "The Chantays" [interview]. *Pipeline*, Summer 1995, pp. 22-29.

——. "The Wailers Interview." *Pipeline*, Winter 1994/95, pp. 8-11.

Cecka, Johnny, and Billy Miller. "Woo Hoo! Rattle with the Rock-a-Teens." *Kicks*, #7, 1992, pp. 30-31.

Ciaffardini, David. "Merrell Fankhauser—The Man from Mu." *Goldmine*, April 26, 1996, pp. 58, 64, 68, 70, 71, 72, 73, 74, 78, 80, 82.

Coleman, Rick. "The Imperial Fats Domino." *Goldmine*, May 17, 1991, pp. 8-13, 20.

Dahl, Bill. "Big Jay McNeely: The Deacon Blows Again." *Goldmine*, November 2, 1990, pp. 22, 126.

Dalley, Bob. "It's Boss—It's The Rumblers." *Kicks*, #5, 1988, pp. 74-76.

——. "Tales from the Fiberglass Jungle!!" [The Crossfires]. *Kicks*, #7, 1992, pp. 38-40.

Del Ray, Teisco. "The Art of Twang" [Duane Eddy]. *Guitar Player*, June 1993, pp. 31-32.

——. "The Twang's the Thang." *Guitar Player*, July 1993, pp. 25, 26, 140.

Elliott, Stuart. "It Isn't All Big Pink Bunnies and Marlboro Men." *The Sunday New York Times*, Week in Review Section, March 10, 1996, p. 7.

Escott, Colin. "Ace Cannon: Tuff Enuff." *Goldmine*, June 17, 1988, pp. 18, 80.

——. "Bill Black—Elvis, Scotty and Who?" *Goldmine*, August 26, 1988, pp. 14, 16.

——. "Bill Haley: Indisputably—The First." *Goldmine*, April 19, 1991, pp. 12-16, 18.

——. "Bill Justis: Raunchy by Choice." *Goldmine*, June 15, 1990, p. 40.

——. "Hi." *Goldmine*, June 2, 1989, p. 16.

Fink, Stu. "Les Paul: A *Goldmine* Interview." *Goldmine*, December 18, 1987, pp. 8-10, 26.

Frevatt, Rentoul. "Here Comes Mr. Acker Bilk and a Whole Platoon of Redcoats." *Billboard*, October 27, 1962, pp. 5, 37.

Gaar, Gillian G. "Rock 'n' Roll Dreams: The Beatles in Hamburg." *Goldmine*, November 25, 1994, pp. 14-20, 22, 26, 28.

Gari, Brian. "Hal Blaine: Rock 'n' Roll's House Drummer." *Goldmine*, October 5, 1990, pp. 40, 42, 44, 146.

Geddes, George. "Chet Atkins: A Man and His Music." *Pipeline*, Autumn 1992, pp. 27-35.

Gershuny, Diana. "Dick Dale: The Big Kahuna Surfs Again." *Guitar Player*, August 1993.

Gill, Chris. "Profile: Link Wray." *Guitar Player*, November 1993, pp. 19, 20, 22, 26.

Goldstein, Henry. "'Trad' Fad Rocking Isles; Even Staid BBC Airs Jazz Trend." *Billboard*, August 28, 1961, pp. 6, 42.

Grendysa, Peter. "King/Federal." *Goldmine*, September 7, 1990, p. 29.

Grimes, William. "Antonio Carlos Jobim, Composer, Dies at 67" [obituary]. *The New York Times*, December 9, 1994, p. D20.

Hammond, Tom. "The Tornados" [interview]. *Pipeline*, Winter 1996, pp. 26-35.

Heath, Ed. "Bo Diddley: The Originator." *Goldmine*, July 27, 1990, pp. 8-11, 88.

Holden, Stephen. "An All-Star Tribute to Both Jobim and a Style." *The New York Times*, March, 1995, p. C16.

Holland, Bernard. "What Jobim Knew: Small Is Beautiful." *The New York Times*, December 2, 1995.

Hopkins, Jerry. "Lou Adler." *Rolling Stone*, December 21, 1968.

Jancik, Wayne. "Gerry Grananhan Talks about Dicky Doo and the Don'ts, the Fireflies and More." *Goldmine*, December 28, 1990, pp. 42, 44.

Kidd, Tom. "The Chantays: The Story of 'Pipeline.'" *Goldmine*, December 16, 1988, pp. 97, 100.

Koda, Cub. "Chuck Berry—and the Joint Was Rockin'." *Goldmine*, December 13, 1991, pp. 8-16, 18, 20, 22.

——. "An Appreciation of Link Wray: Godfather of the Power Chord." *Goldmine*, October 4, 1991, pp. 36, 40, 42.

Kubernik, Harvey Robert. "Jack Nitzsche: Phil Spector's Arranger Remembers the Classic Hits." *Goldmine*, June 17, 1988, pp. 73, 74.

Leigh, Spencer. "Hank Marvin Interview." *Pipeline*, Autumn 1993, pp. 9-15.

MacNeish, Jerry. "The Fireballs: Petty Proteges." *Goldmine*, December 16, 1988, pp. 6-8, 10, 12, 14, 83.

Maher, Jack. "Blue Note Brings on Jazz Reserves to Stay Potent." *Billboard*, May 11, 1963.

——. "Bossa Nova the New Twist?" *Billboard*, October 13, 1962, pp. 4, 43.

——. "Home and Abroad, Bossa Clicks On." *Billboard*, December 1, 1962, pp. 5, 35.

——. "Hot Rod Trend Catches On." *Billboard*, November 25, 1963, pp. 3, 14.

——. "Instrumental Boom Sends Scouts Peering into Strange Corners." *Billboard*, September 15, 1962.

——. "It's a Great Big Bossa-Filled World We Live In, Says Almost Everybody." *Billboard*, November 1962, p. 4.

——. "Jazz Indies Making Those Charts Sing." *Billboard*, April 20, 1963. pp. 1, 8.

——. "Jazz Is a Four-Letter Word: Z-O-O-M!" *Billboard*, August 11, 1962.

——. "Trade Still Riding That Bossa Beat." *Billboard*, May 4, 1963, pp. 1, 8.

McCue, Danny. "Steve Cropper—Playing His Thang." *Goldmine*, June 15, 1990, pp. 18, 20, 22.

McNutt, Randy. "Fraternity." *Goldmine*, September 7, 1990, p. 28.

Nevill, Brian R. "Downey." *Goldmine*, September 20, 1991, pp. 12, 13, 26.

Ohlschmidt, Jim. "Chet Atkins: Certified Guitar Player." *Goldmine*, January 13, 1989, pp. 7, 8, 10, 12, 14, 71.

Pareles, Jon. "Surfin' Again" [interview with Dick Dale]. *The New York Times*, May 1, 1994, p. C5.

Paton, Bob, and Steve Rager. "Rockin' R's." *Kicks* #6, 1988, pp. 50-52.

Perlmutter, Donna. "Tijuana Brass, Right? Don't Ask" [interview with Herb Alpert]. *The New York Times*, May 11, 1995, pp. C1, 11.

Phillips, Lloyd N. "Dave Brubeck: Collecting a Jazz Innovator." *Goldmine*, May 18, 1990, pp. 24-26, 28, 90.

Powers, Jim. "Mondo Melodic Exotica." *Goldmine*, April 26, 1996, pp. 20-23,26, 28, 32, 34, 184.

Propes, Steve. "The Champs: The 'Tequila' Story." *Goldmine*, August 12, 1988, pp. 29, 77.

Reinhart, Charles. "Beatles without Words: A Discography of Beatle Instrumentals." *Goldmine*, October 19, 1990, pp. 46, 48, 111.

Rolontz, Bob. "Kai Winding's 'More' Hit Has Long Jazz Tradition." *Billboard*, August 3, 1963, p. 12.

Santelli, Robert. "Scotty Moore: The Guitar That Changed the World." *Goldmine*, August 23, 1991, pp. 8-12.

Simonds, Roy. "Steve Douglas." *Pipeline*, Autumn 1993, p. 62.

Skelly, Richard. "Jimmy McGriff—King of the Blues Organ." *Goldmine*, March 20, 1992, pp. 57, 60, 64, 113.

Slim, Almost. "James Booker." *Goldmine*, December 30, 1988, p. 8.

——. "Slim Harpo: He Knew the Blues." *Goldmine*, March 11, 1988, pp. 13, 117, 124.

Sokoloff, Vicky. "The Everly Brothers: Their Solo Careers." *Goldmine*, August 11, 1989, pp. 97, 100, 108.

Tamarkin, Jeff. "Buck Owens: All He's Gotta Do Is Act Naturally." *Goldmine*, February 9, 1990, pp. 7, 8, 12, 14, 16, 18, 93.

Tiegel, Eliot. "Tijuana Brass Hot Group." *Billboard*, March 13, 1965, p. 12.

Watrous, Peter. "Bill Doggett, 80, Keyboard Player and Rhythm-and-Blues Innovator" [obituary]. *The New York Times*, November 20, 1996, p. D21.

Wedge, Don. "Elgar Estate Spikes Rock Version of 'Pomp.'" *Billboard*, July 31, 1961, p. 19.

Whiteis, David. "The Hi Records Story." *Goldmine*, May 12, 1995, pp. 24, 26, 28, 30, 32, 82, 191.

Zhito, Lee. "Capitol Snags Dick Dale after Hot Bidding." *Billboard*, February 23, 1963, pp. 1, 8.

——. "Surfing Craze Ready to Splash across Country to East's Youth." *Billboard*, June 29, 1963, pp. 26, 31.

Discography

RECOMMENDED LISTENING
(All titles are on CD, unless otherwise noted.)

CHAPTER 1: DREAM MUSIC AND THEME MUSIC
Mondo Mambo! The Best of Perez Prado & His Orchestra. Rhino Records R2 7889.
Les Paul with Mary Ford: The Best of the Capitol Masters. Capitol C4-99617 (cassette).

CHAPTER 2: WAILING SAX, POUNDING DRUMS
Big Jay McNeely: Road House Boogie. Saxophonograph RBD 505.
Earl Bostic: All His Hits. King KCD-5010.
Bill Doggett and His Combo: All His Hits. King KCD-5009.
The Champs: Greatest Hits. Backline Records BLCD 9.02040 L.
The Fabulous Wailers: The Boys from Tacoma. Etiquette Records ETCD 012693.

CHAPTER 3: TWANGY GUITARS
Twang Thang: The Duane Eddy Anthology. Rhino Records R2 71223 (double CD).
Link Wray and the Raymen: Mr. Guitar. Norton Records CED 242 (double CD).
Walk Don't Run: The Best of the Ventures. EMI CDP-7-93451-2.
The Best of the Fireballs: The Original Norman Petty Masters. Ace CDCHD 418.

CHAPTER 4: LET'S DANCE!
Tom Shannon Presents . . . the Rockin' Rebels. Ace CDCHD 426.
Dave "Baby" Cortez: Happy Organs Wild Guitars and Piano Shuffles. Ace CDCHD 386.
Johnny and the Hurricanes: Come On Let's Rock—20 Greatest Hits. Black Tulip 266072.
Sandy Nelson: King of the Drums: His Greatest Hits. See for Miles Records SEECD 423.
——. *Rock 'N' Roll Drum Beat*. Ace CDCHD 586.
B. Bumble and the Stingers: Nut Rocker. Ace CDCHD 577.

CHAPTER 5: THE EUROPEAN CONNECTION
It's Hard to Believe: The Amazing World of Joe Meek. Razor & Tie RE 2080-2.
Telstar: The Original Sixties Hits of the Tornados. Music Club MCCD 161.
The Very Best of Bent Fabric. Taragon Records TARCD-1028.

CHAPTER 6: ALL THAT JAZZ
Dave Brubeck's Greatest Hits. CBS 32046.
Vince Guaraldi: Greatest Hits. Fantasy MPF-4505/FCD 8431.
Stan Getz and Charlie Byrd: Jazz Samba. Polydor 810061-2CD.
Jimmy Smith: Jazz Masters 29. Verve 314 521 855-2.

CHAPTER 7: SURFER'S STOMP

King of the Surf Guitar: The Best of Dick Dale and His Del-Tones. Rhino Records R2 75756.

Wipe Out! The Best of the Surfaris. Varese Sarabande VSD-5478.

——. *Surfaris Stomp.* Varese Sarabande VSD-5588.

The Chantays: Pipeline. Varese Sarabande VSD-5491.

——. *Waiting for the Tide.* Rocktopia R11129.

Al Casey: Jivin' Around. Ace SC CDCHD 612.

The Crossfires: Out of Control. Sundazed SC 6062.

Penetration! The Best of the Pyramids. Sundazed SC 11023.

Intoxica! The Best of the Revels. Sundazed SC 11020.

Big Surf (featuring the Lively Ones, Dave Myers and the Surftones, the Centurions, the Impacts, and the Sentinals). Ace CDCHD 319.

Wax, Board and Woodie: A Collection of Rare and Unreleased Surf and Hot Rod Songs. Varese Sarabande VSD-5726.

CHAPTER 8: MEMPHIS SOUL STEW

Bill Black's Combo: Greatest Hits and Bill Black's Combo Play Tunes by Chuck Berry. Hi Records UK CD 115.

King Curtis: Trouble in Mind and It's Party Time with King Curtis. Ace CDCHD 545.

——. *Instant Soul: The Legendary King Curtis.* Razor & Tie RE 2054.

Booker T. and the MG's: Soul Dressing. Atlantic 7 82337-2.

——. *The Very Best of Booker T. and the MG's.* Rhino Records R2 71738.

——. *Uptight.* Stax CDSXE 024.

——. *That's the Way It Should Be.* Columbia CK 53307.

CHAPTER 9: COUNTRY LICKS

Chet Atkins: Gallopin' Guitar (The Early Years: 1949-1954). Bear Family BCD 15714 (4 CDs).

The Instrumental Hits of Buck Owens and His Buckaroos. Sundazed SC 6049.

CHAPTER 10: POP GOES THE INSTRUMENTAL

Herb Alpert and the Tijuana Brass: Classic, Volume 1. A & M Records CD 2501.

COLLECTIONS AND ANTHOLOGIES

Axes & Saxes: The Great Instrumentals. The Rock 'N' Roll Era series, Time-Life Music 2RNR-36.

Instrumental Gold. MCA MSD2-35317 (double CD).

'50s Instrumentals. Time-Life Music HPD-30.

'60s Instrumentals. Time-Life Music HPD-34.

'60s Instrumentals: Take Two: Your Hit Parade Series. Time-Life Music HDP-39.

Rock Instrumental Classics (5 vols.: vol.1,the 50s; vol. 2, the 60s; vol. 3, the 70s; vol. 4, Soul; vol. 5, Surf). Rhino Records R2 71601-5.

Teen Beat: 30 Great Rockin' Instrumentals (3 vols.). Ace CDCHD 406, 522, 602.

Those Wonderful Instrumentals. K-Tel 3091-2.

Appendix

Seventy of the Best Rock and Pop Instrumentals

his is, as all "best of" lists are, a highly personal choice, but might be useful to someone looking for a place to start listening to and collecting classic rock and pop instrumentals. So for what it's worth, here, in alphabetical order according to artist, are this author's seventy favorite instrumentals from the golden age of rock (1955-66) with one new one from a classic surf group.

"Walking with Mr. Lee" . . . . Lee Allen

"A Taste of Honey" . . . . Herb Alpert and the Tijuana Brass

"Peter Gunn" . . . . Ray Anthony

"Baja" . . . . the Astronauts

"Slow Walk" . . . . Sil Austin

"Midnight in Moscow" . . . . Kenny Ball

"The Poor People of Paris" . . . . Les Baxter

"Stranger on the Shore" . . . . Acker Bilk

"Smokie-Part 2" . . . . Bill Black's Combo

"Green Onions," "My Sweet Potato," "Time is Tight" . . . Booker T. and the MG's

"Night Train" . . . . James Brown

"Take Five" . . . . the Dave Brubeck Quartet

"Nut Rocker" . . . . B. Bumble and the Stingers

"Bust Out" . . . . the Busters

"Tequila" . . . . the Champs

"Pipeline," "Killer Dana" . . . . the Chantays

"Topsy II" . . . . Cozy Cole

"Wiggle Wobble" . . . . Les Cooper and the Soul Rockers

"Rinky Dink" . . . . Dave "Baby" Cortez

"Soul Serenade," "Ode to Billy Joe" . . . . King Curtis

"Misirlou" . . . . Dick Dale and the Del-Tones

"Quiet Village" . . . . Martin Denny

"Aztec" .... Bo Diddley
"Honky Tonk, Part 2" .... Bill Doggett
"Stickshift" .... the Duals
"Rebel-'Rouser," "Ramrod" .... Duane Eddy
"Theme from *A Summer Place*" .... Percy Faith
"Theme from *The Apartment*" .... Ferrante and Teicher
"Torquay" .... the Fireballs
"Desafinado" .... Stan Getz and Charlie Byrd
"Cast Your Fate to the Wind" .... Vince Guaraldi
"Rudy's Rock" .... Bill Haley and the Comets
"Apache" .... Jorgen Ingmann
"Sandstorm" .... Johnny and the Hurricanes
"The In Crowd" .... the Ramsey Lewis Trio
"Memphis" .... Lonnie Mack
"Last Night" .... the Mar-Keys
"Balboa Blue," "Out of Limits" .... the Marketts
"Teen Beat," "Let There Be Drums" .... Sandy Nelson
"The Lonely Surfer" .... Jack Nietzsche
"Manhattan Spiritual" .... Reg Owen
"Our Winter Love" .... Bill Pursell
"Penetration" .... the Pyramids
"Yakety Sax" .... Boots Randolph
"Woo Hoo" .... the Rock-a-Teens
"Wild Weekend" .... the Rockin' Rebels
"The Stripper" .... David Rose
"Poor Boy" .... the Royaltones
"Sleepwalk" .... Santo and Johnny
"Walk on the Wild Side" .... Jimmy Smith
"Moonglow and Theme from *Picnic*" .... Morris Stoloff
"Wipe Out" .... the Surfaris
"Telstar" .... the Tornadoes
"You Can't Sit Down" .... Phil Upchurch Combo
"A Swingin' Safari" .... Billy Vaughn
"Walk-Don't Run,'" Perfidia" .... the Ventures
"Harlem Nocturne" .... the Viscounts
"Tall Cool One" .... the Wailers
"Cleo's Mood" .... Junior Walker and the All Stars
"Canadian Sunset" .... Hugo Winterhalter and Eddie Heywood
"Rumble," "Jack the Ripper" .... Link Wray and the Raymen

Index

Note: **boldface** type indicates photograph

BillboardBooks

THE BEST ON CD SERIES:
THE JAZZ CD LISTENER'S GUIDE by Howard Blumenthal
The jazz fan's consumer's guide to 600 of the best jazz CDs available from 100 of the best-loved and most influential artists of the 20th century. Entries include biographies, CD title, record label, catalogue number, and explanation of what makes the recording stand out. Each CD is cross-referenced to a recording of similar appeal to point shoppers to possible future purchases. *208 pages. 150 photos. Paperback. $14.95. 0-8230-7662-8*

THE BEST ON CD SERIES:
THE WORLD MUSIC CD LISTENER'S GUIDE by Howard Blumenthal
A valuable resource for fans of world music wanting to find 600 of the best CDs available by 100 artists from around the globe. (See above entry for details.) *208 pages. 150 photos. Paperback. $14.95. 0-8230-7663-6*

THE BIG BOOK OF SHOW BUSINESS AWARDS by David Sheward
A handy resource guide covering the Oscar, Tony, Emmy, and Grammy awards as well as other major show business honors. Also provided is a wealth of historical information, gossip and trivia relating to the awards, and a gallery of lively photographs. *352 pages. 100 photos. Paperback. $21.95. 0-8230-7630-X*

THE BILLBOARD BOOK OF AMERICAN SINGING GROUPS:
A History, 1940-1990 by Jay Warner
The definitive history of pop vocal groups, from the doo wop of Dion and the Belmonts, to the Motown hits of the Supremes, to the surf sound of the Beach Boys, to the country rock of Crosby, Stills and Nash. More than 350 classic acts spanning five decades are profiled here, with fascinating information about each group's career, key members, and musical impact as well as extensive discographies and rare photos. *544 pages. 80 photos. Paperback. $21.95.*

THE BILLBOARD BOOK OF NUMBER ONE ALBUMS:
The Inside Story Behind Pop Music's Blockbuster Records by Craig Rosen
A behind-the-scenes look at the people and stories involved in the enormously popular records that achieved Number One album status in the Billboard charts. Inside information on over 400 albums that have topped the chart since 1956, plus new interviews with hundreds of superstar record artists as well as a wealth of trivia statistics and other facts. *448 pages. 425 photos. Paperback. $21.95.*

THE BILLBOARD BOOK OF NUMBER ONE HITS,
Fourth Edition, Revised and Enlarged by Fred Bronson
The inside story behind the top of the charts. An indispensable listing of every single to appear in the top spot on the Billboard Hot 100 chart from 1955 to 1997, along with anecdotes, interviews, and chart data. *912 pages. 850 photos. Paperback. $24.95.*

THE BILLBOARD BOOK OF TOP 40 ALBUMS,
Third Edition, Revised and Enlarged by Joel Whitburn
The complete guide to every Top 40 album from 1955 to 1994. Comprehensive information on the most successful rock, jazz, comedy, country, classical, Christmas, Broadway, and film soundtrack albums ever to reach the top of the Billboard charts. Includes chart positions, number of weeks on the chart, and label and catalog number for every album listed. *416 pages. 150 photos. Paperback. $21.95.*

THE BILLBOARD BOOK OF TOP 40 COUNTRY HITS:
Country Music's Hottest Records, 1944 to the Present by Joel Whitburn
From the classic recordings of Hank Williams and Bob Wills, to enduring artists Patsy Cline and Tammy Wynette, to today's young superstars Garth Brooks and Shania Twain, the rich history of country music is documented in this comprehensive compilation of Billboard's Country Singles charts. Provides exhaustive data on every record to score at least one Top 40 hit. *562 pages. 96 photos. Paperback. $21.95*

THE BILLBOARD BOOK OF TOP 40 HITS,
Sixth Edition, Revised and Enlarged by Joel Whitburn
A perennial favorite, listing every single to reach the Top 40 of Billboard's weekly Hot 100 charts since 1955. Includes new chart data and expanded biographical information and trivia on artists listed. *800 pages. 300 photos. Paperback. $21.95*

THE BILLBOARD BOOK OF ONE-HIT WONDERS,
Second Edition, Revised and Expanded by Wayne Jancik
A one-of-a-kind rock and roll reference guide that charts the flip side of the pop music story. Uncovers the fascinating circumstances surrounding the rise to fame—and occasional rapid return to obscurity—of performers who had only one hit in Billboard's Top 40 charts. Contains over 100 new entries and a wealth of data and entertaining information that just can't be found elsewhere. A must for pop music fans and record collectors. *512 pages. 235 photos. Paperback. $21.95.*

THE BILLBOARD GUIDE TO HOME RECORDING,
Second Edition, Revised and Updated by Ray Baragary
The complete do-it-yourself reference to recording techniques and equipment options. Provides a step-by-step approach to producing high-quality tapes, demos, and CDs in a home studio. Includes information on recorders, mixers, microphones, and signal processors; recording basic tracks and overdubbing; expanding the home studio with MIDI; the development of General MIDI standards; and the use of computers in sequencing. *272 pages. 97 illustrations. Paperback. $19.95.*

THE BILLBOARD GUIDE TO MUSIC PUBLICITY,
Revised Edition by Jim Pettigrew, Jr.
A clear-headed reference providing career-minded musicians and their representatives with key information about such vital activities as getting media exposure, preparing effective publicity materials, and developing short-term and long-range publicity. New to the revised edition is coverage of desktop publishing, compact disks, basic copy-editing tips, and a recommended reading list. *176 pages. 16 illustrations. Paperback. $18.95.*

THE BILLBOARD GUIDE TO PROGRESSIVE MUSIC by Bradley Smith
From historic pioneers Pink Floyd and jazz fusion's Brand X to electronic artists Tangerine Dream and new groups like Djam Karet, new fans and longtime followers of progressive music will welcome this wide-ranging consumer's guide to cutting-edge artists and their recordings. *320 pages. 50 photos. Paperback. $18.95. 0-8230-7665-2*

THE REAL DEAL:
How to Get Signed to a Record Label From A to Z by Daylle Deanna Schwartz
A new music industry primer offering crucial information and advice that any musician playing popular music and desiring a record deal needs to have. Includes an explanation of the roles of an agent, attorney, A&R person, producer, and manager; what copyright and music publishing are; the importance of doing live performance; ways to build a following; how to use networking to reach the right people; and the pros and cons of releasing an independent recording. Also contains advice from top creative and business professionals and a resource section. *256 pages. Paperback. $16.95.*

THE ROCK AND ROLL READER'S GUIDE by Gary M. Krebs
An indispensable consumer guide for book collectors and music fans alike. The first comprehensive bibliography of books about, and by, rock and pop stars in addition to works written about the music scene itself. Focuses on both selected general reference works—such as artist profiles, chart data, pictorials, concert events, women and rock, and magazines—and all publications on artists A-Z. *464 pages. Paperback. $21.95.*

THIS BUSINESS OF ARTIST MANAGEMENT,
Revised and Enlarged Third Edition by Xavier M. Frascogna, Jr. and H. Lee Hetherington
Firmly established as the standard reference work in the field of artist management in music, and winner of the 1980 Deems Taylor Book Award. Now revised and updated to include interviews with top record executives, coverage of new forms of business, updates on the legal framework of the music business, and contemporary investment and money management advice. *304 pages. Hardcover. $21.95.*

THIS BUSINESS OF MUSIC,
Seventh Edition by M. William Krasilovsky and Sidney Shemel
The bible of the music business, with over 250,000 copies sold. A practical guide to the music industry for publishers, writers, record companies, producers, artists, and agents. Provides detailed information on virtually every economic, legal, and financial aspect of the complex business of music. *736 pages. Hardcover. $29.95.*

BILLBOARD'S HOTTEST HOT 100 HITS,
Revised and Enlarged Edition by Fred Bronson
The Ultimate music trivia book. An illustrated compendium of 40 years of Billboard's chart data broken down into 175 categories, including artists, writers, producers, and record labels. Plus, a definitive list of the Top 5000 hits from 1955 through 1995. *512 pages. 250 photos. Paperback. $21.95*

THE ENCYCLOPEDIA OF DAYTIME TELEVISION by Wesley Hyatt
The definitive daytime television resource! Covers all series aired for three weeks or more on a commercial network between 1947 and 1996. Plus 100 nationally syndicated programs from the same period. Each entry provides dates of airing,, the principal cast, and other pertinent information. *528 pages. 100 photos. $24.95. 0-8230-8315-2.*

HOW TO BE A WORKING MUSICIAN
A Practical Guide to Earning Money in the Music Business by Mike Levine
An invaluable handbook of commonsense career advice to anyone wanting to earn money as a working musician. Includes guidance on performing at bars, clubs, celebrations, and business functions; providing accompaniment in theaters and cabarets; playing recording sessions; and composing for T.V. and radio ads. *224 pages. $16.95. 0-8230-8329-2*

KISS AND SELL: The Making of A Supergroup by C.K. Lendt
A riveting expose of the machinations and manipulations of what's involved in making it to the top of the rock world, written by the man who traveled with Kiss for 12 years as their business manager. Both a case study of the harsh realities of how the business of music works and a unique perspective on the lives, lifestyles, and indulgences of rock stars. *352 pages. 18 photos. Paperback. $18.95.*

MORE ABOUT THIS BUSINESS OF MUSIC,
Fifth Edition, Revised and Enlarged by Sidney Shemel and M. William Krasilovsky
A completely updated companion to This Business of Music, this book presents a practical guide to areas of the music business such as jazz, religious music, live performances, the production and sale of printed music, background music and transcriptions, and the impact of technology from CDs and DATs to VCRs. *224 pages. Hardcover. $18.95.*

The above titles should all be available from your neighborhood bookseller. If you don't find a copy on the shelf, books can also be ordered either through the store or directly from Watson-Guptill Publications. To order copies by phone or to request information on any of these titles, please call our toll-free number: 1-800-278-8477. To order copies by mail, send a check or money order for the cost of the book, with $2.00 postage and handling for one book and $ .50 for each additional book, plus applicable sales tax in the states of CA, DC, IL, OH, MA, NJ, NY, PA, TN, and VA, to:

WATSON-GUPTILL PUBLICATIONS
PO Box 2013
Lakewood, NJ 08701-9913